Louis Becke, Walter Jeffery

Admiral Phillip

The founding of New South Wales

Louis Becke, Walter Jeffery

Admiral Phillip
The founding of New South Wales

ISBN/EAN: 9783337386795

Printed in Europe, USA, Canada, Australia, Japan

Cover: Foto ©ninafisch / pixelio.de

More available books at **www.hansebooks.com**

BUILDERS OF GREATER BRITAIN

Edited by H. F. WILSON, M.A.

Barrister-at-Law
Late Fellow of Trinity College, Cambridge
Legal Assistant at the Colonial Office

b

BUILDERS OF GREATER BRITAIN

Builders
of
Greater Britain

ADMIRAL PHILLIP

ADMIRAL PHILLIP

THE FOUNDING OF NEW SOUTH WALES

BY

LOUIS BECKE

AND

WALTER JEFFERY

LONDON
T. FISHER UNWIN
PATERNOSTER SQUARE
MDCCCXCIX

PREFACE

ANOTHER Boswell would fail if he attempted to tell, in the words of Arthur Phillip himself, the story of 'Governor' Phillip's life. Only some half-a-dozen years of his career are fully known to us, and in that time Phillip worked harder and talked and wrote less about himself than most men would have done under such trying circumstances. From 1786, when he was chosen to found the settlement of New South Wales, till his return to England in 1792, his despatches and a few contemporary chronicles—now become rare books—are the only sources from which a knowledge of the man can be gathered. The chroniclers were all officers of the settlement, and their books, like the despatches, are but the dry bones of history. The Government of New South Wales has been for some time searching for information relating to the first Governor of the colony ; but with such small result that even his burial place remained unknown till the end of 1897, when the tomb was unexpectedly discovered in the ancient parish church of St Nicholas at Bathampton, near the City of Bath, by the vicar, the Reverend L. J. Fish. And the authors believe that it may be taken for granted that, beyond what personal detail is given in this volume and its appendices, there is little else to be found. The discovery of the hitherto unpublished record of Phillip's service under the Portuguese Government was made through the persistent efforts of the Editor ; the writers having, after several attempts, failed to obtain more than the bald fact that Phillip had served in the Portuguese Navy. Even his descendants could throw no light whatever upon the point.

This book, therefore, is rather a narrative of the founding of New South Wales than a biography of the colony's first Governor. It ought not to lack interest on this account ; for it tells the story of the beginning of Greater Britain in the South.

Of the personality of Phillip, as we have said, little is really known. He was an obscure naval captain selected by the Government of the time to establish a penal settlement at the other side of the world. He landed on the shores of a country which, to all his companions, appeared a most forbidding and unpromising land—one that 'would never be worth anything to anyone.' Phillip, a few months after his arrival, wrote to England to assure his superiors that it would prove 'the most valuable acquisition Great Britain ever made.'

For these prophetic words alone, the man who uttered them, so far as we can come to a knowledge of him, is worth knowing. Such an understanding of his character as can be gathered by industry of research, this book endeavours to furnish.

The writers are, of course, greatly indebted to the old chroniclers, to the *Historical Records of New South Wales*, and the *Official History* by Mr G. B. Barton ; and (for the use of papers and 'clues') to Mr

David Scott Mitchell, the well-known collector of Australian literature. The Editor's acknowledgments to those who have supplied him with the materials for the two Appendices dealing with Phillip's collateral descendants, and his service in the Portuguese Navy, are separately made. The portrait of Phillip is taken from the frontispiece to his *Voyage*, a volume published in 1789 ; and the two maps represent respectively the area of the first British Government in Australia, and the site of the earliest settlement at Sydney.

LOUIS BECKE.
WALTER JEFFERY.

June 1899.

CONTENTS

CHAPTER V

CHAPTER VI

CHAPTER VII

CHAPTER VIII

CHAPTER IX

CHAPTER X

CHAPTER XI

CHAPTER XII

CHAPTER XIII

CHAPTER XIV

CHAPTER XV

CHAPTER XVI

LIST OF ILLUSTRATIONS

Admiral Phillip

CHAPTER I

CAPTAIN ARTHUR PHILLIP was the first Governor of the first Australian colony, and this narrative of his life is the story of the pioneers in that great Southern Continent where to-day nearly every English family has a kinsman, and where the race has already built a 'Greater Britain' across the seas.

The man who, one hundred and ten years ago, founded New South Wales is almost forgotten, yet the country now in such vigorous manhood was for the first half-dozen years of its existence a miserable starveling, and but for Phillip's tender nursing, its life would have ended in the year of its birth.

Arthur Phillip was born on 11th October 1738, in Bread Street, Allhallows, within the City of London. His father, Jacob Phillip, was a native of Frankfort, in

Germany, who, having settled in England, maintained his family as a teacher of languages, although his former occupation appears to have been that of a steward. His mother was Elizabeth Breach, and Phillip's father was her second husband. Her first husband was a Captain Herbert of the Royal Navy, who was, it is said, a relative of Lord Pembroke, and it is possible that Phillip's career in the navy may have been influenced in some degree by his mother's former marriage.

Destined for the sea, he was sent at the age of thirteen to Greenwich School, in an old list of the boys of which his entrance is recorded as follows :—

'Date of admission, 24th June 1751 ; occupation of father, steward ; name of applicant, Arthur Phillip ; age, 12¾ years ; date when left, 1st December 1753 ; period bound for, seven years ; to whom bound, William Readhead ; ship, *Fortune*, 210 tons burden, trading to Greenland.'

Evidently, however, young Phillip remained but a short time in the *Fortune*, for at seventeen, according to his *Voyage*, a work published in 1789, he was, at the commencement of hostilities in 1755, serving under Captain Michael Everet, and learning 'the rudiments of his profession under that able officer.'

Six years later, at the age of twenty-three, he was serving as lieutenant of the *Stirling Castle* under Sir George Pococke, one of the best officers of the period. It seems, however, that he found no opportunity of distinguishing himself in the King's service, for about 1763 he. 'found leisure to marry' and to settle at Lyndhurst, in the New Forest, where he devoted himself to farming and the usual pursuits of a country gentleman. Here for some years he lived quietly, though doubtless awaiting the opportunity to again engage in an active life afloat. But finding that his own country made no call upon his services, he offered them to the kingdom of Portugal when that nation engaged in its struggle with Spain. His offer was eagerly accepted, and, as the writer of his *Voyage* says, such was his conduct and such his success that when the interference of France in 1778 made it his duty to relinquish his position as post-captain in the Portuguese navy and fight the enemies of his own country, 'the Portuguese Court regretted his departure, but applauded his motive.'

No precise information as to the nature of his services to Portugal is given by any of his chroniclers, but it is very probable that much of his work consisted in organising the Portuguese fleet to cope successfully with its antagonist. A decree of the King of Portugal, dated from Lisbon on 16th January 1775, and signed 'The King, Dom Joas,' and countersigned by the Marquis of Tancos, commands 'all who shall see this, my letter patent, that in view of the merits and qualifications to be found in the person of Arthur Phillip, and feeling sure that he will faithfully discharge any duties which may be entrusted to him, and also on account of the confidence which I place in him on all the aforesaid grounds : I hereby appoint him according to my good will and pleasure (as by this letter I do appoint him) post-captain of the ships of the line of my navy, in which post he will serve at my good will and pleasure ; and he is to receive double the amount of pay corresponding with his rank. He will moreover enjoy all the honours, privileges, liberties, exemptions and immunities that may duly appertain to him : I therefore command Dom Joas, my dearly beloved and esteemed cousin, a member of my Councils of State and War, and Captain-General of my Royal Navy of my galleons navigating the high ocean, that after placing him in possession of his post (provided he shall have first taken the oath to faithfully discharge his duties) he will allow him to serve and discharge his respective duties. The Admiral of my Navy, as well as the chief and superior officers, shall recognise him as post-captain, and my officers, soldiers and others under his orders shall duly obey him and carry out his directions in everything concerning my service as they ought to be and are in duty bound. His aforesaid pay is to be entered and registered in the proper books, in order that it may be paid to him at the proper dates. In testimony of which I have caused this letter, which is signed by me and sealed with the great seal of my arms, to be issued.'

Upon his return to England he was, in September 1779, gazetted master and commander of the *Basilisk* fireship. Again, as it seems, no chance was afforded him of proving his worth ; but his superiors were now evidently beginning to recognise his merits as an able and diligent officer, for on the 13th November 1781, when he was upwards of forty-three years of age, he was made post-captain of the *Ariadne* frigate, being transferred in December to the *Europe*, a sixty-four. During the exciting events of 1782 he was actively employed, and in the following year he sailed with a reinforcement to the East Indies, 'where superior bravery contended against superior force, till the policy of our negotiators put an end to unequal hostilities by a necessary peace.'

Phillip, during these services abroad, appears not to have troubled himself with private correspondence. His personal friendships, if he had any, were few, and there is no record of his experiences and adventures in a stirring time, beyond the dry-as-dust and scanty official records of his movements. And it is probable, from what we know of the man's character as displayed in later years, that he would shrink from, if not abhor, talking or writing about himself even to his own relatives ; in fact, during his long exile in Australia he never alludes to family ties, nor even complains of the fact that for the first two years he did not receive a letter from his wife. His officers suffered from the same anxiety as to the welfare of those they had left behind them, and that was doubtless enough for Phillip. If his subordinates liked to complain to their friends and relatives in England of the apathy of the Government in not sending even a mail to the new settlement, they could do so ; he was too proud and self-contained a man to make domestic anxieties a peg on which to hang even a just grievance, and thus set an example which would have been contagious, and might have led to the disintegration and even the decay of the community.

One who met him in 1796 thus describes his personal appearance :—

'Well I remember his little figure, smothered up in his brown camlet cloak lined with green baize, his face shrivelled, and thin aquiline nose, under a large cocked hat, gathered up in a heap, his chin between his knees, sitting under the lee of the mainmast, his sharp and powerful voice exclaiming, "I cannot bear this, I am as sick as a dog !"'

This description of the man is not very impressive; but remember the situation.   Phillip was seated in the stern of a small boat which was beating out of Mutton Cove, at Plymouth, in a strong squall and nasty sea, and, to tell the truth, was — as the best of sailors sometimes are—overcome with sea-sickness !

Had Phillip made enemies as did one of his successors in the Governorship of New South Wales—Bligh—this incident would, perhaps, have been made the occasion of saying that the founder of Australia was notoriously unfitted for a naval command.   The military traducers of Bligh slandered his reputation by asserting that he tried to hide himself under his bed when the officers of the infamous New South Wales Corps deposed him.

Phillip was forty-eight years of age when he began the work which entitles him to an honoured place among the Builders of Greater Britain. Up to the year 1786, notwithstanding that the Portuguese Court had expressed a high appreciation of the services rendered to their nation by the British officer, his naval career is scarcely worth remembering. His opportunities for winning distinction with his sword were few, and if he had had them, it is likely that he would have only done well where men with less brains and more dash would have done brilliantly. This book contains nothing but the story of half a dozen years of the man's life ; yet in those six years he founded Australia.

CHAPTER II

THE causes which led to the colonisation of New
South Wales—Cook's voyages, the overcrowded state
of the English gaols (one consequence of the American
revolution), the proposals of Matra, Sir George Young,
and Sir Joseph Banks for forming colonies—can only
be briefly referred to here.

Phillip has no place in the prologue to the story of the
establishment of Greater Britain under the Southern
Cross, and it is with Phillip only that this book has
to do. Yet, for a proper appreciation of Phillip as a
Builder, it is necessary to give some account of the
share which those who were the architects of the
structure actually had in the undertaking.

Ask ninety-nine out of every hundred persons,
'Who discovered Australia?' They will answer,
'Captain Cook.' The answer is, in a sense, correct,

but the brilliancy of the great navigator's fame will lose nothing by the truth, and the truth is that he never even saw the site of the first settlement in the Antipodes. What the name of Columbus is to America, that should the name of Cook be to Australia, and although Phillip and his transports can scarcely be compared with the Pilgrim Fathers and the *Mayflower*, yet, as the pioneers of settlement in Australia, the officers of the First Fleet ought to be remembered as colonisers, with something of the same admiration we have for those sturdy Puritan adventurers.

Leaving out of the story the Portuguese and Dutch explorations on the western coast of Australia, something of the eastern coast was known (although not to Englishmen) a couple of hundred years before Cook's voyage. But Cook surveyed it and made it British territory ; and the publication of the narrative of his voyage suggested schemes for its colonisation. One James Maria Matra in 1783, thirteen years after Cook's return from his Botany Bay voyage, submitted a proposal for colonising the new territory with American loyalists. Sir Joseph Banks, the naturalist who accompanied Cook, was, however, the man who not only had most to do with the matter, but until the day of his death in 1820 took the keenest interest in the colony's progress. Banks gave evidence before a Committee of the House of Commons which had been appointed in

1779 to inquire into the question of transportation, and spoke strongly in favour of Botany Bay as a place suitable for the purpose. Admiral Sir George Young was also consulted, and after many plans had been submitted and much time consumed, the Government decided to take action, and then left it to Lord Sydney, at this time Secretary of State for the Home Department, to carry out a modification of the various proposals which had been made.

That minister had to choose an officer to command the fleet of transports and govern the new territory, and little is known of the actual reasons for Phillip's selection. Presumably, however, he was appointed on his merits, as he appears to have had no private influence whatever with his superiors. On the 31st August 1786, Lord Sydney wrote to the Lords of the Admiralty a voluminous letter, dated from Whitehall, notifying them that His Majesty had been pleased to signify his royal commands that 750 convicts then under sentence of transportation and lying in the various gaols 'should be sent to Botany Bay, on the coast of New South Wales, in the latitude of 33° south, at which place it is intended that the said convicts should form a settlement.' Then followed an intimation that the Lords of the Treasury would provide means of conveyance, together with provisions and other supplies to keep these wretched outcasts of society alive, 'as well as tools to enable them to erect habitations, and also implements for agriculture.' A ship of war 'of a proper class'—how Phillip must have writhed when he learnt that it was the wretched *Sirius*—with a sufficient complement of officers and men, and another vessel of 200 tons as a tender, was to be ready simultaneously with the convict transports to act as convoy, and to prevent the prisoners overpowering the military guards on board the chartered vessels of the fleet. The letter is too long to be given here in detail, though the great results that attended this despatch of the 'First Fleet' lend it an importance that would not be accorded to a mandate of the Government ordering a fleet away on some warlike enterprise. The instructions to the Admiralty were explicit and complete, but Phillip was destined to gain to the full his bitter experience of red-tapeism before he sailed. The prisoners were to be put on board the various transports at sundry points in the Thames, whence Phillip was to convoy them to Plymouth, and at that port he was to pick up another ship with its load of felons. Further instructions were given that the fleet should, at the discretion of the officer commanding the expedition, call in at certain ports to provision and water the ships, the Cape of Good Hope being especially named as a place where fresh supplies could be obtained.

To secure due obedience and subordination from the convicts, and for the defence of the settlement against attacks by the natives, it was considered expedient to provide a small force of disciplined men, and '160 private marines, with a suitable number of officers and non-commissioned officers,' were to be so furnished. Solemn assurance was given that this force would be properly victualled after their landing—a promise which was not fulfilled—and another cheering intimation was given that such tools, implements and utensils as this body of men would have occasion for 'to render their situation comfortable . . . at the new intended settlement,' would be duly forthcoming. Then came the official chestnut—perhaps unintentional—for the marine cats to pluck, stating that the period of service, 'it is designed, shall not exceed a period of three years.'

With this letter was enclosed the 'Heads of a Plan' upon which the new settlement was to be formed, together with the proposed establishment for its regulation and government. It is unnecessary to reproduce this document in full, but some quotations from it may be given. The ships were to take on board as large a quantity of provisions as could be stowed—sufficient at any rate to last for two years. 'Supposing,' wrote Lord Sydney, 'one year to be issued at whole allowance, and the other year's provisions at half allowance, which will last two years longer.' The Government 'presumed' that by the end of that time the settlement, with the live stock and grain which might be raised by the common industry, would be able to maintain itself as far as food was concerned. The difference of expense, however, it was added, between this mode of disposing of the convicts of the country and that of the usual ineffectual one, was too trivial to be a consideration with His Majesty's Government, 'at least in comparison with the great object to be attained by it, especially now the evil' (the convict element) 'is increased to such an alarming degree, from the inadequacy of all other expedients that have hitherto been tried or suggested.'

The advantages likely to result to the new settlement from the cultivation of the New Zealand hemp or flax plant were then alluded to. The supply of hemp was of great consequence to Great Britain as a naval power—the production of hemp by felons has a certain suggestive humour—and already English manufacturers of rope and canvass believed that the New Zealand material made better canvass than that grown in Europe, and reported that a ten-inch cable of New Zealand hemp was superior in strength to one of eighteen inches made of the European plant. The Government had also no doubt but that 'most of the Asiatic productions'—none were specified—could be cultivated in the new colony, and that, in a few years after its foundation, recourse to European countries by England for such commodities would be unnecessary. The possibility of exploiting the vast kauri forests of New Zealand for masts and other ship-building purposes was next mentioned, such material being designed for the use of the navy in the Indian seas. The anticipations in regard to the cultivation of flax in the new colony, it may be stated, were never realised, but the export of timber from New Zealand soon became a great and profitable industry, and has so remained.

Lord Howe, First Lord of the Admiralty, duly replied to this letter, and in his reply said:—

'I cannot say the little knowledge I have of Captain Philips (*sic*) would have led me to select him for a service of this complicated nature. But as you are satisfied of his ability, and I conclude he will be taken under your direction, I presume it will not be unreasonable to move the King for having His Majesty's pleasure signified to the Admiralty for these purposes as soon as you see proper, that no time may be lost in making the requisite preparations for the voyage.'

This correspondence throws no light on the reasons for the appointment of Phillip. The position was one which it was scarcely likely many importunate friends of the Government would clamour for, and as the management of the colonisation scheme was practically left by Pitt and his Cabinet in the hands of their colleague, the Home Secretary, in the absence of evidence to the contrary, Lord Sydney should have the credit of having selected Phillip solely on his merits.

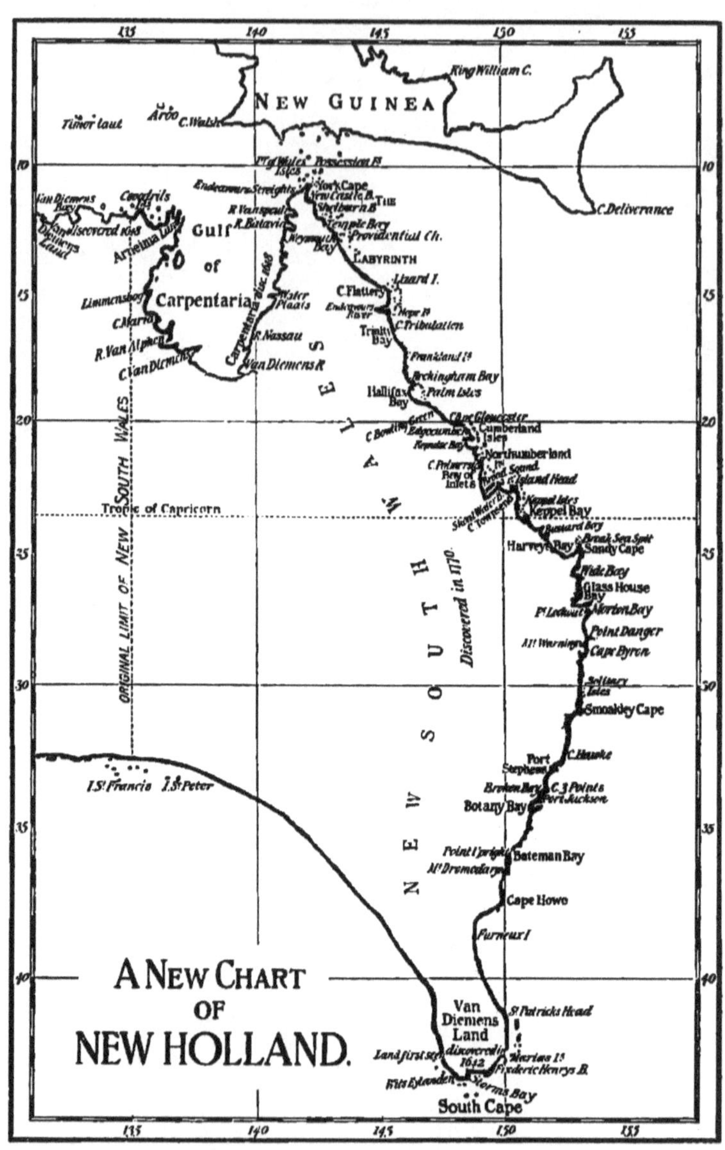

Map of the Eastern Half of Australia, shewing extent of Phillip's Government, 1787.

On the 12th October, the Lords of the Admiralty informed the Home Office that 'in obedience to His Majesty's commands, we immediately ordered the *Sirius*, one of His Majesty's ships of the sixth rate, with a proper vessel for a tender, to be fitted for this service ; and . . . the ship will be ready to receive men by the end of this month.'

On the same date Phillip received a short commission appointing him Governor of New South Wales, but this was afterwards replaced by a longer and more formal document.

This last commission, dated 2d April 1787, appointed Arthur Phillip, Esquire, 'to be our Captain-General and Governor-in-Chief in and over our territory called New South Wales, extending from the Northern Cape or extremity of the coast called Cape York, in the latitude of 10 degrees 37 minutes south, to the southern extremity of the said territory of New South Wales or South Cape, in the latitude of 43 degrees 39 minutes south, and of all the country inland westward as far as the 135th degree of east longitude, reckoning from the meridian of Greenwich, including all the islands adjacent in the Pacific Ocean, within the latitudes aforesaid, etc., etc.'

A reference to the map of Australia will show that the territory which Phillip was appointed to govern included about half the continent. It was not until ten years later that Van Diemen's Land (now Tasmania) was proved by Bass to be an island, and the 'South Cape' named in the commission, and still the name of the southernmost point of Tasmania, when Phillip's commission was drawn, was supposed to be part of the continent.

The commission, which gave Phillip all the usual powers, a short Act of Parliament, an Order in Council, the Letters Patent constituting the Courts of Law, and a Letter of Instructions, were all that the Governor had to guide him in conducting the enterprise to a successful issue.

The 'Instructions' order the Governor ' to fit himself with all convenient speed,' and land the 600 male and 180 female convicts, intended to form the new colony, as soon as possible at Botany Bay. Teneriffe, Rio de Janeiro, and the Cape of Good Hope are named as places where the ships were to refresh on their way out, and seed-grain and live stock were to be taken on board. The Governor is enjoined to be expeditious in getting the land into cultivation, to practise economy, to explore the coasts, to reserve ample land for further batches of convicts which were to follow, to protect the natives and endeavour to conciliate them, and to do many other things, which, when they are of interest, will be referred to hereafter. The concluding paragraph says :—

' And whereas it is our royal intention that every sort of intercourse between the intended settlement at Botany Bay, or other place which may be hereafter established on the coast of New South Wales

and its dependencies, and the settlements of our
East India Company, as well as the coast of China,
and the islands situated in that part of the world, to
which any intercourse has been established by any
European nation, should be prevented by every
possible means : It is our royal will and pleasure
that you do not on any account allow craft of any
sort to be built for the use of private individuals
which might enable them to effect such intercourse,
and that you do prevent any vessels which may at
any time hereafter arrive at the said settlement
from any of the ports before mentioned from having
communication with any of the inhabitants residing
within your Government, without first receiving
especial permission from you for that purpose.'

This was penned only one hundred and twelve
years ago. Now, besides the Orient, the Peninsular
and Oriental, and the many other steamship lines
running magnificent vessels to 'the settlement,'
there are two German companies, a French and a
Japanese company carrying on a regular service,
and 10,000 ton steamers are dry-docked and floated
again within twenty-four hours at a part of 'the
settlement' which, long after Phillip landed in it,
remained unpeopled.

CHAPTER III

PHILLIP was not long in getting to work, and his capacity for detail early began to show itself. A month after his appointment he is found writing letters to the Admiralty asking for small things essential to success, which only the man held directly responsible for results appears to have remembered.

Here for instance is his first letter, spelling and all (a practice which will generally be followed in future) as he wrote it :—

'[LONDON,] *Oct.* 31*st*, 1786.

'SIR,—The Right Honourable the Lords Com-missioners of the Admiralty having ordered His Majesty's ship *Sirius*, under my command, to be supply'd with six caronades and four six-pounders, I am to request that you will please to move their Lordships to order ten more of the six-pounders to be put on board, with the ironwork necessary for the cariages. Having the ironwork, the guns can at any time be mounted, and may, I presume, in future be of great use to us, on board or on shore, as the service may require,—I have, etc.,

'A. PHILLIP.'

This letter is of itself too trivial to be worth reprinting, but this formidable armament formed the colony's first fortress battery, and one of the guns still remains, a forgotten relic, mounted near the South Head Light (which is the best coast light in the world) at Sydney. By way of contrast to this, let us see how the authorities provided for things of importance. Lieutenant Philip Gidley King, second lieutenant of the *Sirius*, afterwards himself a Governor of New South Wales, kept a journal. This officer's grandson is now a member of the Legislative Council of New South Wales, and the hon. member has placed his grandfather's journal at the disposal of the public.

The *Sirius* was of 20 guns, 612 tons, and 160 men. She was commissioned on 24th October 1786, Phillip being appointed to the chief command as first captain, while John Hunter acted as second captain. The last officer was so appointed that he might command the ship when Phillip took up his shore duties. Says King :—

'The construction of a King's ship not being deemed proper for this service, the *Berwick* storeship was pitched on by the Admiralty, and her name changed to the *Sirius*, so called from the bright star in ye southern constellation of the Great Dog. She had been purchased on the stocks by the Government in 1781, and was sent once to America as a storeship during ye war, and once after the peace to ye W't Indies, since which time she had layn in ordinary at Deptford, till named for this service, when she was taken into dock, and, as the yard people said, thoroughly overhaul'd; however, we have frequently had reason to think otherwise in the course of our voyage. The *Supply*, armed tender of 170 tons, 8 guns, and 50 men, commanded by Lieutenant H. L. Ball, was formerly a navy transport; her size is much too small for so long a voyage, which, added to her not being able to carry any quantity of provisions, and her sailing very ill, renders her a very improper vessel for this service.' But, bad as were the sailing qualities of the *Supply*, she was a faster ship than the *Sirius*.

A constant stream of letters from Phillip to the Admiralty went on from October 1786 to the sailing of the fleet from Spithead in the following May. All these letters show that to Phillip alone is due the credit of properly preparing the expedition. The Government left everything to Lord Sydney, and he left the details of equipment entirely to Phillip, who did not pass on the responsibility to his subordinates. The circumlocution branch of the Admiralty must have been maddened by his persistence. For example, in December he writes a letter containing fourteen questions relating to what, to officialdom, no doubt appeared most trivial matters, but which the questioner's instinct told him it would be wise to have settled before he left England. The contractors, dockyard officials and others charged with the task of preparing the expedition seem to have neglected their duties, and their superiors to have exercised no supervision over them. Yet, owing to his wonderful foresight and his steady 'pegging away' at the officials, Phillip did succeed in getting many things that he wanted. Just before leaving England, he wrote a memorandum on the general conduct of the expedition and the treatment of the convicts. Some paragraphs of this document are worth printing, for they depict him in another character than that of an excellent man of business :—

'During the passage, when light airs or calms permit it, I shall visit the transports to see that they (the convicts) are kept clean and receive the allowance ordered by Government; and at these times I shall endeavour to make them sensible of their situation, and that their happiness or misery is in their own hands,—that those who behave well will be rewarded by being allow'd to work occasionally on the small lotts of land set apart for them, and which they will be put in possession of at the expiration of the time for which they are transported. . . .

'As I would not wish convicts to lay the foundations of an empire, I think they should ever remain separated from the garrison, and other settlers that may come from Europe, and not be allowed to mix with them, even after the 7 or 14 years for which they are transported may be expired.

'The laws of this country will, of course, be introduced in [New] South Wales, and there is one that I would wish to take place from the moment His Majesty's forces take possession of the country: That there can be no slavery in a free land, and consequently no slaves.'

In other letters he asked for specific instructions on important questions which his good sense warned him would demand an answer before long, but which do not seem to have occurred to the Home Government until he thought of them. He made a primary and most fortunate suggestion that the choice of a selection for the site of the new settlement should be left to his own judgment; that the terms by which lands were to be granted should be pointed out by the article which conferred on him the authority for granting such lands; that he should have the right to exile to New Zealand or any of the neighbouring islands any convict who might be condemned to death; that he should have the power of emancipation; and that he should be able to suspend and send home any officer who from his situation could not be tried by court-martial. He further asked that he should be authorised to despatch one of the ships of the fleet to

Charlotte Sound in New Zealand to procure flax-plants; and his, and indeed the Government's, lack of knowledge of the climatic conditions of the new territory is evinced by his request that he should also be allowed to send a ship to the Friendly Islands (the Tongan Archipelago) for the purpose of importing thence the bread-fruit plant. And the worthy people who do not consider the exigencies of empire-building and the laws of nature, will be shocked to learn that Phillip, a man of the most stringent morality, mentioned the fact that at the Friendly Islands 'women could be procured.' In the same letter he asked that the Secretary of State should empower him, in case the *Sirius* should return to England, to take command of any other ships that might remain on the coast, by hoisting a distinguishing pendant on such ships, so that he might retain the command at sea and be able to explore the coast. And to this request he adds that he has no desire to claim the pay of a commanding officer for hoisting such pendant. His forethought and humanity are shown by such demands as that he should 'have power to change the species of provisions served to the marines and convicts, for if salt meat is issued, without any proportion of flour, as has been hitherto done by the contractor to the marines embarked on board the *Alexander*, the scurvy must prove fatal to the greatest part. Of the marines already embarked two months, one in six are sent to the hospital since that ship's arrival at Spithead.'

The Government, as a matter of fact, was too busy with the impeachment of Warren Hastings to trouble itself with trifles of this kind—for the despatch of a fleet of convict transports, even though it was to colonise new territory, was regarded as a trifle at this time. No single page of history recorded it, even the *Annual Register* did not think it worth an entry.

To some of Phillip's wise and well-considered suggestions, the Government responded that upon the death or suspension of any civil officer he was at liberty to appoint any 'proper person' in his place until His Majesty's pleasure was known; that he could send a suspended officer to England by the first opportunity—with his reasons for such suspension; that the Government would not object to his choice for the site of the principal settlement, but he was to understand that he was not to be allowed to delay the disembarkation of the establishment upon his arrival on the coast upon the pretence of searching after a more eligible place than Botany Bay.

If Phillip felt insulted at this dictum he was too good a disciplinarian himself to show it. The Government's chief anxiety was to get rid of a batch of convicts—it was Phillip's desire to effect that riddance in a humane manner, to treat them as human beings, and to endeavour to make them reclaim themselves when they reached their destination.

In this same letter Lord Sydney told Phillip that Parliament would be moved to fix his salary as Governor at £1000 per annum nett, which, 'with the pay of the *Sirius*, is judged to be a proper allowance for the support of the stations you are appointed to fill.' The astounding generosity of the Government was further exemplified by allowing him a contingent charge of five shillings a day for the pay of a secretary, and the magnificent sum of £20 per annum for stationery. His request to be granted table money was curtly refused.

Two letters, written at the last moment, show how much was left undone when the fleet sailed. On the 12th of March Phillip wrote to Lord Sydney, telling him that the Navy Board had informed him that no alterations could be made as regarded the victualling of the Marines during the passage, despite his earnest entreaties. 'It is,' he wrote, 'to prevent my character as an officer from being called in question, should the consequences I fear be realized that I once more trouble your Lordship on this subject.' The contracts for the garrison and convicts, he remarked, were made without even his advice or opinion being asked, and he had repeatedly pointed out the serious consequences that might be looked for from so many men being crowded in such a small space for so long a period and from the wretched scale of victuals. Flour, which was always allowed marines in the navy, was refused him. 'This,' he pleaded, 'must be fatal to many, and the more so as no anti-scorbutics are allowed on board the transports for either marine or convict; in fact, my Lord, the garrison and convicts are sent to the extremity of the globe as they would be sent to America—a six weeks' passage.' Then in dignified words he went on to say that he could foresee the critical situation he might be in after losing part of the garrison, which even then he considered to be very weak for the arduous service it was to undergo; but he was prepared, he said, to meet difficulties, and had but one fear—that it might be said some day that he should have known that it was more than probable that he would lose half the garrison and convicts, crowded as they were, and so badly victualled for such a long and trying voyage. 'And,' he concluded, 'the public, believing it rested with me, may impute to my ignorance or inattention what I have never been consulted in, and which never coincided with my ideas, to avoid which is the purport of this letter; and I flatter myself your Lordship will hereafter point out the situation in which I have stood thro' the whole of this business should it ever be necessary.'

In the second letter he begs for more 'cloaths' for the unfortunate convicts; and that as more prisoners were to be sent on board the different ships the Government would give orders that before leaving the gaols or hulks they should be 'washed and cloathed.'

Then he alludes in indignant terms to the condition of the unfortunate female convicts on board the transport *Lady Penrhyn*. 'The situation in which the magistrates sent the women on board . . . stamps them with infamy—almost naked and so very filthy that nothing but clothing them could have prevented them from perishing.' The clothing for these women he provided himself from the stores on the *Sirius*, and asked that the Navy Board would replace it, for their deplorable state filled him with horror and indignation. As it was, a fever had already broken out among them. Many of them were suffering from special complaints which, he wrote, 'must spread in spite of every precaution I may take hereafter, and will be fatal to themselves. There is a necessity for doing something for the young man who is on board that ship as surgeon, or I fear that we shall lose him, and then a hundred women will be left without any assistance, several of them with child. Let me repeat my desire that orders immediately may be given to increase the convict allowance of bread; 16 lb. of bread for 42 days is very little. . . .

'This is a long letter, but it is my duty to repeat complaints that may be redressed, and which I am certain you desire equally with myself.'

It was the same old story, better remembered in connection with a greater man—Wellington fighting his campaigns in spite of the Government, and without the assistance which he legitimately required.

On the 7th May, the senior officer joined the First Fleet at Portsmouth. The ships were lying off the Motherbank, a spot where little more than a hundred years later, on the 26th June 1897, the naval might of the greatest Empire the world has ever known was displayed in five lines of modern warships which, anchored closely together as they were, covered a distance of five-and-twenty miles! Within a stone's throw of Phillip's little fleet lay the weed-covered timbers of the *Royal George*; from the same spot, twenty years after Phillip left for Australia, Nelson sailed on his last fateful but glorious voyage in the *Victory*. The *Victory* remains afloat in Portsmouth harbour, a speaking memento of Nelson's career; and the British community of the Australasian colonies is a great and living tribute to the work of the obscure naval officer who laid the foundations of a new Empire beyond the seas.

Contrary winds and other obstacles kept the fleet at its anchorage for another five days. One cause of the delay, and how Phillip removed it, is thus described by Collins :—

'The sailors on the transports refused to proceed to sea unless they should be paid their wages up to the time of their departure, alleging as a ground for their refusal that they were in want of many articles necessary for so long a voyage. The custom of their employ, however, being against a demand which yet appeared reasonable, Captain Phillip directed the different masters to put such of their people as refused to proceed with them to sea on board the *Hyæna* frigate, and to receive an equal number of her seamen, who should afterwards be re-exchanged at sea, her captain being directed to accompany the fleet to a certain distance.'

Here is a list of the expedition—according to one of its officers—as it sailed from Spithead :—

The *Sirius* and the *Supply*, King's ships (already described), and the following transports :—*Alexander*, 452 tons, 30 seamen, 35 marines, 194 convicts; *Lady Penrhyn*, 333 tons, 30 seamen, 3 officers of marines, 101 females; *Charlotte*, 335 tons, 30 seamen, 42 marines, 86 male and 20 female convicts; *Scarborough*, 430 tons, 30 seamen, 44 marines, 205 male convicts; *Friendship*, 274 tons, 25 seamen, 46 marines, 76 male and 21 female convicts; *Prince of Wales*, 350 tons, — seamen, 29 marines, 2 male and 47 female convicts; *Fishburn*, victualler and agent's ship, 378 tons, 22 men; *Golden Grove*, victualler and agent's ship, 335 tons, 22 men; and the *Borrowdale*, victualler and agent's ship, 275 tons, 22 men.

In a last letter, dated from the *Sirius*, on the Motherbank, 11th May 1787, and addressed to the Under-Secretary for the Home Department, Phillip says good-bye in words which show that he had a good heart for the future :—

'Once more I take my leave of you, fully sensible

of the trouble you have had in this business, for which at present I can only thank you ; but at a future period, when this country feels the advantages that are to be drawn from our intended settlement, you will enjoy a satisfaction that will, I am sure, make you ample amends.'

On the 12th of May the fleet passed the Needles and began its long voyage.

CHAPTER IV

THE saloon passenger on a sixteen-knot Orient or P. and O. liner, during the six weeks of *ennui* enforced by a passage from London to Sydney, can sometimes, if he tries very hard, find something to growl about ; the bedroom steward may bring his morning coffee a moment or two late, and so forth ; but such trifles are not great hardships compared with those which attended the method of carrying emigrants followed in the 'favourite clippers' that brought out the bulk of Australian settlers before trade unionism and 'one-man-one-vote' politics put a stop to emigration. Everyone has read stories of how emigrants were accommodated. The foul-smelling, unpainted, deal-boarded part of the ship's hold where passengers were stowed, bred a just discontent among the half-starved exiles, and the captain of an emigrant ship was kept pretty well occupied in allaying the irritation of his passengers, who were generally of a class not to bear their woes silently.

Between a convict transport and an emigrant ship, the difference in accommodation was little enough— notwithstanding the nonsense that has been written about the horrors of all Australian convict transports. The true reason of the dreadfulness of some of these voyages lay in the fact that the 'tween decks of a convict transport generally carried, necessarily crowded together, for a long spell of idleness, a hundred or more of the worst class of criminals, often as physically diseased as they were unhealthily minded.

Upon Phillip lay the task of conducting, in a fleet of transports on a six months' voyage to a country practically unknown, about a thousand passengers, of whom more than seven hundred were probably in every respect the worst that could have been selected in the gaols of England. Many of them were desperate wretches whose presence on board the ships was a more constant and greater menace to their safety than all the dangers known and unknown of the sea. The conduct of this voyage is, therefore, no unimportant test of the senior officer's fitness to command, and it naturally forms a chapter in his life.

Phillip had under him intelligent and loyal subordinates, and from nearly all of them he received valuable aid from the beginning. But here again all was not plain sailing. Major Ross, the commandant of marines and Lieutenant-Governor, stands out as the one malcontent on the Governor's staff, and from the time of his appointment until his return to England, Ross generally hampered and never assisted Phillip. Hunter, the captain of the *Sirius*, King, the second lieutenant, Collins, lieutenant of marines, doing duty as Judge Advocate, are the three men whose names will be longest remembered in the history of the expedition. The two first afterwards became in turn Governors of New South Wales, while Collins subsequently served as Lieutenant-Governor of Van Diemen's Land. Hunter and Collins both published accounts of the settlement, and these works, with others by their brother officers,—Tench (of the marines), and White (the principal surgeon),—and the journals of King are to-day the storehouses from which Australian historians draw most of their materials. Phillip, during his command, was on good terms with all these men—but King was his especial friend.

The fleet arrived at Santa Cruz, Teneriffe, on the 3d of June 1787. Since its sailing on 13th May, the surgeon's report showed that 8 persons had died, 81 were on the sick list, and 1015 were the total number on the victualling list of the fleet.

The voyage so far had been without notable incident. Some of the prisoners on the *Scarborough* formed a plot to take the ship. Two of the ringleaders were taken on board the flagship and given each two dozen lashes by the boatswain's mate, and were then placed on board another transport.

· This punishment of two dozen lashes is worth the reader's attention, as we shall, later on, refer to a charge made by one of the historians of the First Fleet that Phillip's punishments were 'not frequent, but prompt and terrible.' Says Collins, referring to the cause of this mutiny : 'Captain Phillip had very humanely, a few days previous to this scheme, directed that the irons with which most of the male convicts had hitherto been confined should be taken off them generally, that they might have it more in their power to strip their clothes off at night when they went to rest, be also more at their ease during the day, and have the further advantage of being able to wash and keep themselves clean. This indulgence had left it more in the power of those who might be so disposed to exert their ingenuity in so daring an attempt.'

Before the fleet sailed, Major Ross had taken care that his men's comfort should not be entirely over-looked. The Government had omitted to supply wine or spirit rations for use after arrival in the colony to the detachment. Phillip interested himself in the matter, and worried the authorities into complying with its urgent request for a 'moderate distribution of the above-ment'd article.' The Major did not similarly report the lack of a much more important part of the equipment of the force ; for Phillip, writing to Lord Sydney from Teneriffe, complains that the marines have next to no ammunition ! Yet he does not blame Ross, who was really responsible. ' I understood,' he wrote, 'that they would be furnished with ammunition, but, since we sailed, find that they were only supplied with what was necessary for immediate service while in port ; and we have neither musquet balls nor paper for musquet cartridges ; nor have we any armourer's tools.' He begs his lordship to send out supplies of ammunition by the first ship, and also some women's clothing which was left behind and for want of which 'we shall be much distressed.' In another letter from the same place he says :—

'In general the convicts have behaved well. I saw them all yesterday for the first time' (since leaving England). 'They are quiet and contented, tho' there are amongst them some compleat villains.'

And no musket balls ! Some months to be passed yet at sea, the new country peopled by strange blacks ; the new colonists, for the greater part, more to be guarded against than these savages, and the garrison of 200 marines without cartridges ! Well was it for the safety of the expedition that the convicts did not know of Ross's carelessness.

One incident happened at Santa Cruz, tragical enough, of the kind some of us remember at the old Surrey Theatre. A convict escaped and got into a boat lying astern of one of the transports. His flight was soon discovered ; and then began a man hunt which lasted a whole day. By-and-by the fugitive was found lying at the foot of a rock on the west shore of the bay. From the ship's side he had been seen trying to climb the steep rocks, and at every attempt falling back exhausted, bruised and bleeding.

A boat, with armed searchers, rowed towards the spot. The convict made desperate attempts to get out of his pursuers' reach, and the people on the ships watched the scene as from the 'front of the house'— a gallery audience. The poor wretch was taken at the muzzle of a levelled musket. A flogging and heavy leg irons was all he got out of his dash for liberty.

Here is a story of another kind. The seamen of one of the transports clubbed together and handed their metal spoons to a 'coiner' among the prisoners. The fellow turned the spoons into good imitations of the silver dollars of the Brazils, and the sailors tried to pass the counterfeit money. At the first attempt the fraud was detected, and the sailors, to save themselves, confessed. Their grog was stopped, and the coiner was flogged.

The fleet stayed a week at Teneriffe exchanging courtesies with the Governor of the island, and receiving on board fresh provisions and water. On the 5th of August the ships reached Rio de Janeiro, where Phillip took in a great quantity of stores, including 10,000 musket balls.

From Rio he wrote several letters to Lord Sydney

and Nepean, and in them gave a detailed account of his progress thus far. The English captain's former service under the Portuguese Government obtained for him from the Viceroy many civilities, and the generous reception of the fleet at the Brazils was very different to its treatment at the hands of the Dutch Governor at the Cape of Good Hope, the next port of call.

During the stay of the ships at Rio, Phillip caused an observatory to be established on shore, and a party of navigating officers were landed to make observations, test the rate of the timepieces and so forth, while the ships were cleaned inside with disinfectants, and the convicts minutely inspected. Fresh meat, vegetables and oranges were freely given to them as precautions against scurvy, and Phillip himself went among them, threatening severe punishment to the unruly, and speaking a few words of encouragement to those who evinced any signs of a disposition to redeem their characters.

Just before the *Sirius* sailed, a Portuguese soldier stowed away. The man was discovered and brought before Phillip. He said that having been absent from his duty some time he feared to return, and begged to be received on board and carried to New Holland. 'Put him in one of our boats and take him ashore,' was Phillip's curt order.

The man, as the sailors led him towards the gangway, turned pale and trembled at the prospective punishment.

'And,' added Phillip, 'land him at some spot where he can get back to barracks without his absence being discovered.'

A similar instance occurred at the Cape, when a Dutch soldier tried to get a passage on one of the transports, and Phillip returned him to his regiment, first obtaining a promise of pardon from the authorities.

Soon after the vessels cleared Rio, they met with their first bad weather, and the five weeks and four days which they occupied in reaching the Cape were on this account very trying to the closely confined prisoners. But the care taken to observe cleanliness, and the stock of wholesome food procured from Rio, preserved them in good health, and the sick list was a small one.

A letter to Nepean from Phillip, written while at Rio, and dated 2d September 1787, shows that he kept his eyes open to other matters besides the one he had in hand :—

'This is my last letter, as I hope to sail to-morrow. You know how much I was interested in the intended expedition against Monte Vedio, and that it was said that the Spaniards had more troops than I supposed. The following account I have from a person who was there (through) all the war, and I am certain that the account is exact: One Regiment under 700 ; Four Companys of Artillery, 400 ; Dragoons, 400 ; Two Battalions of Infantry, 700. These were divided on the north and south shores, and in different towns.

Monte Vedio would not have been defended, as half these troops could not have been drawn together. Of this you will be so good as to inform the Lords Sydney and Landsdown ; it will corroborate what I mentioned before I left town. The 21st being the Prince of Portugal's birthday, and the Vice-King receiving the compliments of all the officers, I waited on him with those I had presented to him on our arrival. The *Sirius* fired 21 guns, having the flag of Portugal hoisted at the fore-topmast-head, and the Union at the mizen. He seemed much pleased with this compliment, and we part perfectly satisfied with each other.'

One of Phillip's despatches from Rio contains these words :—

' One hundred and fifteen pipes of rum has been purchased for the use of the garrison, when landed, and for the use of the detachment at this port.'

This purchase was to be the cause of much trouble in the future. To this day some of the oldest inhabitants of the colony will tell you that they can recall the time when an acre of land could be bought for a bottle of rum. Such transactions were common enough early in the century, and one of the principal and oldest buildings in Sydney is still remembered as portion of the old Rum Hospital, a title it earned as a store in the days of the Rum currency.

The fleet arrived at the Cape on the 13th of October 1787, and sailed from Table Bay on the

12th of the following month. During the time, in spite of a very cool reception from the Dutch Governor, Phillip secured plenty of fresh provisions and a great quantity of plants, seeds and live stock, but on account of the heavy charges and the want of room to stow them, the amount purchased was very much less than it should have been. What Australians now rightly speak of as 'our great pastoral industry' was started with fewer than fifty sheep, half a dozen cows, a couple of bulls, six horses, and some pigs and goats. It is perhaps superfluous to state that many Australian sheep-breeders of to-day could not off-hand tell you within a thousand or two how many sheep they own.

The enthusiastic projectors of the new colony had great faith in its future as a rival to the Spice Islands, and Phillip, obedient to instructions, did not forget to take on board at Rio all sorts of seeds and plants with this end in view, but the selection turned out unsuitable to the new country, and what was embarked at the Cape proved to be much more useful, probably because Phillip was aided in his choice by a botanist —Mason—who was residing there.

The fleet left Table Bay, as already stated, on the 12th of November, and on the 25th of the same month Phillip decided to go on board the *Supply*, which sailed better than the *Sirius*, with the view of reaching Botany Bay first and making some preparations for the landing of the colonists. The *Alexander*,

Scarborough and *Friendship* accompanied the *Supply*, and the fleet, thus divided into two squadrons, continued the voyage without noteworthy incident until their arrival within a couple of days of each other at Botany Bay.

'Thus,' writes Collins, the Judge-Advocate, 'under the blessing of God was happily completed in eight months and one week, a voyage which before it was undertaken the mind hardly dared venture to contemplate, and on which it was impossible to reflect without some apprehensions as to its termination. . . . We had sailed five thousand and twenty-one leagues . . . without meeting any accident, in a fleet of eleven sail, nine of which were merchantmen that had never before sailed in that distant and imperfectly explored ocean. . . . Only thirty-two persons had died since leaving England, among whom were to be included one or two deaths by accident; although previous to our departure it was generally conjectured that before we should have been a month at sea one of the transports would have been converted into a hospital ship. But it fortunately happened otherwise. The high health which was apparent in every countenance' (when Botany Bay was reached) 'was to be attributed not only to the refreshments we met with at Rio de Janeiro and the Cape of Good Hope, but to the excellent quality of the provisions with which we were supplied by Mr Richards, junior, the contractor; and the spirits visible in every eye was to be ascribed to the general joy and satisfaction which immediately took place on finding ourselves arrived at that port which had been so much and so long the subject of our most serious reflections, the constant theme of our conversations.'

In similar language Tench and White describe the satisfactory termination of the voyage.

If there are now living any descendants of 'Mr Richards, junior, the contractor,' let them treasure this certificate to the honesty of their ancestor, for his was a virtue rare among the contractors of his day.

A youngster named Southwell, a master's mate on the *Sirius*, from whose letters much of interest can be extracted, has a word of praise for Phillip's care of the people in his charge.   He says :—

'The Commodore's conduct has endeared him to most of them, and, indeed, I believe few could have been found better calculated for the occasion than our commander. He is a man who has seen much of the Service and much of the world, and has studied it. He is possessed of great good sense, well informed, indefatigable upon service, is humane and at the same time spirited and resolute ; for of his courage, fame allows him to have given honorable proofs on former occasions.'

And again :—

'The Governor is certainly one of a thousand, and is very considerate in everything, and extraordinary

clever in every contrivance and method to render the
ships healthy and airy.'

This same Southwell afterwards quarrelled with
Phillip, and what he has to say against the Governor
will be duly recorded ; meanwhile let Phillip have the
full benefit of his favourable testimony :—

'I have to add that on coming on board, after so long
a cessation from duty, I thought it would look better
not to sue for any indulgence in that respect, and,
indeed, was so much mended that there was no very
great merit to me on that acc't. Accordingly, I kept
the deck, and acted in my station, but for very few
hours, for we had hardly got the anchors up before the
Governor told me by no means to keep watch or to
expose myself to the weather till I found myself fully
recovered in health and strength, for he cou'd perceive
I was much reduced and very different from when he
saw me in town. This was very kind and considerate,
and I made my best acknowledgements ; and as I really
thought a few nights' recess would ensure the matter
and compleate my health, I told him I would make
use of the indulgence for a few nights, but he most
obligingly told me to lay by both day and night till I
felt myself perfectly well, and that I need only come
on deck when I thought I might derive advantage
from air and exercise. He frequently asks me how I
do, and has desired me to want for nothing that he has
on board, and to send to his steward for it without ceremony, for that anything he has is quite at my service,

and he shou'd be happy it would do me good. I am
the more particular on this head, as I know it will be
of a pleasing savour to your affectionate solicitude for
my welfare—indeed, he is very kind to all, and we
are very happy in our worthy commander.'

That the modern voyager may the better understand
why Collins rejoices at the successful conduct of this
sea journey, here is an extract from a letter from
Port Jackson on the voyage of the Second Fleet of
transports :—

'Oh ! if you had but seen the shocking sight of
the poor creatures that came out in the three ships
it would make your heart bleed. They were almost
dead. Very few could stand, and they were obliged
to sling them like goods and hoist them out of the
ships, they were so feeble, and they died ten or twelve
a day when first landed. There died in three ships
alone on the way out 347 men and women. They
were not so long as we' (the First Fleet) 'were coming
here, but they were confined, and had bad victuals
and stinking water. Governor Phillip was very angry,
and scolded the captains a great deal, and, I heard,
intended to write to London about it, for I heard him
say it was murdering them.'

Eleven sail of ships in the First Fleet, 700 convicts,
many of whom embarked ill, but only 32 deaths.
What a terrible contrast was afforded by the Second
Fleet !

CHAPTER V

FOR Phillip the sea-captain, the anxieties of a long voyage under unusual and trying circumstances were ended, and his weather-beaten ships safely anchored; for Phillip the Governor (not in its present quasi-ornamental interpretation, but what is signified by the word's real meaning), the work was now to begin. 'The commander over men; he to whose will our wills are to be subordinate and loyally surrender themselves, and find their welfare in doing so, may be reckoned the most important of Great Men.'

If Phillip, in his small way, so governed that his subjects *did* loyally surrender themselves, and found their welfare in so doing, then he may take rank with the 'most important of Great Men.' But as yet he

had other things to consider than methods of governing—chief among them the site of the settlement—
for Botany Bay, he found, would not do. The very
appearance of the country must have been disheartening, for Botany Bay is about as unlovely a
spot as can be imagined; and indeed the whole coast
line of New South Wales, even at that season of
the year — the middle of summer — presented a
monotonously repellent and forbidding aspect to
people whose eyes were used to the soft beauties
of the scenery of their native land.

Phillip went expeditiously to work. There was no
shifting of responsibilities upon the authorities; no
waiting for instructions from the Home Office. He
had to decide at once, at the very beginning of the
business, where, after his eight months' voyage, he
should land his thousand subjects. And no doubt
he congratulated himself that he had taken care
before he left England to have liberty to change
the intended site of the settlement.

His first despatch, dated Sydney Cove, 15th May
1788, tells Lord Sydney his reasons for making the
change. Almost as soon as the *Supply* had anchored,
he began to examine Botany Bay, which, though an
extensive expanse of water, afforded no shelter from
easterly winds—the 'disaster' wind of the eastern
Australian seaboard. Then, too, the water was
shallow, for the most part, except near the entrance,
and his seaman's eye was quick to note that ships

would be exposed to a heavy sea when easterly weather set in. Creeks of fresh water were plentiful (until quite recently the greater part of the water supply of Sydney was derived from the Botany Bay swamps), but the lowlands were spongy and swampy, and Phillip did not see 'any situation to which there was not some very strong objection,' though there were spots whereon a small number of people might have been settled. Yet even the most eligible situation, he considered, would be unhealthy by reason of the swamps, and he decided to examine Port Jackson, fifteen miles to the northward. But so that no time should be lost, in case his search for a better harbour and site for a settlement should prove fruitless, he at once gave orders for a certain area of ground 'near Point Sutherland, to be cleared, and preparations made for landing under the direction of the Lieutenant-Governor.'

The story of his discovery of the site of the future settlement may well be left to himself:—'I went round' (from Botany Bay) 'with three boats, taking with me Captain Hunter and several officers, that by examining different parts of the port at the same time less time might be lost. We got into Port Jackson early in the afternoon, and had the satisfaction of finding the finest harbour in the world, in which a thousand sail of the line may ride in the most perfect security, and of which a rough survey, made by Captain Hunter and the officers of the *Sirius* after the ships came round, may give your Lordship some idea. The different coves were examined with all possible expedition. I fixed on the one that had the best spring of water, and in which the ships can anchor so close to the shore that at a very small expence quays may be made at which the largest ships may unload. This cove, which I honoured with the name of Sydney, is about a quarter of a mile across at the entrance, and half a mile in length.'

Three days later he returned to Botany Bay, and immediately made preparations to leave. Ordering Hunter to follow him with the transports, he sailed in the *Supply* for Port Jackson on 25th January—seven days after he had first anchored in Botany Bay—and on the following evening all the transports were safely moored in Sydney Cove.

Whilst the ships were lying at Botany Bay, the *Boussole* and the *Astrolabe*, two French exploring ships commanded by the ill-fated La Pérouse, appeared and dropped anchor. Learning that La Pérouse was anxious to send letters to Europe by the returning transports, Phillip sent an officer over to him to receive the despatches. This meeting with La Pérouse was the last occasion on which the Frenchmen were seen, and the despatches sent by the French Admiral through the English exiles contained the last news the French received of their exploring expedition until forty years later, when the relics of the unfortunate ships were discovered on the island of Vanikoro.

The task of clearing the ground and erecting store-houses was begun as soon as the ships arrived in Port Jackson—'a labour of which it will be hardly possible,' says Phillip, 'to give your Lordship a just idea.' Then troubles came thick and fast; yet he does not dilate upon the worry and incessant strain he must have undergone from the day he landed his people to the date of his letter to Lord Sydney, a period of sixteen weeks. Here is a long extract :—'The people were healthy when landed, but the scurvy has, for some time, appeared amongst them, and now rages in a most extraordinary manner. Only sixteen carpenters could be hired from the ships, and several of the convict carpenters were sick. It was now the middle of February; the rains began to fall very heavy, and pointed out the necessity of hutting the people; con-victs were therefore appointed to assist the detachment in this work.

'February the 14th the *Supply* sailed for Norfolk Island, with Philip Gidley King, second lieutenant of His Majesty's ship *Sirius*, for the purpose of settling that island. He only carried with him a petty officer surgeon's mate, two marines, two men who understood the cultivation of flax, with nine men and six women convicts. . . . I beg leave to recommend him as an officer of merit, and whose perseverance in that or any other service may be depended upon. . . .

'Your Lordship will not be surprized that I have been under the necessity of assembling a Criminal Court. Six men were condemned to death. One, who was the head of the gang, was executed the same day; the others I reprieved. They are to be exiled from the settlement, and when the season permits I intend they shall be landed near the South Cape, where, by their forming connexions with the natives, some benefit may accrue to the public. These men had frequently robbed the stores and the other convicts. The one who suffered and two others were condemned for robbing the stores of provisions the very day they received a week's provisions, and at which time their allowance . . . was the same as the soldiers, spirits excepted; the others for robbing a tent, and for stealing provisions from other convicts.

'The great labour in clearing the ground will not permit more than eight acres to be sown this year with wheat and barley. At the same time the immense number of ants and field-mice will render our crops very uncertain. Part of the live stock brought from the Cape, small as it was, has been lost, and our resource in fish is also uncertain. Some days great quantities are caught, but never sufficient to save any part of the provisions; and at times fish are scarce.'

'The very small proportion of females makes the sending out an additional number absolutely necessary, for I am certain your Lordship will think that to send for women from the Islands, in our present situation, would answer no other purpose than that of bringing them to pine away in misery.

'Your Lordship will, I hope, excuse the confused manner in which I have in this letter given an account of what has past since I left the Cape of Good Hope. It has been written at different times, and my situation at present does not permit me to begin so long a letter again, the canvas house I am under being neither wind nor water proof.'

In reading these extracts, it should be remembered that all previous knowledge of Port Jackson is summed up in these words from Cook's *Voyages*: 'At this time (noon, 6th May 1770) we were between two and three miles distant from the land and abreast of a bay or harbour in which there appeared to be a good anchorage, and which I called Port Jackson.'

Phillip was not the man to waste words in his despatches, and so he says nothing of the interesting ceremony at the inauguration of the settlement. On this subject latter-day historians have not been so reticent, and one writer in a book published thirty-five years ago put an up-to-date speech into the mouth of the Governor, in which, among other things equally remarkable, he is made to discourse of the country's 'fertile plains, tempting only the slightest labours of the husbandman to produce in abundance the fairest and richest fruits ; its interminable pastures, the future home of flocks and herds innumerable ; its mineral wealth, already known to be so great as to promise that it may yet rival those treasures which fiction loves to describe. Enough for any nation, I say, would it be to enjoy those honours and those advantages, but others, not less advantageous, but perhaps more honourable, await the people of the state of which we are the founders.'

Collins, Tench, White, and the author of the semi-official publication, *Phillip's Voyage*, all supply full accounts of the ceremony, and young Southwell gives in one of his letters what appears to be a *verbatim* report of Phillip's speech :—

'On the 26th of January' (still observed as a public holiday in the colony), 'the day after the arrival of the ships from Botany Bay, the Union Jack was hoisted at the head of Sydney Cove, the marines saluted and fired three volleys, and the Governor, the centre of a little group of officers, proposed the toasts of "The King and the royal family," and "Success to the new colony."'

On the 7th February, everyone belonging to the settlement having been landed from the ships, the colonists to the number of 1030 were all assembled, the convicts seated in a half circle, the marines paraded in front of them, and the officers in a group in the centre. Then Collins, the Judge-Advocate, read the Governor's commission, the other officers' commissions, the Act establishing the colony and the rest of the formal documents, the marines fired three volleys, and silence was commanded.

Phillip stepped forward, and in a hearty, simple manner thanked the marines for their good conduct, and then turning towards the convicts, according to Southwell, he thus addressed them :—

'You have now been particularly informed of the nature of the laws by which you are to be governed, and also of the power with which I am invested to put them into full execution. There are amongst you, I am willing to believe, some who are not perfectly abandoned, and who, I hope and trust, will make the intended use of the great indulgence and lenity their humane country has offered ; but at the same time there are many, I am sorry to add, by far the greater part, who are innate villains and people of the most abandoned principles. To punish these shall be my constant care, and in this duty I ever will be indefatigable, however distressing it may be to my feelings. Not to do so would be a piece of the most cruel injustice to those who, as being the most worthy, I have first named ; for should I continue to pass by your enormity with an ill-judged and ill-bestowed lenity, the consequence would be, to preserve the peace and safety of the settlement, some of the more deserving of you must suffer with the rest, who might otherways have shown themselves orderly and useful members of our community. Therefore you have my sacred word of honour that whenever you commit a fault you shall be punished, and most severely. Lenity has been tried ; to give it further trial would be vain.   I am no stranger to the use you make of every indulgence.   I speak of what comes under my particular observation ; and again I add that a vigorous exercise of the law (whatever it may cost my feelings) shall follow closely upon the heels of every offender.'

After some other words tending to this effect, they had liberty to disperse, and the Governor then passed up and down through the ranks of the marines upon parade, and having been saluted by them with due honours, went, together with the principal officers, to partake of a cold repast that had been previously prepared in a marquee.   During the whole ceremony, at intervals, the band played, and 'God Save the King' was performed after the commissions were read.

According to *Phillip's Voyage*, the Governor concluded his speech by particularly noticing 'the illegal intercourse between the sexes as an offence which encouraged a general profligacy of manners and was in several ways injurious to society.'   To prevent this, he strongly recommended marriage, and promised 'every kind of countenance and assistance to those who by entering [1] into that state should manifest their willingness to conform to the laws of morality and religion.'   He formally declared 'his earnest desire to promote the happiness of all who were under his

---

[1] Collins reports that before the end of the month several couples were 'announced for marriage.'

government, and to render the settlement in New South Wales advantageous and honourable to his country.'

It is clear that Phillip had ample reason to complain of the conduct of the prisoners.

'Many of them,' says Collins, 'tried to desert to the French ships' (the *Boussole* and *Astrolabe*) 'before they left Botany Bay, and it was soon found that they secreted at least one-third of their working tools, and that any sort of labour was with difficulty procured from them. The want of proper overseers principally contributed to this. . . . Petty thefts among themselves began soon to be complained of. The sailors from the transports brought spirits on shore at night, though often punished for so doing, and drunkenness was the consequence.'

The first despatch of the Governor has already given some idea of the progress of the settlers for the first few weeks after they landed. Before that letter left for England in one of the returning transports, it was becoming apparent to Phillip that the colony would not be self-supporting for a long while to come.

Phillip kept a regular journal, sending a copy of it, brought up to date, by each transport as the ship left for England by way of China. In July he despatched a very long letter to Lord Sydney, and these extracts from it will be of interest :—

'Thus situated, your Lordship will excuse my

observing a second time that a regular supply of provisions from England will be absolutely necessary for four or five years, as the crops for two years to come cannot be depended on for more than what will be necessary for seed. . . . I should hope that few convicts will be sent out this year or the next, unless they are artificers, and . . . I make no doubt but proper people will be sent to superintend them. The ships that bring out convicts should have at least the two years' provisions on board to land with them, for the putting the convicts on board some ships and the provisions that were to support them in others, as was done . . . much against my inclination, must have been fatal if the ship carrying the provisions had been lost.

'I have the honour to enclose your Lordship the intended plan for the town.[1]   The Lieutenant-Governor has already begun a small house, which forms one corner of the parade, and I am building a small cottage on the east side of the cove, where I shall remain for the present with part of the convicts and an officer's guard.   The convicts on both sides are distributed in huts, which are built only for immediate shelter.   On the point of land which forms the west side of the cove an Observatory is building, under the direction of Lieutenant Dawes,

---

[1] This plan was altered by Phillip's successors, and in consequence, instead of being wide open thoroughfares, the streets of Sydney are as narrow as those of London.

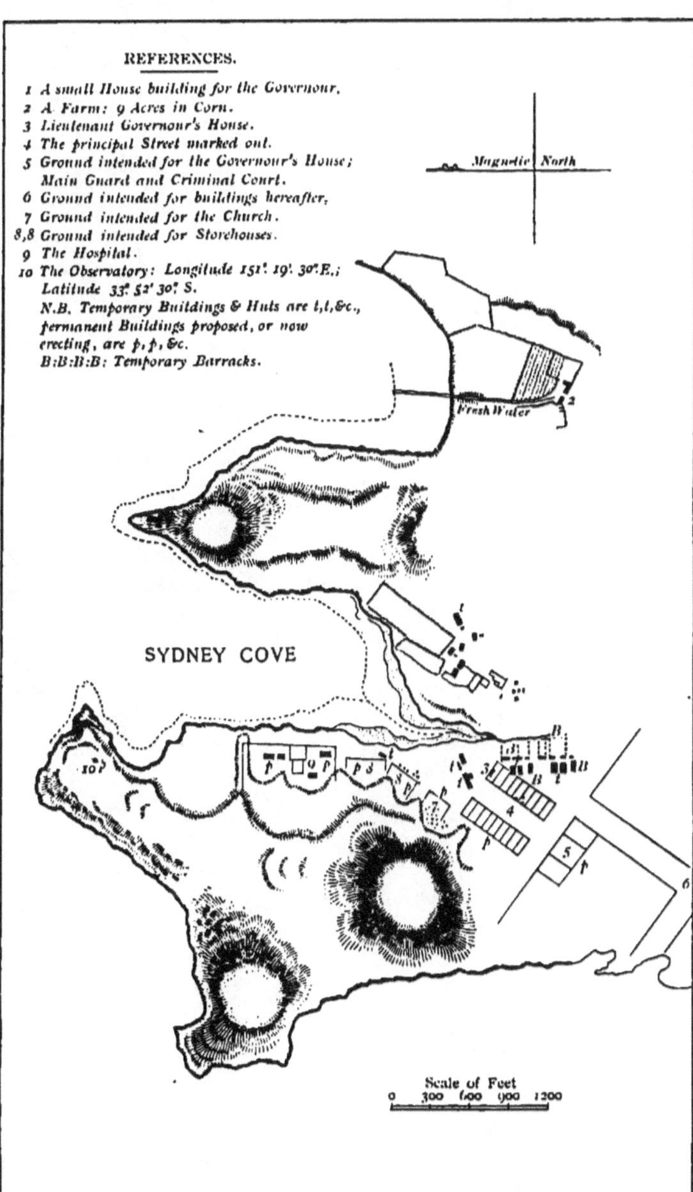

Sketch of Sydney Cove, Port Jackson, 1788.

who is charged by the Board of Longitude with observing the expected comet. The temporary buildings are marked in black ; those intended to remain, in red. We now make very good bricks, and the stone is good, but do not find either lime-stone or chalk. . . . The principal streets are placed so as to admit a free circulation of air, and are two hundred feet wide. . . .' Then follows a detailed account of the progress made so far in building operations generally.

'Of the convicts,' he writes, ' 36 men and 4 women died on the passage, 20 men and 8 women since land-ing—11 men and 1 woman absconded ; 4 have been executed, and 3 killed by the natives. The number of convicts now employed in erecting the necessary buildings and cultivating the lands only amounts to 320—and the whole number of people victualled amounts to 966—consequently we have only the labour of a part to provide for the whole. . . .

'I could have wished to have given your Lordship a more pleasing account of our present situation ; and am persuaded I shall have that satisfaction hereafter ; nor do I doubt but that this country will prove the most valuable acquisition Great Britain ever made ; at the same time no country offers less assistance to the first settlers than this does ; nor do I think any country could be more disadvantageously placed with respect to support from the mother country, on which for a few years we must entirely depend.'

From a private letter of the same date to Under-Secretary Nepean, we may extract the following passages :—

'I am very sorry to say that not only a great part of the cloathing, particularly the women's, is very bad, but most of the axes, spades, and shovels the worst that ever were seen. The provision is as good. Of the seeds and corn sent from England, part has been destroyed by the weevil ; the rest in very good order. . . .

'If fifty farmers were sent out with their families, they would do more in one year in rendering this colony independent of the mother country, as to provisions, than a thousand convicts. There is some clear land, which is intended to be cultivated, at some distance from the camp, and I intended to send out convicts for that purpose, under the direction of a person that was going to India in the *Charlotte* transport, but who remained to settle in this country, and has been brought up a farmer, but several of the convicts (three) having been lately killed by the natives, I am obliged to defer it untill a detachment can be made.'

Here is another complication, and a description of the climate :—

'The masters of the transports having left with the agents the bonds and whatever papers they received that related to the convicts, I have no account of the time for which the convicts are sentenced, or the dates of their convictions. Some of them, by their own account, have little more than a year to remain, and, I am told, will apply for permission to return to England, or to go to India, in such ships as may be willing to receive them. If lands are granted them, Government will be obliged to support them for two years; and it is more than probable that one-half of them, after that time is expired, will still want support. Until I receive instructions on this head, of course none will be permitted to leave the settlement; but if, when the time for which they are sentenced expires, the most abandoned and useless were permitted to go to China, in any ships that may stop here, it would be a great advantage to the settlement.

'The weather is now unsettled, and heavy rains fall frequently; but the climate is certainly a very fine one, but the nights are very cold, and I frequently find a difference of thirty-three degrees in my chamber between 8 o'clock in the morning and 2 o'clock in the afternoon, though the sun does not reach the thermometer, which is at the west end of my canvas house.'

Notwithstanding all his troubles, the Governor still kept a good heart, for he ends with a cheery declaration that neither patience nor perseverance, in the laborious task before him, will be wanting on his part. It will be seen in what follows how well this promise was fulfilled.

CHAPTER VI

IN a paragraph of Phillip's 'Instructions,' he was enjoined to use every possible means 'to open an intercourse with the natives, and to conciliate their affections.' If any of them were ill-treated or wantonly destroyed by the whites, he was to bring the offenders to punishment ; and was to report his opinion to one of the Secretaries for State as to the way in which intercourse with these people could be turned to the advantage of the colony.

The manner and spirit in which he carried out this part of his duties supplies us with an interesting if not altogether agreeable chapter in the narrative of the Governor's administration. Light and pleasant reading is none too common, naturally enough, in the annals of the penal settlement.

Phillip very often turned from the disheartening duty of trying to civilise his prisoners to the more promising task of tutoring the native savages, either as a relaxation, or because he really believed that the blacks could be taught to work, and so add to the wealth of his poor territory; for either or both of these reasons, there was nothing in which the first Governor of Australia took a greater, or more intelligent interest.

A great number of people, many of whom have never met him or who have only made his acquaintance through the medium of a bottle of rum, have asserted that the Australian aboriginal belongs to the lowest type of humanity, and his warmest admirers will admit that he is a long way below the American Indian, the African negro, or the Polynesian.

But even in recent times the Australian blacks, as the rank and file in exploring expeditions, as trackers in the police force, or as ordinary day-labourers on cattle and sheep stations, have earned from their masters the best of characters. However, in this book we have no concern with the present day blacks— the civilising process has well nigh got rid of them, and the majority of the few that remain, have either become good Christians, regularly under the missionary influence, or are cheerfully drinking themselves to death.

Phillip's first meeting with the natives was at Botany Bay, and he wrote of them as follows :—

' With respect to the natives, it was my determination from my first landing that nothing less than the most absolute necessity should ever make me fire upon them.'

La Pérouse had been obliged to fire on them at Botany Bay ; and this, coupled with the bad behaviour of some of the transport seamen and convicts, caused the natives to avoid the settlers at Port Jackson for a time.   Phillip himself, while at Botany Bay, had very quickly made friends with them by going among them alone and unarmed, and no disputes occurred with them during his stay there. They were all naked, but quickly ornamented themselves with the beads and pieces of red baize given to them.   When Phillip's boat party entered Port Jackson, many armed blacks met them upon landing, and were ' very vociferous.'   One of them, who appeared to be the master of the family, was induced by the Governor to accompany him to where the marines were boiling some meat, and examine what was in the pot. ' He exprest his admiration,' says Phillip, ' in a manner that made me believe he intended to profit from what he saw. . . .   I believe they know no other way of dressing their food but by broiling, and they are seldom seen without a fire, or a piece of wood on fire, which they carry with them from place to place, and in their canoes, so that I apprehend they find some difficulty in procuring fire by any other means with which they are acquainted.[1]   The boats, in passing near a point of

---

[1] Phillip was wrong in this conclusion. The Australian blacks are adepts in producing fire by the friction of two sticks.

land in the harbour, were seen by a number of men, and twenty of them waded into the water unarmed, received what was offered them, and examined the boats with a curiosity that gave me a much higher opinion of them than I had formed from the behaviour of those seen in Captain Cook's voyage, and their confidence and manly behaviour made me give the name of Manly Cove to this place. The same people afterwards joined us where we dined; they were all armed with lances, two with shields and swords—the latter made of wood, the gripe small, and I thought less formidable than a good stick. As their curiosity made them very troublesome when we were preparing our dinner, I made a circle round us. There was little difficulty in making them understand that they were not to come within it, and they then sat down very quiet. The white clay rubbed on the upper part of the face of one of these men had the appearance of a mask ; and a woman that appeared on some rocks near which the boats passed was marked with white on the face, neck and breasts, in such a manner as to render her the most horrid figure I ever saw. They are not often seen marked in this manner, and it is only done on some particular occasions.'

The women, he noticed, appeared to be less cheerful than the men, and under great subjection, though at Broken Bay several of them met Phillip's landing party, and 'one of them, a young woman, was very talkative and remarkably cheerful. . . . The talkative lady, when she joined us in her canoe the day after we first landed, stood up and gave us a song that was not unpleasing. As most of the women have lost the two first joints of the little finger on the left hand, so most of the men want the right front tooth in the upper jaw, and have the gristle that separates the nostrils perforated, frequently having a piece of stick or a bone thrust through, and which does not add to their beauty. This is general, but I saw some very old men that had not lost the tooth, and whose noses were not perforated for this ornament. On my showing them that I wanted a front tooth, it occasioned a general clamour, and I thought gave me some little merit in their opinion.'

On another occasion, at Broken Bay, an old black appeared and guided the boats to a safe landing-place, and then rendered assistance in clearing the ground 'for a camping-place. His behaviour was so friendly that Phillip gave him a hatchet and other presents, but, when it was dark, he returned and stole a spade. The Governor, to show his displeasure, 'gave him two or three slight slaps on the shoulder' with his open hand. . . . 'Seizing a spear, he came close up to me, poised it, and appeared determined to strike. . . . This circumstance is mentioned to show that they do not want personal courage, for several officers and men were then near me. . . .

'They cannot be called a very cleanly people, yet I have seen one of them, after having in his hand a piece of pork, hold out his fingers for others to smell, with strong marks of disgust ; and tho' they seldom refused bread or meat if offered them, I have never been able to make them eat with us, and when they left us they generally threw away the bread and meat ; but fish they always accepted, and would broil and eat it.' Phillip estimated the number of blacks living about Botany Bay, Broken Bay, Port Jackson and the immediate coast as not less than fifteen hundred.

Soon after landing, Captain Hunter, with the first lieutenant of the *Sirius*, set about making a survey of Port Jackson and exploring the bays and arms of Sydney Harbour. Hunter often came across the natives while at this work, and the shyness of the blacks was beginning to wear off when the trouble with the Frenchmen at Botany Bay and a similar incident in Sydney Cove put a temporary stop to friendly relations.

The natives were accustomed to leave their possessions—clubs, spears, fire sticks and so on—lying on the beach, and the Europeans received a strict order never to touch them. The whites, of course, disobeyed this order—they wanted curios—and thus began a quarrel. The natives, determined to have some return for their lost property, to the number of about a score, landed on an island and seized some European tools. The blacks were only driven into their canoes after the two or three white men in charge of the island opened fire on them, wounding several with small shot.   The scene of this encounter was Garden Island, so called from its being set apart as a vegetable garden for the people of the *Sirius*.   It is now the Imperial Naval Depôt in Sydney, the head-quarters of the squadron on the Australian station, and is one of the most important naval establishments outside of Great Britain.

This outbreak of hostilities was followed soon afterwards by more serious disturbances.   Convicts who straggled away from the settlement were often attacked and seriously wounded, and later on some were killed.   In all these cases there was evidence that some provocation had, either through wantonness or ignorance of native susceptibilities, been given.

Phillip, anxious to put a stop to these disorders, determined as a first means to that end to capture a native and teach him some English, or learn from him enough of his language to establish communication between the two races.

Accordingly, a young man was seized and placed in charge of a trustworthy convict, the two being lodged in a hut near the main guardhouse.   The black took it very coolly, and the convict reported that he slept and ate and drank with perfect indifference.

Captain Hunter, whose account of what he saw and did is invaluable for the reason that his narrative is always in the unembellished log-book style of a plain sailor, thus tells the story :—

' As soon as the ship was secured, I went on shore

to wait on the Governor, whom I found in good
health.   He was sitting by the fire drinking tea
with a few friends, among whom I observed a native
man of this country, who was decently cloathed, and
seemed to be as much at his ease at the tea-table as
any person there ; he managed his cup and saucer as
well as though he had been long accustomed to such
entertainment.   This man was taken from his friends,
by force, by Lieutenant Ball, of the *Supply*, and
Lieutenant George Johnston, of the marines, who
were sent down the harbour with two boats for that
purpose. . . .   His name was Arabanoo, and he was
taken . . . in the following manner.   After having
been a short time in conversation with some of the
gentlemen, one of the seamen, who had been previously directed, threw a rope round his neck, and
dragged him in a moment down to the boat.   His
cries brought a number of his friends into the skirts
of the wood, from whence they threw many lances,
but without effect.   The terror this poor wretch
suffered can better be conceived than expressed.   He
believed he was to be immediately murdered ; but
upon the officers coming into the boat, they removed
the rope from his neck to his leg, and treated him
with so much kindness that he became a little more
chearful.   He was for some time after his arrival at
the Governor's house ornamented with an iron shackle
about his leg, to prevent his being able to effect his
escape with ease ; this he was taught to consider as

bang-ally, which is the name given in their language
to every decoration ; as he might well believe it a
compliment paid to him, because it was no uncommon
thing for him to see several (of the most worthless of
the convicts, who had merited punishment) every day
shackled like him, the cause of which he could not of
course understand. However, he was very soon reconciled to his situation by the kind treatment he received
from every person about him, and the iron growing
uneasy, it was taken off, and he was allowed to go
where he pleased. He very soon learnt the names of
the different gentlemen who took notice of him, and
when I was made acquainted with him, he learnt
mine, which he never forgot, but expressed great
desire to come on board my " *nowée*," [1] which is their
expression for a boat or other vessel upon the water.
. . . . I found him to be a very good-natured, talkative
fellow ; he was about thirty years of age, and tolerably
well-looked. I expressed, when at the Governor's, much
surprize at not having seen a single native on the shore,
or a canoe as we came up in the ship, the reason of
which I could not comprehend, until I was informed
that the smallpox had made its appearance a few
months ago amongst these unfortunate creatures, and
that it was truly shocking to go round the coves of
this harbour, which were formerly so much frequented
by the natives, where, in the caves of the rocks which
used to shelter whole families in bad weather, were

[1] Compare the Latin ' *navis* ' and the Greek ' *vaûs*.'

now to be seen men, women and children lying dead.'

After the death of Arabanoo, who fell a victim to the smallpox, Phillip determined to repeat his civilising experiment, and in November 1789 two more natives were captured, Coleby and Bennilong; the last named is entitled to some notice here, for he was the first *true* Australian to visit England.

Mrs Macarthur, wife of Captain Macarthur, who introduced the merino sheep to the colony in 1790, in a letter to friends in England, says :—

'Amongst the unhappy objects' (*i.e.*, those suffering from the smallpox) 'who were discovered were a boy and a girl; these were brought in, and from the humanity of the clergyman, who took the girl, and of the principal surgeon, Mr White, who took the boy, they were both saved. After they began to learn English and to make us understand them, it was imagined . . . that if a man or two could be brought to reside with us, that some valuable information might be obtained respecting the interior parts of the country.

'With this view the Governor left no means untried to effect an intimacy with them, but every endeavour of that sort, as before, prov'd ineffectual.... Despairing to gain their confidence by fair means, the Governor ordered that two men should be taken by force. This was done. The poor fellows . . . exhibited the strongest marks of terror and consternation at this proceeding, believing they were certainly meant to be sacrificed. When they were taken to the Governor's house, and immediately clean'd and clothed, their astonishment at everything they saw was amazing. A new world was unfolded to their view at once. For some days they were much dejected, but it soon gave way to cheerfulness. They were then admitted to the Governor's table, and in a little time ate and drank everything that was given them.

'The oldest of the two, Coleby, however, soon tired of his honourable captivity, and in a very artful manner one night made his escape. Bennilong stayed till May 1790, and then took himself off without any known reason, having been treated with the most uniform kindness.'

He had taken very kindly to the white men, and was given a hut on the eastern point of Sydney Cove, which was known for many years after, and is even now sometimes spoken of, as Bennilong Point. Fort Macquarie covers the site of the hut, and Government House is within a stone's throw of the place.

In one of her letters Mrs Macarthur tells of Bennilong's reappearance, and how that event nearly led to Phillip's death. On the 7th of September Captain Nepean and some other officers were on their way to Broken Bay when the boats put in at Manly Cove—now the most favourite seaside resort of the inhabitants of Sydney. Some 200 natives were there observed feeding on the carcase of a whale which had floated ashore. They seemed very friendly, and Nanberry (the boy above mentioned), who was in one of the boats, was told to inquire for Bennilong and Coleby, 'when, behold! both gentlemen appeared, and advancing with the utmost confidence, asked in broken English for all their old friends in Sydney.' Nepean at once sent a messenger to Phillip, who would, he knew, be pleased at the news.

Without losing time the Governor, accompanied by Mr Collins and Lieutenant Waterhouse, at once set out and reached Manly Cove. To show his friendly intentions, Phillip landed unarmed, and Bennilong approached and shook hands with him. Coleby, however, had disappeared. The Governor took care not to embarrass Bennilong by asking the reason of his flight, and the black appeared much pleased and thankful for some presents given him by Captain Nepean, and asked Phillip for a hatchet. This the Governor promised to bring him the next day. 'Then,' says Mrs Macarthur, 'Mr Collins and Mr Waterhouse now joined them, and several natives also came forward; they continued to converse with much seeming friendship until they' (the white men) 'had insensibly wandered some distance from the boat, . . . none of the gentlemen had the precaution to take a gun. . . . This the Governor

perceiving, deemed it prudent to retreat, and after
assuring Bennilong that he would remember his
promise, told him he was going. At that moment
an old-looking man advanced, whom Bennilong said
was his friend, and wished the Governor to take
notice of him. At this he approached the old man
with his hand extended, when on a sudden the
savage started back, and snatched up a spear from
the ground and poized it to throw. The Governor,
seeing the danger, told him in their tongue that it
was bad, and still advanced, when, with a mixture
of horror and intrepidity, the native discharged the
spear with all his force at the Governor. It entered
above his collar-bone, and came out at his back,
nine inches from the entrance, taking an oblique
direction. The natives from the rocks now poured
in their spears in abundance, so that it was with
the utmost difficulty and the greatest good fortune
that no other hurt was received in getting the
Governor into the boat.'

Phillip's personal coolness needs not this incident
to prove its existence, but Mrs Macarthur's statement of his behaviour ought to have a place here.
She says :—

'As soon as they returned to this place an
universal solicitude prevail'd, as the danger of the
wound could by no means be ascertained untill the
spear was extracted, and this was not done before
His Excellency had caus'd some papers to be ar-

rang'd, lest the consequence might prove fatal, which happily it did not, for in drawing out the spear it was found that no vital part had been touch'd. . . . The wound perfectly heal'd in the course of a few weeks. . . . Bennilong came many times to see the Governor during his confinement, and expressed great sorrow; but the reason why the mischief was done could not be learnt.'

This incident happened in 1790, and Mr Southwell, the young man from whose letters we have before quoted, was at that time a very discontented master's mate, still without promotion. Let us hope that the change in his sentiments towards the Governor was not brought about too much by his disappointments, for his opinions on this adventure of Phillip's and on other matters to be quoted savour somewhat of bitterness.

'I cannot sufficiently express my approbation of your good sense in forbidding those who perused it to publish my insignificant narrative; or my chagrin at their improper conduct who have, notwithstanding, taken the liberty to do so. I saw it, being the concluding part, in the *Hampshire Chronicle and Portsmouth and Chichester Journal*, Sept'r 7, 1789. Mr Morgan, since we were at sea, came across it, and from peculiarity of stile immediately recognized it, as did most of our principals on board. I add that I am vexed at it for several reasons, and pray you to take care who you honour with a sight of my cobweb productions, if this is the way they honour

them.   Apropos, that date is the anniversary of the
Governor's misfortune of the year 1790, when he
was speared by a native in Manly Bay, in a manner
which savours much of imprudence next to folly.
Bennilong, as I said in my letters, had made his
escape, and this was the first interview since that
incident.   It, however very near fatal, proved by no
means so, as he soon recovered, and it was followed
by the fullest intercourse with these people, insomuch
that they eat, drink and sleep in the camp with the
most perfect sangfroid ; and some of their dames, like
too many of ours, gladly forego that dear pleasure of
nursing their own bratts, and leave them in perfect
security to the care of several of the convict women,
who are suitably rewarded by the Governor.'

By degrees the natives on the shores of the harbour grew more familiar with the whites, and in
the course of two or three years, the aboriginals in
the immediate neighbourhood of Sydney ceased to be
a serious menace to the colonists, except in cases
where individuals suffered through their own mis-
conduct.

Phillip had so thoroughly won the affection of
Bennilong that the black, by his own especial request,
accompanied the Governor to England, taking with
him a fellow-countryman, who before Phillip left had
'regularly joined His Excellency's household.'

Poor Bennilong succumbed to the benefits of
civilisation.   A letter from Hunter, written just

before he sailed from Plymouth on his return to the colony in January 1795, alludes to him as follows :—

' Bennilong is with me, but I think in a precarious state of health. He has for the last twelve months been flattered with the hope of seeing again his native country—a happiness he has fondly looked forward to, but so long a disappointment has broken his spirit, and the coldness of the weather here has so frequently laid him up that I am apprehensive his lungs are affected—that was the cause of the other's death. I do all I can to keep him up, but still am doubtful of his living.'

The grave of ' the other,' to whom Hunter refers, is in the churchyard[1] of the village of Eltham, in Kent. Poor Hunter was put to considerable expense over these two aboriginals, who were a trying charge ; and he did his best, though without result, to make the Government refund him his outlay.

During his stay in England, Bennilong did not apparently attract much attention. On his return to the colony he passed the remainder of his life drifting aimlessly about between the little township of Sydney and the native camps in its vicinity. Phillip's immediate successors apparently took but

[1] The stone bears the following inscription :—' In memory of Yemmerrawanyea, a native of New South Wales, who died the 18th May 1794, in the 19th year of his age. Stone renewed 1882.'

a languid interest in the native question, and beyond occasional squabbles between the two races and fragmentary stories of their customs, more or less inaccurately reported, little worth printing is recorded.

Of Bennilong himself we hear again from time to time, and he is always in disgrace, until at last the early chroniclers mention his name no longer.

Phillip's policy towards the natives, save in one instance, during his administration was to win their friendship by kindness. Even after he was wounded, he allowed no attempt at reprisals to be made, but, on the contrary, took a great deal of trouble to make Bennilong understand and inform his countrymen that the Governor regarded the outrage as arising from their fear of capture—a fear justified by the previous abduction of some of their number. The importance of preserving the crops from the thieving propensities of the blacks was the only excuse permitted for firing upon the aborigines.

Tench relates an incident which illustrates both the danger from the blacks, and the one occasion when Phillip got out of patience with them. In December 1790, a sergeant of marines, with three convicts, among whom was M'Entire, the Governor's gamekeeper, a man of whom Bennilong had always shown the utmost hatred and terror, went out to shoot kangaroos in the vicinity of Botany Bay. About midnight two natives were observed by the sergeant creeping towards the camp with spears in

their hands ; and M'Entire spoke to them in their
own language, when one of them, without the least
warning, sent a spear into his left side. The wound
was pronounced by the surgeons to be mortal ; then,
writes Tench :—

'The poor wretch . . . began to utter the most
dreadful exclamations, and to accuse himself of the
commission of crimes of the deepest dye, accompanied with such expressions of his despair of God's
mercy as are too terrible to repeat. He lingered until the 20th of January, and then expired.
From the aversion uniformly shewn by all the
natives to this unhappy man, he had long been
suspected by us of having in his excursions shot
and injured them. To gain information on this
head from him, the moment of contrition was seized.
On being questioned with great seriousness, he, however, declared that he had never fired but once on a
native, and then had not killed, but severely wounded
him, and this in his own defence. Notwithstanding
this death-bed confession, most people doubted the
truth of the relation, from his general character and
other circumstances.'

Believing that the murder of M'Entire was quite
unprovoked, the Governor was determined to inflict
a stern punishment upon the natives. He, like many
other cultured men, no doubt thought that that
instinctive desire to kill strangers, so predominant in
savage races, and termed bloodthirsty treachery by

civilised people, was deserving of severe reprisals—not realising that fear and horror are the primary motives of attack. The party sent consisted of two captains, two subalterns, and forty privates with non-commissioned officers, and Tench was pitched upon to command it.

'His Excellency informed me,' says Tench, 'that . . . if practicable, we were to bring away two natives as prisoners; and to put to death ten; that we were to destroy all weapons of war but nothing else; that no hut was to be burned; that all women and children were to remain un-injured, not being comprehended within the scope of the order; that our operations were to be directed either by surprize or open force; that after we had made any prisoners, all communication, even with those natives with whom we were in habits of intercourse, was to be avoided, and none of them suffered to approach us; that we were to cut off and bring in the heads of the slain, for which purpose hatchets and bags would be furnished; and finally, that no signal of amity or invitation should be used in order to allure them to us; or if made on their part (was) to be answered by us; for that such conduct would be not only present treachery, but give them reason to distrust every future mark of peace and friendship on our part.'

Then Phillip gave his reasons.

'He said that since our arrival in the country, no less

than seventeen of our people had either been killed or
wounded by the natives; that he looked upon the tribe
living on the before-mentioned peninsula, and chiefly
on the north arm of Botany Bay, to be the principal
aggressors; that against this tribe he was determined
to strike a decisive blow, in order at once to convince
them of our superiority, and to infuse an universal
terror, which might operate to prevent farther mischief. . . . That his motive for having so long
delayed to use violent measures had arisen from
believing that in every former instance of hostility,
they had acted either from having received injury, or
from misapprehension. To the latter of these causes,
added he, "I attribute my own wound; but in this
business of M'Entire, I am fully persuaded . . . the
barbarity of their conduct admits of no extenua-
tion . . . and I am resolved to execute the prisoners
who may be brought in, in the most public and
exemplary manner, in the presence of as many of
their countrymen as can be collected, after having
explained the cause of such a punishment, and my
fixed determination to repeat it whenever any future
breach of good conduct on their side shall render it
necessary."'

Hunter—all honour to him—proposed that, instead of destroying ten persons, the capture of
six would better answer all the purposes for which
the expedition was to be undertaken; as out of this
number a part might be set aside for retaliation; and

the rest at a proper time liberated, after having seen
the fate of their comrades, and being made sensible of
the cause of their own detention.

'This scheme His Excellency was pleased instantly
to adopt, adding, "If six cannot be taken, let this
number be shot. Should you, however, find it practicable to take so many, I will hang two, and send
the rest to Norfolk Island for a certain period, which
will cause their countrymen to believe that we have
despatched them secretly."

'At four o'clock on the morning of the 14th we
marched ; . . . provided with three days' provisions,
ropes to bind our prisoners with, and hatchets and bags,
to cut off and contain the heads of the slain. . . .'

Tench and his men spent two or three days in this
attempt, but the natives eluded capture, and says the
narrator :—

'At one o'clock we renewed our march, and at
three halted near a fresh water swamp, where we
resolved to remain until morning ; that is, after a
day of severe fatigue, to pass a night of restless in-
quietude, when weariness is denied repose by swarms
of mosquitoes and sand-flies, which in the summer
months bite and sting the traveller without measure
or intermission. Next morning we bent our steps
homeward ; and, after wading breast-high through
two arms of the sea, as broad as the Thames at
Westminster, were glad to find ourselves at Sydney
between one and two o'clock in the afternoon.'

This expedition against the natives, when compared with that undertaken by Governor Arthur in Tasmania in 1830, was a very mild affair. Settlers in the pursuance of private quarrels have murdered more blacks than were killed by English officials during the whole of their administration of the Colony. Even modern methods in Africa, when compared with Phillip's treatment of the natives, suffer by comparison.

Soon after this incident a serious rupture between the two races occurred in this manner. A native named Ballooderry was accustomed to catch fish and exchange them with the settlers at Parramatta. Some convicts one day destroyed this man's canoe. Ballooderry watched his opportunity, and retaliated by spearing a convict, although Phillip had already punished the first aggressors. The Governor would not allow Ballooderry to be punished for this, but issued an order that he and his tribe were not to come near the settlement. From that day the natives in the vicinity never visited Parramatta.

After Phillip left the colony, no serious endeavour was made to civilise the aborigines. The race, as we have said, is now fast dying out. Whereas in the first Governor's time it was estimated, as stated above, that on the shores of Port Jackson, Botany Bay, and Broken Bay alone[1] there were at least 1500 blacks; only a stray one is ever seen in these localities now.

---

[1] The Aborigines Protection Board, which sends aboriginal children to school and supplies the blacks with blankets and rations, in the annual report for 1896, states that the total number of 'blacks' in New South Wales was 6984, 'of whom 3481 are half-castes.'

THE ANTAGONISM OF MAJOR ROSS—THE MARINES—
THE QUARREL BETWEEN ROSS AND HIS OFFICERS
—PHILLIP'S ACTION—ROSS'S OPINION OF THE
COLONY'S PROSPECTS — HIS COMPLAINTS — THE
'WATCH' DISPUTE—PHILLIP'S FORBEARANCE—
THE COURT-MARTIAL ON MEREDITH—PHILLIP'S
DETRACTORS—SOUTHWELL AND HIS LETTERS

PHILLIP's administration possessed from the first what is said to be one of the peculiar advantages of Parliamentary forms of government—a strong Opposition, and the Lieutenant-Governor was the leader thereof.

In his letters to his superiors in England, Ross condemned all Phillip's acts and contradicted all the Governor's assertions as to the colony's future. Posterity is the only true judge between the 'ins and the outs,' and now that more than a hundred years have elapsed since these two men did their duty, each according to his lights, time has proved that Phillip was right and Ross was wrong.

That branch of the service to which Ross belonged has, ashore and afloat, earned for itself such fame that the very sight of a marine's uniform in the streets of

Sydney is to an Englishman there what standing upon
the deck of the old *Victory* at Portsmouth must be to
an Englishman at home. But there was no glory to
be won in the service which the marines were called
upon to perform in the colonisation of Australia.

Their work was mere routine garrison duty, the
'sentry go' of barrack life, certainly with less food
and more discomforts than usual; but these were
hardships suffered equally by everyone, from Phillip
to the youngest ship's boy.

If, through no fault of their own, the part of the
marines was an insignificant one, their commandant
might well have played his own in such a way as to
make the piece run smoothly. But instead of this,
from Major Ross, we hear more of hardships suffered,
of offended dignity, and of a dozen other trivial grievances than from all the other members of the expedition put together.

The men of the marine detachment volunteered on
the conditions that the non-commissioned officers and
men should be given their discharge, if they desired
it, on their return to England, after they had been
relieved, at the expiration of three years ; or could be
discharged abroad upon the relief, and be permitted
to settle in the country if they preferred it.   And
they were to be victualled by a commissary, and to
be given such tools, implements and utensils as they
needed whilst employed for the protection of the new
settlement.

In a letter from Ross to Nepean just before the fleet left England, the Major wrote reminding him that he was leaving behind him his wife and a 'very small tho' numerous' young family; that his pay was his only means; and asked, in the event of his death, that the Under-Secretary's interest would be given towards procuring for his widow and fatherless children 'some compensation from the public,' winding up by appealing to that gentleman's own feelings as a husband and father.

Then he tenders his thanks for 'the generous opinion you have shown in favour of the corps,' and goes on to say, 'every nerve shall be strain'd in the faithful and diligent discharge of our duty, and I entertain not a doubt but that the conduct of the whole will be such as will not only do credit to your recommendation' (of the marines for the service), 'but give satisfaction to the Administration. These much-wished-for objects obtain'd, I shall then ardently hope that what you once hinted to me might be the consequence, will, with your assistance, take place, and that we shall no more return to our original obscurity, but become an active corps of your own creation.' This was very judicious letter-writing indeed.

The Admiralty sent instructions to Ross before he embarked, and these instructions naturally contained no very detailed statement of the work expected of them. They were 'not only to enforce due sub-

ordination and obedience among the settlers, but
were also for the defence of the settlement against
incursions by the natives,' and the officer commanding the detachment was informed that he must
'follow such orders and directions as you shall from
time to time receive from His Majesty through one
of his Principal Secretaries of State, or the Governor
of the settlement for the time being.'

Phillip writing home a few months after landing,
says :—

'As most of the officers have declined any kind of
interference with the convicts, except when immediately employed by themselves, the little progress made
in clearing land that requires so much labour will be
accounted for. A letter sent from the Admiralty to
the commanding officers of marines at Portsmouth
and Plymouth is what the officers say they govern
themselves by, and in which they say no extra duty
is pointed out. What I asked of the officers was so
very little, and so far from being what would degrade
either the officer or the gentleman in our situation, that
I beg leave once more to report to your Lordship the
request I made soon after we landed, and which was
made in the following words : " That officers would,
when they saw the convicts diligent, say a few words
of encouragement to them ; and that when they saw
them idle, or met them straggling in the woods, they
would threaten them with punishment." This I only
desired when officers could do it without going out

of their way; it was all I asked, and was pointedly refused. They declared against what they called an interference with convicts, and I found myself obliged to give up the little plan I had formed in the passage for the government of these people.'

The first serious difficulty with the marines, however, arose between Ross and his officers. A court-martial had been held upon one of the men for striking a comrade, and the officers comprising the court found that the accused was guilty, and sentenced him 'either to ask public pardon before the battalion of William Dempsey, the soldier whom he struck and injur'd, or to receive one hundred lashes on his bare back, by the drummers of the detachment, and where the commanding officer shall appoint.'

Ross ordered the court to reconsider this decision, on the ground that the sentence of two punishments, with the choice left to the prisoner which he would have inflicted, was illegal.

The members of the court, after reconsideration, said they were of the same mind, whereupon Ross told them to consider themselves under arrest. But as there were not enough officers in the settlement to form a general court-martial to try the members of the court, Phillip, after endeavouring to settle the dispute amicably, ordered them to return to their duty, on the ground that their services were necessary to the public.

The five officers (among whom was Tench) who composed this court wrote to Phillip thanking him warmly for his endeavour to reconcile the difference between them and Major Ross, but added that so violent was the treatment they had received, and so disgraceful their present situation, that they could not consent to have their arrest taken off 'until a public reparation should have been made for the indignity we have been used with.'

But much more serious than this dispute was the refusal of one of the marine officers, and the reluctance of others, to sit as a Criminal Court. By their act, had it been persisted in, the Governor's authority would have been set at defiance by any convict who chose to break the regulations of the settlement. Pounds weight of despatches resulted from this affair, and it was not until the opinion of the Law Officers of the Crown arrived from England in 1791 that it was finally settled.

The Attorney-General and Solicitor-General, in expressing the opinion that officers were bound by the Act establishing the Criminal Court to do as Phillip requested them, wound up their letter with these common-sense remarks :—

'A military officer serving in New South Wales is bound to perform the duty of a member of the Criminal Court when duly summoned for that purpose . . . and will be guilty of a misdemeanour by refusing to perform a duty imposed upon him by the King's authority, derived from an Act of Parliament passed for the purpose of giving that authority. We should, however, conceive that persons of the liberal principles which belong to the character of military officers, and who must know that the whole criminal justice of the settlement will stand still if they should refuse to serve in the Criminal Court, would be too much influenced by a sense of the service which they can render to their country by performing this civil function, in addition to their military duty, to render it necessary to remind them of the nature of their duty in this instance, as pointed out by charter and by Act of Parliament.'

The refusal of one of the officers to sit ended by Phillip sending for them all, 'in order,' he writes, 'to point out to them the consequences which would follow their refusal of so essential a part of their duty, and the officers I saw on that occasion assured me that they had never doubted its being a part of their duty after they heard the Act of Parliament and the commission read, which established that court; but Major Ross, afterwards, on the 6th of May, telling me that he was still of opinion that many of the officers did not think the sitting as members of the Criminal Court any part of their duty, I desired that he would assemble the officers, that their separate opinions might be taken on that head.'

In the despatch from which the above is extracted there are some further statements which show how much Ross was responsible for hampering the public service, and adding to the already almost overwhelming anxieties of the Governor. The matter was adjusted for the time by the officers taking Phillip's view of their position, but Ross did all he could to prejudice them against Phillip by stigmatising his conduct as unfair, saying that he 'thought it hard officers should be obliged to sit as members of the Criminal Court, and oppressive to the highest degree.'

'The consequences,' writes Phillip, 'which must have followed had the officers in general been of that opinion will be obvious to your Lordship; but as no legal inquiry could be made respecting the conduct of the officer to whom, as the Lieutenant-Governor and commandant of the detachment, I was naturally to look for support, and from whom the situation of this colony at the time call'd for an address of a very different nature, I did not think it proper to direct any more officers to be sent for on that subject,'—namely, that of learning their separate opinions on the point at issue.

What Ross thought of the colony and its future prospects, and what manner of man he was, is disclosed under his own hand. In a letter to the Secretary of the Admiralty, written only six months after landing, he has much to complain of and much to condemn.

In another letter to Under-Secretary Nepean, he says :—

'Take my word for it, there is not a man in this place but wishes to return home, and indeed they have no less than cause, for I believe there never was a set of people so much upon the parrish as this garrison is, and what little we want, even to a single nail, we must not send to the Commissary for it, but must apply to His Excellency, and when we do he allways sayes there is but little come out, and of course it is but little we get, and what we are obliged to take as a mark of favor. If you want a true description of this country, it is only to be found amongst many of the private letters sent home; however, I will, in confidence, venture to assure *you* that this country will never answer to settle in, for although I think corn will grow here, yet I am convinced that if ever it is able to maintain the people here, it cannot be in less time than probably a hundred years hence. I therefore think it will be cheaper to feed the convicts on turtle and venison at the London Tavern than be at the expence of sending them here.'

Writing again to the Secretary of the Admiralty, Ross ventures to 'intrude an opinion on their Lordships as to the utility of a settlement on this coast.' 'This part of it, at least,' he writes, 'never can be made to answer the intended purpose or wish of the Government, for the country seems totally destitute of everything that can be an object for a commercial nation, a very fine harbour excepted, and I much fear that the nature of the soil is such as will not be brought to yield more than sufficient sustainance for the needy emigrants whose desperate fortunes may induce them to try the experiment. Here I beg leave to observe to their Lordships that the above is but a private opinion. The Governor's I am unacquainted with, as he has never done me the honor of informing me ot his, or asking me for mine; neither has he made me or any other person that I know of acquainted with any part of the intentions of Government, nor have I been let into any part of his plan, which will, I hope, be a sufficient apology for the very lame accounts in my power to give their Lordships, independant of what I have already said. The face of the country round us produces dreadful proofs of the devastation caused by the frequent lightnings, besides our having been already visited by a shock of an earthquake, which happened on the 22d of June.'

Then, after a woful tale about some of his live stock being killed by lightning, he says: 'While I am on this subject I shall take the liberty of mentioning to their Lordships the quantity of provisions served to myself, the officers and men of the detachment, in which there is now no difference between us and the convicts, but in half a pint per day of Rio spirits, which in taste and smell is extremely offensive. Indeed, I may say that nothing short of absolute necessity could induce men to use it. What makes this the more severely felt by many of us is our not having known what we were to be supplied with till it was much too late to make any other provision for ourselves.'

Fortunately for the future prosperity of the colony, the other officers did not whine about their hardships, though Ross no doubt gave them every encouragement to do so. Phillip sometimes came near to losing his temper with the Major, who seemed to miss no chance of harassing the Governor in every possible way. In a despatch to Lord Sydney, dated 1st February 1790,[1] Phillip complains in a dignified manner that 'as every obstacle thrown in the way of the civil government is rendered doubly embarrassing from our situation . . . I am under the disagreeable necessity of laying the following particulars before your Lordship.' Then he states that for many months past robberies had taken place, and he found it necessary to establish a watch, the regulations of which he sent to Ross for his opinion thereon. Ross approved, the watch was established, and did its work so well that in three months not a single robbery was committed in the night.

The watch consisted of twelve convicts—men selected for their good behaviour. Immediately after tattoo had beat they began their patrol. 'No complaint was ever made of them,' remarks Phillip, and they were expressly cautioned to avoid disputes

---

[1] Phillip was not aware that Grenville had at this date succeeded Sydney at the Home Office.

with soldiers or seamen (many of whom were as great
thieves as the convicts themselves). Soldiers and
sailors when stopped by the watch at night were
taken to the guardhouse, from where they were
delivered by the officers if there was no criminal
charge against them. This had been done on several
occasions. One night, however, a soldier was found
in the convicts' camp, and placed in the custody of the
guard. On the following morning, Ross sent the
adjutant to the Judge-Advocate (under whose immediate control Phillip had placed the watch) with a
message 'that he considered a soldier being stopped,
when not committing any unlawful act, as an insult
offered to the corps ; that they would not suffer
themselves to be treated in that manner or be con-
trouled by the convicts while they had bayonets in
their hands.'

Phillip at once sent for the Major and discussed the
matter, and tried to convince him of the necessity of
the order, but Ross sulked, and reiterated 'that it was
an insult to the corps.' Then for the sake of peace
Phillip withdrew the order, 'for,' he wrote, 'it was
not to be supposed that soldiers would quietly suffer
themselves to be stopped by a convict watchman after
such declarations from their commandant.' But Phillip
would not have yielded had Ross's message to the
Judge-Advocate been repeated to him in full : 'I beg
leave to observe to your Lordship that the last sentence,
respecting the bayonets, was never mentioned to me

till after this business was settled, for if it had, I should not have been induced to have withdrawn the order.' So pointed a menace, he adds, could not tend to the good of the service or the preservation of peace in general. Some idea of the unpleasant condition of affairs is shown by another extract from the same letter.

'Officers have been put under arrest by their commandant, and courts-martial have been demanded, and which have likewise been requested by the officers in defence of their conduct, but no inquiry into the conduct of any individual above the rank of a non-commissioned officer can take place, and the consequences will be obvious to your Lordship where so little harmony prevails between the commandant and his officers. The strength of the detachment consists of only eighteen officers, one of whom is on duty at Norfolk Island, and a second has never done any duty since he was appointed by Major Ross; of the sixteen remaining for the duty of this settlement, five have been put under arrest by the commandant, and are only doing duty till a general court-martial can be assembled, in consequence of a sentence passed by them at a battalion court-martial; a sixth officer is suspended in consequence of a representation made by the corps of his unofficerlike behaviour; a seventh is suspended by his commandant for unofficerlike behaviour in taking a soldier who had been abused by a convict to make his complaint to the magistrates without having first given information to his commandant; and both adjutant and quartermaster of the detachment have been equally under his displeasure.'

In a subsequent letter to Nepean, the Governor, at this time, as future chapters will show, harassed enough by the famine that was in the land, thus unbosoms himself:—

'The Lieutenant-Governor has complained of that part of my letter in which I requested that the peace of the settlement may not be disturbed; but have I not had sufficient cause to make that request? Has not representation or complaint been too frequent? Was not the answer given to him by a convict followed by a behaviour on the part of that wretch which drew on him a severe sentence from the Criminal Court? Did not the Lieutenant-Governor, when that convict was under examination, behave in such a manner to Captain Hunter and the Judge-Advocate that the former wished to be excused attending one day in the week as a Justice of the Peace, that he might not subject himself in future to such treatment when acting as a magistrate, and the latter wished to resign his office of Judge-Advocate in consequence of the treatment he had received from the Lieutenant-Governor and Captain Campbell in the presence of convicts and others? I quote the words those officers made use of when they represented that matter to me. And did not the Lieutenant-Governor's conduct, as it appears from the evidence of several of his officers, when Captain Campbell refused the duty of the Criminal Court, bring this settlement to touch on the moment of a general confusion.'

Then he alludes to the incessant grumbling of Ross about the bad treatment his detachment had continuously received, and expresses the opinion that the soldiers are much more comfortable than they had reason to expect.

Ross returned to England by the same ship that brought formal acknowledgments of some of these letters. In his reply, Lord Grenville stated his strong disapproval of Ross's conduct, but took the precaution of intimating that this opinion had been formed subject to what the defence might have to say. Phillip, feeling that he had been moderate in his statements, answered the Secretary of State in very plain language :—

'As your Lordship's letter of the 19th of February 1791 has the following words, "The proceedings of Major Ross and Captain Campbell according to your representations," I beg that your Lordship will permit me to say that the representations I have made of the conduct of those officers are just and impartial, and which do not admit of a doubt. I believe Major Ross's or Captain Campbell's friends could not have represented their conduct in a more favorable point of view, without having deviated from truth ; and the representations I made appeared to me to be necessary for the good of His Majesty's service.'

The Government, however, seemed to have formed a just estimate of the case. The marines were relieved in 1791, and Ross upon his return home was not promoted.

The five officers who had been ordered to consider themselves under arrest for refusing to alter their sentence on a prisoner could not be tried in the colony, and on their return to England, owing to the delay, the Admiralty declined to investigate their case. But Captain Meredith, who while in the colony had been put under arrest by Ross for some trivial cause, was tried at Plymouth, and the court-martial brought this finding, which was duly approved by the Admiralty :—

'That the court is of opinion the charge is groundless and malicious—groundless because the charge is not proved in either of its parts, and if it had been, was of a venial nature, and for which ample atonement was made in the apology offered ; and malicious from the long duration of the arrest, and unusual and unnecessary severity of it ; and the court doth therefore honorably acquit the prisoner. We have taken the said proceedings and sentence into our consideration, and do hereby signify to you our approval thereof.'

Ross soon after his return was appointed a recruiting

officer to his corps, and died while doing that duty at Ipswich in August 1793. What has been written of him is the reverse of complimentary, but it must not be lost sight of that the Lieutenant-Governor's faults were the results of his unfitness for the peculiar position in which he was placed—he was merely the regulation pipeclay type of soldier, doubtless brave and honourable, and eminently fitted to lead a company. These qualifications in a soldier are often enough to be found unaccompanied by intelligence or even by common sense. Tact, good temper and a desire to 'make the best of a bad job' were the qualities more needed than any other, and they were not part of the Major's character.

Lieutenant Dawes was another officer of marines with whom the Governor had disagreements. Dawes was an extremely useful man, whose scientific knowledge had led to his appointment as engineer and artillery officer, and to his being placed in charge of the Observatory.

Like others of his brother officers, he did not get on well with the Governor, who had cause to be angry with him for indulging in a practice to which Phillip objected—exchanging provisions with the convicts. A convict who acted as a sort of middleman was detected, and stated that he had given Lieutenant Dawes 40 lbs. of flour for 20 lbs. of sugar. Phillip had before this asked Ross to point out to him the impropriety 'of purchasing pease from the convicts.'

These breaches of the regulations, petty as they appear, were really serious, for the colony was sadly in want of food. On another occasion Phillip ordered Dawes to accompany an expedition against the blacks. Dawes, on the grounds that he had religious objections to punishing blacks, refused to go, and persisted in this refusal—remarkable conduct, to say the least of it, in a soldier !

We have gone at some length into these disputes between the marines and the Governor because, trivial as they may appear, they contained all the elements necessary to create such a disturbance in the settlement as might very easily have led to serious consequences. A very few years later the military actually revolted and deposed Governor Bligh. With what is known of Bligh's character and the circumstances of his deposition, and what is shown in these letters of Phillip, it is not too much to assume that disaster to the young colony from these disputes between the military and civilians was only averted by the even temper and forbearance of the first Governor.

In this chapter we have endeavoured to show what Phillip's contemporaries had to say against him, so that the worst of the man as he appeared to them may be known, set against his services, and balanced by the reader.

His remaining detractor — young Southwell — is amusing, and his cause of quarrel obvious enough.

Lieutenant Dawes seems to have been a particular

friend of his, and he thus writes of that young gentleman :—

'One friend I cannot but mention, and I am sure you will esteem him for my sake, and that is a Mr Dawes . . . . To give you his character in few words, he is a most amiable man, and though young, truly religious, without any appearance of formal sanctity. He is kind to everyone; but I am speaking of his many affabilities to myself.'

Others of his friends he mentions thus :—

'And as it is only between you and me, and I know you like such little fid-fad, I will name a few. Captain Campbell, the commanding officer of marines, and, when here, Major Ross; the author of the printed narrative, Captain Tench, polite and sensible ; several other lieutenants, Mr Worgan, our surgeon, etc., are all very kind, and sometimes, when I can, I visit them.'

We have quoted young Southwell before, it will be remembered, and he had nothing to say against Phillip then. Early in 1790 he was placed in charge of the signal station at the South Head of Sydney Harbour, a somewhat lonely position for a youth of his temperament. He seems about this time to have begun to have doubts about the Governor.

He writes of Phillip as 'the pompous despot.' 'Our austere Governor's behaviour alters not for the better . . . and I can assure you I am not disposed to speak in his praise. . . . I am rather

vexed with myself for being so very lavish of my
encomiums formerly, but while a shadow of appearance remained that could justify my sending
pleasing accounts, I chose to do it for your sakes.'
Then comes a complaint that the Governor tried to
prevent his sending away letters by the *Scarborough*,
and resented his presence at the settlement—likely
enough when Southwell was so far away from his
post. 'He had no better resource than the sly
pretence of fearing my being in camp might be pre-
judicial to my morals : "What did I want with women
and rogues ? " My answer was warm, being nettled,
"nothing," and that I was certain he could have
nothing of that kind to bring against my conduct ;'
and then he goes so far as to pen an accusation of
Phillip's immoral relations with some woman whom he
does not name. The slander was doubtless invented
for Southwell by other people, who were too careful
to put about such a statement themselves. Yet in
this same letter Southwell says :—

'Apropos, the Governor has this forenoon graciously
sent me an invitation to dine, a thing quite out of
date a long time ; but as I was to eat some kid with
Mr Palmer, I sent word I was indisposed, but much
obliged, etc., of course, and also going down to the
lookout to lay by a little. Observe, was it anything
worse than a common cold I wou'd not say anything
about it in this to you ; but I truly assure you that
is all, and I am a careful codger.'

The 'careful codger' soon after tells his mother that 'a more agreeable turn has taken place lately in affairs, and his disagreeable restrictions are taken off. He treats us with more affability, and is all at once so polite as to beg of my only companion, Mr Harris, and self, whenever we come to camp, to let him have our company, and I am to-morrow (having been a long stranger) to wait upon him by particular invitation.'

Next follows a long and tedious account of the hardships he has endured, 'dragged round the world, made shake in our shoes off Tasman's Head, and at length deprived of our poor old bark at Norfolk Island,'—pitiful stuff from a young seaman.

When he said good-bye to the colony and to Governor Phillip, he tells his mother that 'the Governor, at leave-taking, after a few encomiums on my prudent deportment, good sense, parts, etc., lamenting it had not been in his power effectually to serve me, etc., concluded with recommending it to me to quit the service. . . . I gave him no reason to think that I felt myself obliged by that part of the story, and only answered him by begging he would recollect my time lost in the service, my connection by no means affluent, and other difficulties. In reply, I had a repetition of stale compliments, abilities very equal to something respectable in some other way, and [he] wound all up by saying with some warmth (it may be genuine) that should he return, and the gleam of any possibility of his serving me offer, he would most heartily and gladly do it in any part of the world or situation whatever.'

Many such letters as these were written to the Rev. W. Butler, of Cheyne Walk, Chelsea, Southwell's uncle, and in the course of a reply to one of them, that worthy gentleman thus delivers himself:—

'I have not the happiness nor the honour of knowing your Governor, but I never shall forget the expression of my friend Captain John Faithful Fortescue, on talking about the new administration under such good care: "Upon my soul, Butler," said he, "I do think God Almighty made Phillip on purpose for the place, for never did man better know what to do, or with more determination to see it done; and yet, if they'll let him, he will make them all very happy." Such a compliment, and from an officer of like rank, was too striking to escape my remembrance. I have quoted it fifty times, and don't doubt it has been verified a thousand.'

When Southwell got home, he memorialised the Admiralty for promotion, and his uncle asked Sir Joseph Banks to take charge of his nephew's petition.

Sir Joseph, however, courteously declined, on the grounds that if he solicited a boon from the Admiralty, it would be in favour of Captain Cook's son, 'who, tho' his name stands higher in the opinion of the nation than that of any former youngster has ever done, is still a lieutenant of many years' standing.'

Poor young Southwell ! One pictures the youth (for though he was twenty-four, he was quite a child) in the bush at the signal station, seven long miles from the home of the settlers, brooding over his troubles, petty as they were, yet fully as great in his eyes as were those of that 'pompous despot' the 'austere Governor.' No doubt his friends Ross and Dawes in some measure stimulated his grumbling, and it was not altogether his own selfish grievances which made him thus bitter.

But yet the 'pompous despot' did possibly mean well by the young man—those invitations to dinner were perhaps, after all, signs of some kindness of heart and goodwill. And remember, as will presently be shown, that the materials for dinner were at these times very scarce, and asking a friend to share it was no mere everyday politeness.

CHAPTER VIII

In the annals of Australian exploration, the stories
of attempts to find a way over the Blue Mountains,
and of terrible journeys across the deserts in the heart
of the continent, Phillip has no place—these hazardous
adventures came after his day. When he landed in
1788, his only map was Cook's chart of the continent,
and on its eastern boundary line from north to south
the famous navigator had surveyed the whole sea
coast so thoroughly that the names he gave crowd one
another upon the chart. But here, upon the edge,
Cook's work ended and Phillip's began.

. On the map as it was after the first Governor had
marked all his discoveries upon it, the piece cut out
of the big territory is very small indeed, but to win

that little in the time, and in the face of the difficulties encountered by the first explorers, is of itself evidence enough of his tireless energy.

The first and greatest proof of Phillip's sagacity was his selection of a site for the settlement. The city of Sydney is a monument for all time to its founder. How it came about that Port Jackson was chosen in place of Botany Bay is shown in Phillip's first despatch, already quoted.

The Governor lost little time after landing at Port Jackson before still further extending his dominions. On the 15th of February — scarcely more than a fortnight after the ships had entered Sydney Cove— the *Supply* was sent to Norfolk Island. King, who was given the command of the island, was, as has been said, the friend of Phillip. He had served before under the Governor, and although twenty years younger than his chief, the lieutenant of thirty was unquestionably the ablest officer on the staff. By sending King to Norfolk Island, the Governor, actuated by the highest motives, cut himself off from the society of his best friend, but King's energetic and wise administration justified Phillip's choice.

Very soon after landing, Phillip saw the necessity of going further afield for farming land. No land suitable for agriculture was to be found on the shores of Port Jackson, and so he set out to examine Broken Bay. Describing this journey he says :—

'The 2d of March I went with a longboat and

cutter to examine the broken land mentioned by Captain Cook about eight miles to the northward of Port Jackson. We slept in the boat that night within a rocky point, in the north-west part of the bay (which is very extensive), as the natives, though very friendly, appeared to be numerous ; and the next day, after passing a bar that had only water for small vessels, entered a very extensive branch, from which the ebb tide came out so strong that the boats could not row against it in the stream ; and here was deep water. It appeared to end in several small branches, and in a large lagoon that we could not examine for want of time to search for a channel for the boats amongst the banks of sand and mud.'

After describing the other branches of Broken Bay, one of which he 'honoured with the name of Pitt Water,' he goes on as follows : 'We found small springs of water in most of the coves, and saw three cascades falling from a height which the rains then rendered inaccessible. I returned to Port Jackson after being absent eight days in the boats. Some of the people feeling the effects of the rain, which had been almost constant, prevented my returning by land, as I intended, in order to examine a part of the country which appeared open and free from timber.'

A few weeks later he repeated these explorations, and this time found good land.

No mere pleasure excursions these journeys into the interior, although some of the places visited by these early explorers are nowadays favourite picnic grounds. For instance, the large lake he next describes is now known as Lake Narrabeen— a spot which is to the Sydney holiday-maker as familiar as Hampstead Heath or Richmond is to the Londoner.

In one of his many short but careful examinations of the shores near Port Jackson, Phillip found a deep water passage leading into a branch of the harbour that trended north-west. Finding fresh water at the head of the bay, he resolved to make further exploration ; and a few days later set out with a small party of officers and marines. ‘To the northward of this part of the harbour,’ he writes, ‘we found a large lake, which we examined, though not without great labour, for it is surrounded with a bog and large marsh, in which we were frequently up to the middle. There we saw a black swan ; it was larger than the common swan, and when it rose after being fired at, the wings appeared to be edged with white ; there is some red on its bill, and it is a very noble bird. ... In three days we got round the swamps and marshes, from which all the fresh water drains that this harbour is supplied with. The country we past through when we left the low grounds was the most rocky and barren I ever saw ; the ascending and descending of the mountains being practicable only in particular places, but covered with flowering shrubs ; and when about fifteen miles from the sea-coast we had a very fine view of the mountains inland. . . . From the rising of these mountains I did not doubt but that a large river would be found.'

To determine this matter the energetic Governor led another party, consisting of eleven officers and men, with six days' provisions, into the interior. Leaving the settlement in a boat they landed at the head of the harbour, and for three days the little party marched westward through country which Phillip describes as fine as any he had ever seen, clothed with large timber and, except in occasional places where the soil was poor and stony, without any undergrowth. In general the land was level or else undulating, which gave it a very pleasant and picturesque appearance. On the fifth day they reached more elevated country, and saw hills to the southward. So beautiful did the Governor consider this part of the country that he named the place from which he surveyed it Bellevue. Want of provisions now compelled him to return, though water was everywhere plentiful in pools. But the presence of these could not be depended upon as they advanced, and therefore the party always carried their water with them ; this, with the provisions, arms and two tents, obliged every officer and private to carry each a very heavy load. They returned to the head of the harbour in a day and a half, following a marked tree track on their return. Thirty miles of country had been explored—country that in Phillip's opinion could be cultivated with ease. He, and indeed everyone that accompanied him were anxious to return and penetrate further into the interior in the hope of finding a large river, but the exposure undergone by the Governor at Broken Bay was now telling upon him, and his ardent spirit had to submit to a few weeks' rest. His hopes were raised, however, and he wrote that he now knew that there was good country near the settlement, and that it should be settled in the spring.

Tench—the only one or the old chroniclers who in his writings makes a departure from the hard, matter-of-fact, official style of the others—thus writes of one of these exploring expeditions undertaken in April 1791, to ascertain whether or not the Hawkesbury and the Nepean were the same river :—

'The party consisted of twenty-one persons, including the Governor and our friends Colbee (Coleby) and Boladeree (Ballooderry). Their equipment,' he says, 'will convey to those who have rolled along on turnpike roads only,' some idea of what these explorations meant.

Every man carried his own knapsack, which contained provisions for ten days, a gun, blanket and canteen—40 lbs. weight in all ; then to this were added cooking utensils and a hatchet, and they were 'garbed to drag through morasses, tear through thickets, ford rivers and scale rocks.' It will be seen from these few lines alone that Phillip and his officers did not rust in the settlement, and let the country develop itself, as some writers, with but scant knowledge of the early days of the colony, imagine was the case.

This particular expedition started from the Governor's house at Rose Hill — some miles from the main settlement—and first travelled to the N.E. for the greater part of the day, 'after which,' says Tench, 'we turned to N. 34 West . . . until we halted for the night. Our method was to steer by compass, noting the different courses as we proceeded ; and counting the number of paces, of which two thousand two hundred, on good ground, were allowed to be a mile. At night, when we halted, all these courses were separately cast up, and worked by a traverse table . . . so we always knew exactly where we were, and how far from home : an unspeakable advantage in a new country, where one hill and one tree is so 'like another, that fatal wanderings would ensue without it.' Here Tench pays a high compliment to the ardour and skill of Lieutenant Dawes, who worked the traverses. 'The country for the first two miles, while we walked to the northeast, was good, full of grass, and without rock or underwood ; afterwards it grew very bad, being full of steep barren rocks, over which we were compelled to clamber for seven miles, when it changed to a plain country, apparently very sterile. . . . Our fatigue in the morning had, however, been so oppressive that one of the party knocked up. And had not a soldier, as strong as a pack-horse, undertaken to carry his knapsack in addition to his own, we must either have sent him back or have stopped at a place for the night which did not afford water.'

The two blacks who accompanied the party, says Tench, 'walked stoutly, appeared but little fatigued, and maintained their spirits admirably, laughing to excess when any of us either tripped or stumbled. . . . At a very short distance from Rose Hill, we found that they were in a country unknown to them; so that the farther they went, the more dependant on us they became, being absolute strangers inland. We asked Colbee the name of the people who live inland, and he called them Boo-roo-ber-on-gal, and said they were bad; whence we conjectured that they sometimes warred with those on the sea-coast, by whom they were undoubtedly driven up the country from the fishing-ground, that it might not be overstocked; the weaker here, as in every other country, giving way to the stronger. We asked how they lived. He said on birds and animals, having no fish. . . . About an hour after sunset, as we were chatting by the fire side, and preparing to go to rest, we heard voices at a little distance in the wood. Our natives catched the sound instantaneously, and bidding us be silent, listened attentively to the quarter whence it had proceeded. In a few minutes we heard the voices plainly; and wishing exceedingly to open a

communication with this tribe, we begged our natives
to call to them, and bid them to come to us, to
assure them of good treatment, and that they should
have something given them to eat. Colbee no longer
hesitated, but gave them the signal of invitation in
a loud, hollow cry. After some whooping and shout-
ing on both sides, a man with a lighted stick in his
hand advanced near enough to converse with us.
The first words which we could distinctly understand
were, "I am Colbee, of the tribe of Cad-i-gal."
The stranger replied, "I am Ber-ee-wan, of the tribe
of Boo-roo-ber-on-gal." Boladeree informed him also
of his name, and that we were white men and friends,
who would give him something to eat. Still he
seemed irresolute. Colbee therefore advanced to him,
took him by the hand, and led him to us. By the
light of the moon we were introduced to this gentleman, all our names being repeated in form by our
two masters of the ceremonies, who said that we
were Englishmen, and Bud-ye-ree (good), that we
came from the sea-coast, and that we were travelling
inland.'

The strange black stayed some time conversing
with his countrymen, and then left, highly pleased
with a present of provisions. At nine o'clock on
the following morning the party reached the river,
which at the point where it ·was struck was 'about
three hundred and fifty feet wide; the water pure
and excellent to the taste.' The banks were high,

covered with trees, many of which, Tench remarked, were 'bent by the force of the current. . . . Some of them contained rubbish and drift wood in their branches, at least forty-five feet above the level of the stream. . . . Our natives had evidently never seen this river before; they stared at it with surprise. . . . Their total ignorance of the country, and of the direction in which they had walked, appeared when they were asked which way Rose Hill lay, for they pointed almost oppositely to it. Of our compass they had taken early notice, and had talked much to each other about it; they comprehended its use, and called it "Naa - Moro," literally, "To see the way." A more significant or expressive term cannot be found.'

Following the course of the river downwards, and keeping as close as possible to the bank, the party, suffering greatly from fatigue caused by the impediments to walking—scrub and swampy ground —at last reached a deep creek which effectually barred their progress. They therefore followed its course till nightfall, and then halted. 'Our natives,' says Tench, 'continued to hold out stoutly. The hindrances to walking by the river side, which plagued and entangled us so much, seemed not to be heeded by them, and they wound through them with ease; but to us they were intolerably tiresome. Our perplexities afforded them an inexhaustible fund of merriment and derision. Did the sufferer, stung at once with nettles and ridicule, and shaken nigh to death by his fall, use any angry expression to them, they retorted in a moment by calling him by every opprobrious name which their language affords. Boladeree destroyed a native hut to-day very wantonly, before we could prevent him. On being asked why he did so, he answered that the inhabitants inland were bad; though no longer since than last night, when Bereewan had departed, they were loud in their praise. But now they had reverted to their first opinion—so fickle and transient are their motives of love and hatred.

'We set out on the following morning, and continued to trace the creek. The country which we passed through yesterday was good and desirable to what was now presented to us; it was in general high, and universally rocky. "Toiling our uncouth way," we mounted a hill and surveyed the contiguous country. To the northward and eastward the ground was still higher than that we were upon; but in a south-west direction we saw about four miles. The view consisted of nothing but trees growing on precipices; not an acre of it could be cultivated. We saw . . . several vestiges of the natives. To comprehend the reasons which induce an Indian to perform many of the offices of life is difficult; to pronounce that which could lead him to wander amidst these dreary wilds baffles penetration. . . . We reached the head of the creek, passed it, and scrambled with infinite toil and difficulty to the top of a neighbouring mountain, whence we saw the adjacent country, in almost every direction, for many miles. I record with regret that this extended view presented not a single gleam of change, which could encourage hope or stimulate industry to attempt its culture. We had, however, the satisfaction to discover plainly the object of our pursuit, Richmond Hill, distant about eight miles in a contrary direction from what we had been proceeding upon. It was readily known to those who had been up the Hawkesbury in the boats, by a remarkable cleft or notch which distinguished it. It was now determined that we should go back to the head of the creek and pass the night there, and in the morning cut across the country to that part of the river which we had first hit upon yesterday, and thence to trace upward, or to the left. But before I descend, I must not forget to relate that to this pile of desolation on which, like the fallen angel on the top of Niphates, we stood contemplating our nether Eden, His Excellency was pleased to give the name of Tench's Prospect Mount.'

For several pages Tench goes on describing his journey, until at last, after a week spent in this rough travelling, he says :—

'We resolved to abandon our pursuit, and to return home. . . . The country we passed through was for the most part very indifferent, according to our universal opinion. It is in general badly watered; for eight miles and a half on one line we did not find a drop of water.'

The mountains inland of which Phillip 'had a very fine view' were the Blue Mountains, and for nearly a quarter of a century after his departure from the colony they remained an impassable barrier to the westward. He made repeated journeys into the interior, discovered the Hawkesbury River, reached the foot of the Blue Mountains, gave them, from the blue mist which hung over their peaks, their appropriate name, and sent parties to endeavour to penetrate their mysteries. In this they failed, but discovered the Nepean, the source to-day of Sydney's ample water supply.

Topographical details of all these excursions would be wearisome and out of place here, but the main advantage obtained by this thorough examination of the surrounding country was the establishment of the farms at Rose Hill. This agricultural settlement in the neighbourhood of what is now the old town of Parramatta was planned by Phillip, and from the success of its first settler dates the beginning of the young colony's self-dependence.

At headquarters an heroic attempt was made, in spite of the rocky soil, to grow something. A farm was cleared in the cove next to Sydney, and about nine acres of corn planted. The place is now the site of the Botanic Gardens, and the bay formed by its shores, like many another of the inlets of Port Jackson, commemorates by its name—Farm Cove— the earliest times of settlement. To-day in Farm Cove are the moorings of the fifteen modern war-ships which form the Australian Squadron. Other bays named by Phillip are Careening Cove, Sirius Cove, and Neutral Bay, the last named set apart by the first Governor's port regulations as a place where, should foreign vessels enter the harbour, they were to be moored. The great ocean liners of the Peninsular and Oriental and Orient Companies now anchor in this bay, and the surrounding once green hills have been converted into streets of suburban residences.

While Phillip was getting his land into cultivation, King was rapidly converting his ten square miles of territory—Norfolk Island—into a valuable possession for the main settlement.

On his way to Norfolk Island, Lieutenant Ball, the commander of the *Supply*, discovered and named Lord Howe Island, and on the return trip surveyed and annexed it to Phillip's territory. The little island is distant from Sydney about 440 miles, and is now occupied by some seventy or eighty settlers, mostly old whaling seamen and people with a taste for a secluded life, which, as there is little communication with the mainland, their lonely retreat (notwithstanding that it is, for election purposes, within one of the metro-politan electorates) enables them to gratify.

Lieutenant King did not have an altogether pleasant

time of it in his independent command. A few months after landing, the *Supply*, which made regular trips between the island and the mainland, brought the news to Sydney of a daring plot formed by the convicts to capture the island and then make their escape. Their plan was ingenious enough in some respects. It was intended that, on the first Saturday after the arrival of any ship except the *Sirius* at the island, King should be seized. Saturday was chosen, for the reason that on this day it was his practice to visit a farm which he had established in the interior, and the military were also usually away at the same time bringing in cabbage palm from the woods. The commandant was to be kidnapped while on his way to the farm. Then a message in King's name was to entice Mr Jamieson, the surgeon, away ; he was to be captured in the same manner as King ; and the sergeant and small military guard were to be similarly treated. These all being properly disposed of, the ship was to be signalled to send her boat on shore, and the crew were to be made prisoners. This accomplished, some convicts were to go off to the ship in a boat belonging to the island, and tell the captain that the ship's boat had been stove in, and that the commandant requested that another might be sent. The crew of this were also to be captured ; and then the ship was to be boarded and seized, and the mutineers were to sail her to Otaheite (Tahiti) in the South Seas, and there found a settlement. They intended, however, to leave some provisions for Mr King and his command. Fortunately for the commandant, the plot was revealed to his gardener—a seaman belonging to the *Sirius*—by a female convict who was living with him.

' Mr King had hitherto, from the peculiarity of his situation—secluded from society, and confined to a small speck in the vast ocean, with but a handful of people—drawn them round him, and treated them with the kind attentions which a good family meets with at the hands of a humane master ; but he now saw them in their true colours, and one of his first steps when peace was restored was to clear the ground as far as possible round the settlement, that future villainy might not find a shelter in the woods for its transactions.   To this truly providential circumstance, perhaps, many of the colonists afterwards were indebted for their lives.'

In the last days of February, King, whose heart was set on his being able to send Phillip a good report of the place and some supplies as well, had a bitter disappointment.   It began to blow early on the morning of the 26th, and by noon ' the gale increased to a hurricane, with torrents of heavy rain.   Every instant pines and live oaks of the largest dimensions were borne down by the fury of the blast, which, tearing up roots and rocks with them, left chasms of eight or ten feet depth in the earth.   Those pines that were able to resist the wind bent their tops nearly to the ground ; and nothing but horror and desolation everywhere presented itself. . . . The gardens, public and private, were wholly destroyed ; cabbages, turnips and other plants were blown out of the ground ; and those which withstood the hurricane seemed as if they had been scorched. An acre of Indian corn which grew in the vale, and which would have been ripe in about three weeks, was totally destroyed.' Poor King ! But his was not a nature to be daunted by misfortune. He at once began the work so ruthlessly destroyed over again ; and fortunately the health of the people of his little colony was good. There were at this time on Norfolk Island 16 free people, 51 male and 26 female convicts, and 4 children.

Notwithstanding insurrections and hurricanes, King made good progress with his agriculture, for in December 1789 we are told that 'Lieutenant King wrote that he expected his harvest would produce from four to six months' flour for all his inhabitants, exclusive of a reserve of double seed for twenty acres of ground. Beside this promising appearance, he had ten acres in cultivation with Indian corn, which looked very well.'

Not much in all this, it may be said, but remember always that the men responsible were but rough sailors, whose business in life hitherto had not been Empire - building. Remember, too, that Hawser Trunnion and Hatchway are accepted types of the naval officers of the period, created by Smollett only thirty years earlier, and though to some extent exaggerations, still not very far from the truth. Yet, compare Phillip and King with Trunnion and Hatchway !

At Rose Hill (so named after one of the Secretaries to the Treasury) the soil was free from the rock which everywhere prevented cultivation nearer Sydney, and Phillip early in 1790 wrote :—

'As near two years have now passed since we first landed in this country, some judgment may be formed of the climate, and I believe a finer or more healthy climate is not to be found in any part of the world. Of 1030 people who were landed, many of whom were worn out by old age, the scurvy, and various disorders, only seventy-two have died in one-and-twenty months ; and by the surgeon's returns it appears that twenty-six of those died from disorders of long standing, and which it is more than probable would have carried them off much sooner in England. Fifty - nine children have been born in the above time. . . .

'In December the corn at Rose Hill was got in ; the corn was exceeding good. About two hundred bushels of wheat and sixty of barley, with a small quantity of flax, Indian corn, and oats, all which is preserved for seed. Here I beg leave to observe to your Lordship that if settlers are sent out, and the convicts divided amongst them, this settlement will very shortly maintain itself, but without which this country cannot be cultivated to any advantage. At present I have only one person (who has about an hundred convicts under his direction) who is employed in cultivating the ground for the publick benefit, and he has returned the quantity of corn above mentioned into the publick store. The officers have not raised sufficient to support the little stock they have. Some ground I have had in cultivation will return about forty bushels of wheat into store, so that the produce of the labour of the convicts employed in cultivation has been very short of what might have been expected, and which I take the liberty of pointing out to your Lordship in this place, to show as fully as possible the state of this colony, and the necessity of the convicts being employed by those who have an interest in their labour. The giving convicts to the officers has been hitherto necessary, but it is attended with many inconveniences, for which the advantages arising to the officers do not make amends. It will not therefore be continued after the detachment is relieved, unless particularly directed. The plan I should propose for giving the convicts to settlers will be submitted to your Lordship's consideration in another letter. The numbers employed in cultivation will, of course, be increased as the necessary buildings are finished, but which will be a work of time ; for the numbers in this settlement who do nothing towards their own support exceed those employed for the public.'

The Governor was so pleased with his farm that he took up his residence there in order personally to superintend its cultivation.

The labourers on the settlement were in charge of Phillip's man-servant, who came from England with his master. Collins describes the man as one who 'joined to much agricultural knowledge a perfect idea of the labour to be required from, and that might be performed by, the convicts; and his figure was calculated to make the idle and the worthless shrink if he came near them.

A town was laid out at Rose Hill, with a street a mile long, and on the King's birthday—4th June 1791—the place was named Parramatta. In the old cemetery at the town there still stands the tombstone of the man who surveyed it, and the stone bears this inscription :—

'Sacred to the memory of Augustus Theodore Henry Alt, Baron of Hesse Cassel, who died January 9, 1815, aged 84 years; late Surveyor-General of New South Wales, at the first settling of this colony, which situation he held till superannuated. He served in the Guards in George the Second's reign; was Aide-de-Camp to Prince Ferdinand at the battle of Minden (1759), and Captain in the Royal Manchester Volunteers at the Siege of Gibraltar under General [Elliot] (1781), where he distinguished himself in a gallant manner. He died universally regretted by all his friends, who lost in the Baron a Most

Compleat Gentleman, and also one who never told an untruth to the injury of any man. This monument was erected by his Nephew, Matthew Bowles Alt, Lieutenant in His Majesty's Royal Navy, as a Tribute of Respect to the conduct of his respected uncle.'

All this so far is trivial, perhaps uninteresting, but then Australia has no history, and Phillip's farming experiments, and the condition of his crops were of real importance to the infant colony, for grim famine was at this time beginning to loom upon the horizon.

CHAPTER IX

EARLY in 1789 it became apparent to Phillip that something had gone wrong with the storeships, which, with a childlike faith in the Government, he fully believed must have long before left England with supplies for the settlement. If either of the victuallers which sailed with the First Fleet had come to grief on the passage out—and there was no more likely contingency—the colony, months before the arrival of a second supply of stores, would have been actually starving. The possibility of this had been foreseen by Phillip and pointed out to Lord Sydney, but his lordship seems to have been easy in his mind, imagining no doubt that this paragraph in the 'Instructions' would be faithfully carried out :—

'The increase of the stock of animals must depend entirely upon the measures you may adopt on the outset for their preservation, and as the settlement will be amply supplied with vegetable productions, and most likely with fish, fresh provisions, excepting for the sick and convalescents, may in a great degree be dispensed with. For these reasons it will become you to be extremely cautious in permitting any cattle, sheep, hogs, etc., intended for propagating the breed of such animals, to be slaughtered, until a competent stock may be acquired, to admit of your supplying the settlement from it with animal food without having further recourse to the places from whence such stock may have originally been obtained.'

But fish were so scarce that even the blacks were unable to catch them, and were starving, and the 'vegetable productions' were as yet not forthcoming.

In all his despatches home Phillip never once despairs, never even complains. He tells the truth, puts down in figures how many people there are to feed, how little food there is to give them, and what is wanted to keep the colony alive, and ends his letters with the cheerful assurance that they will still pull through all right. We have seen how Major Ross wrote to England and what he had to say of things at this time, and his letters, with other dismal accounts, were published in the London papers. White, the principal surgeon, wrote [1] :—

'Much cannot now be done, limited in food and reduced as the people are, who have not had one ounce of fresh animal food since first in the country ; a country and place so forbidding and so hateful as only to merit execration and curses, for it has been a source of expence to the mother country and of evil and misfortune to us, without there ever being the smallest likelihood of its repaying or recompencing either. From what we have already seen we may conclude that there is not a single article in the whole country that in the nature of things could prove of the smallest use or advantage to the mother country or the commercial world. In the name of heaven, what has the Ministry been about? Surely they have quite forgotten or neglected us, otherwise they would have sent to see what had become of us, and to know how we were likely to succeed. However, they must soon know from the heavy bills which will be presented to them, and the misfortunes and losses which have already happened to us, how necessary it becomes to relinquish a scheme that in the nature of things can never answer. It would be wise by the first

---

[1] This letter was published in the *Public Advertiser* on the 31st December 1790, appropriately addressed to ' Mr Skill, dealer in hams, tongues, salt salmon, etc., in the Strand.'

steps to withdraw the settlement, at least such as are living, or remove them to some other place; this is so much out of the world and tract of commerce' that it could never answer. How a business of this kind (the expence of which must be great) could first be thought of without sending to examine the country, as was Captain Thompson's errand to the coast òf Africa, is to every person here a matter of great surprise.'

Most of these letters were written privately to friends in England, and the friends no doubt thought the best thing to do with them was to send them to the newspapers, where they were generally published as from 'Officers at Botany Bay.' Another letter, identified as coming from Tench, says :—

'By the time this reaches you, the fate of this settlement and all it contains will be decided. It is now more than two years since we landed here, and within a month less than three since we left England. So cut off from intercourse with the rest of mankind are we, that, subsequent to the month of August 1788, we know not of any transaction that has happened in Europe, and are no more assured of the welfare or existence of any of our friends than of what passes in the moon. It is by those only who have felt the anguish and distress of such a state that its miseries can be conceived.

'The little European knowledge that we are

masters of we picked out of some old English newspapers which were brought from the Cape of Good Hope about a twelvemonth back in the *Sirius*, by which ship you may possibly recollect to have received a letter from me, dated 1st October 1788: but as to all family news, all knowledge of our private affairs, or little endearing accounts which no man, I presume, is without a wish to receive, nothing but a blank for the long space of three years has been presented to us. But great as our anxiety on this head is, it falls short of what we suffer on another account. The dread of perishing by famine stares us in the face; on the day I write we have but eight weeks' provision in the public stores, and all chance of a reinforcement under seven months is cut off, unless ships from England should yet, notwithstanding the lateness of the season, come in upon us. The hope of this is, however, very feeble, for, without the most shameful and cruel inattention on your part, ships must have left England by the first of August last to come here: and if so, they have undoubtedly perished on their route. Even this alternative, dreadful as it is, is less inflicting than to believe that our country would send us out here as a sacrifice to famine and the savages of the place, who, if ever they shall by any means learn our situation, will prove extremely troublesome.' . . . Then the writer goes on to say that the 'pride, pomp and circumstance

of war' are at an end with the garrison, for none
of the soldiers have boots! . . . After having
suffered as they have, he says it will be hard for
them on their return to England 'to meet the
sneers of a set of holiday troops, whose only employ
has been to powder their hair, polish their shoes,
etc. . . . though I must admit that our gait and
raggedness will give them some title to be merry
at our expence.' So continuously had they been
employed that no military manœuvre of any consequence had been practised since the detachment
left England. And he concludes by saying :—

'The country is past all dispute a wretched one,
a very wretched, and totally incapable of yielding
to Great Britain any return for colonizing it.
Amidst its native productions I cannot number
one which is valuable as an article of commerce.
There is no wood fit for naval purposes ; no fibrous
grass or plant from which cloth can be made ; no
substance which can improve or aid the labours
of the manufacturer ; no mineral productions ; no
esculent vegetables worth the care of collecting
and transporting to other climes ; and lastly, which
is of the most serious consideration, no likelihood
that the colony will be able to support itself in
grain or animal food for many years to come, so
that a regular annual expence is entailed on the
mother country as long as it is kept.'

Ross we have already quoted. So early as July

1788 he wrote that 'the country would not support itself for a hundred years.' Another writer described it as 'the outcast of God's works.'

The first news from the settlement sent home *via* China by the returning transports did not reach England until March 1789, when letters down to November 1788 all came in together. No storeship had up to that date been ordered for despatch to Botany Bay.

The Home Office was at this time the department for the administration of the Colonies,[1] and Sydney, who was at the head of it, did not even reply to Phillip's despatches, but in April he gave instructions that a man-of-war should be got in readiness to carry provisions to the settlement. At the same time he arranged for the despatch of another batch of convicts, totally disregarding Phillip's statements that clothing, implements and provisions were urgently needed, and that more useless mouths to feed would mean disaster.

In June 1789 Lord Sydney resigned office and was succeeded by Lord Grenville.[2] His first despatch to Phillip was the first communication, after more than three years' absence from England, that Phillip had received from his superiors.

In this letter Grenville informs the Governor of

---

[1] The office of Secretary of State for the Colonies was not created until 1854.

[2] Then the Right Hon. W. W. Grenville.

the receipt of his despatches; that His Majesty has been pleased to approve of his conduct of the 'arduous and important service' committed to his care; and that the ship *Lady Juliana* had been taken up by the Government to convey to Port Jackson about 240 female convicts, with a consignment of implements, clothing and provisions. The convicts upon arrival were to be transferred to Phillip to be employed as would be most conducive to the advantage of the colony. The attention given by the Governor to the separation of the convicts of different sexes on the voyage out of the First Fleet is duly commended, and a 'well-grounded hope' is expressed that he will continue to promote matrimonial connection between the unmarried people.

This unpleasant intelligence concerning the *Lady Juliana's* cargo was, however, followed by the news that the *Guardian*, man-of-war, was to sail a fortnight after the transport with about three times the quantity of stores embarked on the former, 'which,' Grenville adds, 'excepting in the article of provisions, you will find nearly to correspond with the estimates accompanying your letters.' But the Secretary of State was careful to add that the supplies had been procured at a very considerable expense, and it was hoped that Phillip would make the most of them. He was further informed that in the autumn the Government expected to send out another 1000 convicts of both sexes, and the unfortunate man, already worried and overworked, was enjoined to make arrangements 'for their accommodation as well as for their employment' upon their arrival.

His choice of Port Jackson as the site of the settlement was approved of, but as by his own account the soil did not appear to be very fertile, and the numbers and hostility of the natives made cultivation difficult and dangerous, it was thought that Norfolk Island would be the most favourable position, and were it not for the fact of great labour and expense having already been incurred at Port Jackson, Grenville would have recommended that island being made the main settlement.   Phillip, however, was instructed to increase the establishment on the island as far as he conveniently could, and if any similar situation equally advantageous should be discovered, to detach thither a considerable part of the convicts who would be sent out in the next ships.   'The *Guardian* will have on board about twenty-five convicts who are either artificers or persons accustomed to agriculture, and also eight or ten superintendents, who have been engaged in consequence of your recommendation of the measure; to each of the latter an annual salary of £40 will be given in addition to the ration of provisions.'

Captain Cook, it will be remembered, had discovered Norfolk Island, and its size, by a reference to the chart, could have been seen by the youngest clerk in the Home Office, and yet in the opinion of Grenville it was a better place than Port Jackson for the chief settlement !

But before this despatch arrived many things happened. First, Phillip, finding that no storeships came in, despatched the *Sirius* to the Cape of Good Hope for provisions. She returned in May 1789, and on the way back she encountered very heavy weather. Southwell, who was on board, writing to his uncle, says :—

'I will now say a word or two concerning our passage when coming from the Cape of Good Hope. When I last wrote to you, having taken in our cargo, the principal which was six months' full allowance of flour for the colony and twelve months' provisions for the ship, we sailed again for New Holland, and had a very narrow escape from shipwreck, being driven on that part of the coast called Tasman's Head, in thick weather and hard gales of wind, and embayed, being twelve hours before we got clear, the ship forced to be overpressed with sail and the hands kept continually at the pumps, and all this time in the most distressing anxiety, being uncertain of our exact situation and doubtful of our tackling holding, which has a very long time been bad : for had a mast gone or a top-sheet given way, there was nothing to be expected in such boisterous weather but certain death on a coast so inhospitable and unknown. And now to reflect if we had not have reached the port with that seasonable supply, what could have become of this colony ?'

The flour brought by the *Sirius* was not much, and still no storeships came. Phillip accordingly determined to reduce the rations, and on 1st November 1789 a reduction of one-third was made. This reduction applied to everyone, women excepted, in the settlement. Says Collins :—

'The Governor, whose humanity was at all times conspicuous, directed that no alteration should be made in the ration to be issued to the women. They were already upon two-thirds of the men's allowance; and many of them either had children who could very well have eaten their own and part of the mother's ration, or they had children at the breast; and although they did not labour, yet their appetites were never so delicate as to have found the full ration too much had it been issued to them. The like reduction was enforced afloat as well as on shore, the ships' companies of the *Sirius* and *Supply* being put to two-thirds of the allowance usually issued to the King's ships. . . .

'Thus opened the month of November in this settlement; where, though we had not the accompanying gloom and vapour of our own climate to render it terrific to our minds, yet we had that before us, in the midst of all our sunshine, which gave it the complexion of the true November so inimical to our countrymen.'

These reduced rations were issued, Collins adds, to the convicts on Saturdays ; by the following Tuesday night the greater number of the recipients had nothing left to allay the pangs of hunger. Their only resource was persistent thieving from their fellows or the other members of the settlement. The Governor therefore gave instructions to issue provisions on Wednesdays as well as Saturdays. The allowance being thus divided caused even the improvident to be more able to perform the labour required from them ; and that Phillip, in view of their condition, made that labour as light as possible, we can have no doubt.

Tench gives us a picture of the settlement at this time :—

'Our impatience of news from Europe strongly marked the commencement of the year. We had now been two years in the country, and thirty-two months from England, in which long period no supplies, except what had been procured at the Cape of Good Hope by the *Sirius*, had reached us. From intelligence of our friends and connections we had entirely been cut off, no communication whatever having passed with our native country since the 13th of May 1787, the day of our departure from Portsmouth. Famine, beside, was approaching with gigantic strides, and gloom and dejection overspread every countenance. Men abandoned themselves to the most desponding reflections, and adopted the most extravagant conjectures.

'Still we were on the tip-toe of expectation. If thunder broke at a distance, or a fowling-piece of louder than ordinary report resounded in the woods, "a gun from a ship" was echoed on every side, and nothing but hurry and agitation prevailed. For eighteen months after we had landed in the country, a party of marines used to go weekly to Botany Bay to see whether any vessel, ignorant of our removal to Port Jackson, might be arrived there. But a better plan was now devised, on the suggestion of Captain Hunter. A party of seamen was fixed on a high bluff called South Head at the entrance to the harbour, on which a flag was ordered to be hoisted whenever a ship might appear, which should serve as a direction to her, and as a signal of approach to us. Every officer stepped forward to volunteer a service which promised to be so replete with beneficial consequences. But the zeal and alacrity of Captain Hunter and our brethren of the *Sirius* rendered superfluous all assistance or co-operation.

'Here on the summit of the hill, every morning from daylight till the sun sunk, did we sweep the horizon in hope of seeing a sail. At every fleeting speck which arose from the bosom of the sea the heart bounded, and the telescope was lifted to the eye. If a ship appeared here, we knew she must be bound to us : for on the shores of this vast ocean (the largest in the world) we were the only community which possessed the art of navigation, and languished for intercourse with civilised society.

'Vigorous measures were become indispensible. The Governor, therefore, early in February ordered the *Sirius* to prepare for a voyage to China; and a farther retrenchment of our rations, we were given to understand, would take place on her sailing.

'But the *Sirius* was destined not to reach China. Previously to her intended voyage she was ordered, in concert with the *Supply*, to convey Major Ross, with a large detachment of marines, and more than 200 convicts, to Norfolk Island, it being hoped that such a division of our numbers would increase the means of subsistance, by diversified exertions. She sailed on the 6th of March . . . and on the 27th of the same month, the following order was issued from head-quarters : " The expected supply of provisions not having arrived makes it necessary to reduce the present ration, and the commissary is directed to issue, from the 1st of April, the undermentioned allowance to every person in the settlement without distinction, four pounds of flour, two pounds and a half of salt pork, and one pound and a half of rice per week." '

The officer in charge of the look-out was, it will be remembered, young Southwell, and he watched the departure of the two ships as they sailed out between the Heads. Nothing more was seen of either of them, he writes, till the 5th April, when at daybreak he was roused from his slumbers by the look-out man with the news that a sail was in sight. The ship, as she neared the land, was judged by him to be the *Supply*, though he wondered at her returning so soon. Foreboding an accident, he 'desired the gunner to notice if the people mustered thick on her decks as she came in under the headland.'

His misgivings were too well-founded—the ship was the *Supply*, the *Sirius* had left her bones on Norfolk Island.

CHAPTER X

FAMINE was now upon the land. Collins and Tench both tell in simple but moving words the pitiful story of that time, the darkest hour in the colony's young life. Tench writes :—

'On the 5th of April, news was brought that the flag on the South Head was hoisted. Less emotion was created by the news than might be expected. Everyone coldly said to his neighbour, "The *Sirius* and *Supply* are returned from Norfolk Island."'

To satisfy himself that the news was correct, he went to the Observatory and looked through the large astronomical telescope at the flag. He saw it plainly enough, but with sinking heart was at once convinced that the ship was not from England, for

he could see the solitary figure of the signalman
strolling to and fro, unmoved by what he saw. ' I
well knew how different an effect the sight of strange
ships would produce.' Phillip, burning with anxiety,
was ready to go down the harbour, and Tench accompanied him. Half-way down the harbour, just as they
turned a point, they saw a boat which they knew
belonged to the *Supply* rowing towards them. As
the boats neared each other, Tench saw Captain
Ball (of the *Supply*) make a motion with his hand
which indicated that he brought a tale of disaster.
Turning to the Governor, Tench begged him to
prepare himself for bad news. ' A few minutes
changed doubt into certainty ; and to our unspeakable consternation we learned that the *Sirius*
had been wrecked on Norfolk Island on the 19th
of February. Happily, however, Captain Hunter
and every other person belonging to her were saved.
Dismay was painted on every countenance when the
tidings were proclaimed in Sydney. The most dis-
tracting apprehensions were entertained, and all hopes
were now concentred in the little *Supply*.

' When the age of our provisions is recollected, the
inadequacy of our food will more strikingly appear.
The pork and rice were brought with us from England.
The pork had been salted between three and four
years, and every grain of rice was a moving body,
from the inhabitants lodged within it ! We soon
left off boiling the pork, as it had become so old and

dry that it sunk one-half in its dimensions when dressed. Our usual method of cooking it was to cut off the daily morsel and toast it on a fork before the fire, catching the drops which fell on a slice of bread or in a saucer of rice. Our flour was the remnant of what was brought from the Cape by the *Sirius*, and was good. Instead of baking it, the soldiers and convicts used to boil it up with greens.'

Can anyone nowadays imagine the hideous isolation of the place? Railways, telegraphs, steamships have made such a complete cutting off from the world, in these times, a matter of impossibility. Upon Phillip alone rested the duty of finding food and caring for a thousand persons, nine hundred of whom, from ignorance and viciousness, would have died of starvation sooner than have done a hand's turn to help themselves.

Maxwell, one of the lieutenants of the *Sirius*, had gone melancholy mad, was discharged from the ship, and was at this time wandering about the settlement. Says Collins :—

'Mr Maxwell, whose disorder at times admitted of his going out alone, was fortunately brought up from the lower part of the harbour, where he had passed nearly two days, without sustenance, in rowing from one side to the other in a small boat by himself. He was noticed by a sergeant who had been fishing, and who observed him rowing under the dangerous rocks of the Middle Head, where he must soon have been dashed to pieces, but for his fortunate interposition. After this escape he was more narrowly watched. While occupied in listening to the tale of his distress, the *Supply* returned from Norfolk Island with an account that was of itself almost sufficient to have deranged the strongest intellect among us. A load of accumulated evils seemed bursting at once upon our heads. The ships that we expected with supplies were still to be anxiously looked for; and the *Sirius*, which was to have gone in quest of relief to our distresses, was lost upon the reef at Norfolk Island on the 19th of last month. This was a blow which, as it was expected, fell with increased weight, and on every-one the whole weight seemed to have fallen.

'This untoward accident happened in the following manner: Captain Hunter was extremely fortunate in having a short passage hence to Norfolk Island, arriving there in seven days after he sailed. The soldiers and a considerable part of the convicts were immediately landed in Cascade Bay, which happened at the time to be the leeward side of the island. Bad weather immediately ensued, and continuing for several days, the provisions could not be landed, so high was the surf occasioned by it. This delay, together with a knowledge that the provisions on the island were not adequate to the additional numbers that were now to be victualled, caused him' (Hunter) 'to be particularly anxious to get the provisions on shore. The bad weather had separated the *Sirius* from the *Supply*; but meeting with a favourable slant of wind on the 19th, Captain Hunter gained the island from which he had been driven, and stood for Sydney Bay, at the south end of it, where he found the *Supply*; and it being signified by signal from the shore (where they could form the best judgment) that the landing might be effected by any boat, he brought-to in the windward part of the bay, with the ship's head off shore, got out the boats, and loaded them with provisions.' He then describes how the ship began to drift towards the rocks, and how an endeavour was made to put her about, when she missed stays, and striking with violence on the reef, very soon bilged, and was irrecoverably lost. 'Her officers and people were all saved, having been dragged on shore through the surf on a grating. This day, which untoward circumstances have rendered so gloomy to us, was remarkably fine, and at the unfortunate moment of this calamity there was very little wind. On the next or second day after, permission was given to two convicts (one of whom, James Brannegan, was an overseer) to get off to the ship, and endeavour to bring on shore what live hogs they might be able to save; but with all that lamentable want of resolution and consideration which is characteristic of the lower order of people when temptations are placed before them, they both got intoxicated with the liquor which had escaped the

K

plunder of the seamen, and set the ship on fire in two places. A light on board the ship being observed from the shore, several shot were fired at it, but the wretches would neither put it out or come on shore; when a young man of the name of Ascott, a convict, with great intrepidity went off through the surf, extinguished the fire and forced them out of the ship.'

For his good service it is satisfactory to know that Ascott was not forgotten by Phillip, who wrote to England and procured his pardon.

The disaster to the *Sirius* again served to show Phillip's resourcefulness. He assembled his civil and military officers without delay, and the desperate situation of the colony was thoroughly considered. It was decided to reduce still further a ration that was already too low for proper human subsistence. To fish for a living, instead of being a mere expression, became a literal fact, for all private boats were to be surrendered for the general benefit.

The services of the three convicts to whom the duty had been assigned of shooting kangaroos for individuals were now employed for the benefit of the community, but although considered good marksmen, they only succeeded in killing three kangaroos in as many weeks. A fishery, under the control of one of the midshipmen of the wrecked *Sirius*, was established at Botany Bay, but it did not answer, and was soon abandoned. At the present day Botany Bay is one of the main sources of the fish supply of the city of Sydney, but in Phillip's day—doubtless owing to the want of proper gear—the quantity of fish taken was very inconsiderable, and the labour of transporting it by land from thence was greater than the advantage which was expected to be derived from it.

The boats were therefore removed to Sydney, where they were employed with better success, but the straits of the settlement may be imagined when it is recorded that an officer had to go in every boat, night and day, to prevent the fish caught being devoured by the hungry fishermen. Once four hundredweight of fish were caught, but generally the united take of the boats was no more than sufficient to provide the men employed with one pound of fish per man, which was allowed them in addition to their scanty ration. The small, privately owned boats were therefore returned to their owners, and the fishing was conducted in the larger boats belonging to the settlement, under the direction of some seamen belonging to the *Sirius*.

Absolute starvation now stared the community in the face. The proposed voyage of the *Sirius* to China for provisions was at an end, and the long looked for succour from England, though hourly expected, had not arrived. The necessity of procuring relief became every day more pressing. The Governor, therefore, determined to send the *Supply* to Batavia. Ball, the energetic commander of this small vessel, was directed to buy a supply of eight months' provisions for himself, and from the Dutch authorities to hire a vessel and purchase flour, beef, pork and rice, together with some necessaries for the hospital. The expectation of this relief was indeed distant, but yet it was more to be depended upon than that which might be coming from England. A given time was fixed for the return of the *Supply*; but it was impossible to say when a vessel might arrive from Europe. Whatever might be the distress for provisions, it would be some alleviation to look on to a certain fixed date when it might be expected to be removed. Lieutenant Ball's passage lay through the region of fine weather, and the hopes of everyone were fixed upon the little vessel which was to convey him. The *Supply* sailed from Sydney on the 17th of April; on board was Lieutenant King, the late commandant of Norfolk Island, charged with Phillip's despatches for the Secretary of State. The emotions of the settlers, free and bond, as they saw the small craft, the last link that bound them to the world beyond, disappear from their view, may be readily imagined.

Collins narrates that 'the Governor, from a motive that did him immortal honour in this season of general distress,' gave up three hundredweight of flour which was his private property, 'declaring that he wished not to see anything more at his table than the ration which was received in common from the public store, without any distinction of persons ; and to this resolution he resolutely adhered, wishing that if a convict complained, he might see that want was not unfelt even at Government House.'

The ration at 'Government House' and the military and convict quarters was then, Collins tells us :—

'To each man for 7 days, or to 7 people for one day : flour, $2\frac{1}{2}$ pounds ; rice, 2 pounds ; pork, 2 pounds.'

The pease were all expended. Was this a ration for a labouring man ? The two pounds of pork, when boiled, from the length of time it had been in the store, shrunk away to nothing ; and when divided among seven people for their day's sustenance, barely afforded three or four morsels each.

'The inevitable consequences of this scarcity of provisions ensued. Labour stood nearly suspended for want of energy to proceed ; and the countenances of the people plainly bespoke the hardships they underwent. The convicts, however, were employed for the public in the afternoons ; and such labour was obtained from them as their situation would allow.'

Meanwhile, what was happening at Norfolk Island ? Ross's opportunity had come to show how *he* could govern. Possibly Phillip had sent him to the island to get rid of him. It was time for someone to carry to the Home Government urgent representations of the colony's great need, and Phillip had no officer so well fitted for this service as King. The lieutenant could be trusted to do his best to procure the much-needed supplies, and at the same time he was not the man to join forces with the 'opposition,' and recommend that the settlement should be abandoned on the ground that 'it would not support itself for a hundred years.'

The military, if not the administrative spirit, is shown in what followed the wreck of the *Sirius*. King retained command of the island until he left it in the *Supply*, and did so at the request of Ross, yet according to Hunter's *Narrative*, immediately after the ship was lost, 'Lieutenant-Governor Ross ordered the drums to assemble all the mariners and convicts; martial law was then proclaimed, and the people were told that if anyone killed any animal or fowl, or committed any robbery whatever, they would be instantly made a severe example of. The officers and marines were ordered to wear their field arms; guards were set over the barn and storehouses, and some other necessary regulations were ordered by the Lieutenant-Governor.'

It will be seen that Ross, who was unable to sanction his officers taking part in judicial proceedings at Port Jackson under Governor Phillip, speedily discovered a means by which a court could be formed at Norfolk Island under Lieutenant - Governor Ross. At Port Jackson the marines declared that a general court-martial could not assemble unless thirteen officers were present, and could not act then unless under a warrant from the Admiralty. At Norfolk Island, by proclaiming martial law, Ross conceived that his warrant for convening a court was sufficient for all purposes. The condition of affairs at the island when the *Sirius* went on shore is, of course, some justification for Ross's 'panic legislation,' although Mr Barton, the ablest Australian historian, has arrived at an opposite conclusion. Mr Barton quotes authorities to show that the only justification recognised by English law for proclaiming martial law ' is necessity, a necessity demonstrated by facts, not an imaginary one.' But Ross was in the position of a captain of a ship with his vessel in the breakers, who loads his revolvers in readiness to shoot the first man who attempts to rush the boats.

Ross's crew were of a kind very likely to rush the boats, and if he was a little hasty in getting his revolvers ready, small blame to him on that account : but it is a pity that when acting under Phillip he should have shown such extreme regard for red-tape formalities in the matter of the court-martial.

All this time the people on the mainland are left nearly starving, and so Norfolk Island must take care of itself as best it can for a while. No news of it can reach Port Jackson, for the *Sirius* is slowly breaking up on the reef, and the *Supply* has gone to Batavia for help.

'I early and late look with anxious eyes toward the sea, and at times, when the day was fast setting and

the shadows of the evening stretched out, have been
deceived with some fantastic little cloud, which, as
it has condensed or expanded by such a light, for a
little time has deceived impatient imagination into a
momentary idea that 'twas a vessel altering her sails
or position while steering in for the haven, when in
a moment it has assumed a form so unlike what the
mind was intent upon, or become so greatly· extended,
as fully to certify me of its flimsy texture and fleeting
existence. Surely our countrymen cannot have altogether forgotten us, or been vainly led from any silly,
sanguine representations hence, to trust we could make
it out tolerably well without their assistance.'

One can well imagine young Southwell, who thus
wrote to his uncle, straining his eyes seaward from
the cliffs at South Head, and looking in vain for a
sail on the solitary Pacific — the ocean, for many
hundreds of miles further than the range of his
telescope, a desert of water.

Meanwhile, what must have been the feelings of
the lonely man upon whom the welfare of the entire
settlement depended—a burden no wise lessened by
the whinings of his small-souled subordinates, each
preoccupied with his own individual grievances?

Tench tells how at length the clouds of misfortune
began to separate, and on the evening of the 3rd of
June, the joyful cry of 'the flag's up,' resounded in
every direction.

'I was sitting in my hut, musing on our fate, when

a confused clamour in the street drew my attention. I opened my door, and saw several women with children in their arms running to and fro with distracted looks, congratulating each other, and kissing their infants with the most passionate and extravagant marks of fondness. I needed no more; but instantly started out, and ran to a hill, where, by the assistance of a pocket-glass, my hopes were realized. My next door neighbour, a brother officer, was with me; but we could not speak; we wrung each other by the hand, with eyes and hearts overflowing. Finding that the Governor intended to go immediately in his boat down the harbour, I begged to be of his party. As we proceeded, the object of our hopes soon appeared— a large ship, with English colours flying, working in between the heads which form the entrance of the harbour. The tumultuous state of our minds represented her in danger, and we were in agony. Soon after, the Governor, having ascertained what she was, left us, and stepped into a fishing boat to return to Sydney.

' The weather was wet and tempestuous; but the body is delicate only when the soul is at ease. We pushed through wind and rain, the anxiety of our sensations every moment redoubling. At last we read the word " London " on her stern. " Pull away, my lads, she is from old England; a few strokes more, and we shall be aboard; hurrah for a belly-full, and news from our friends ! " Such were our exhortations to the boat's crew. A few minutes completed our wishes, and we found ourselves on board the *Lady Juliana* transport, with two hundred and twenty-five of our countrywomen, whom crime or misfortune had condemned to exile. We learned that they had been almost eleven months on their passage, having left Plymouth, into which port they had put, in July 1789. We continued to ask a thousand questions in a breath. Stimulated by curiosity, they inquired in turn ; but the right of being first answered, we thought, lay on our side. " Letters ! letters ! " was the cry. They were produced, and torn open in trembling agitation. News burst upon us like meridian splendor on a blind man.   We were overwhelmed with it ; public, private, general and particular. Nor was it until some days had elapsed that we were able to methodize it, or reduce it into form. We now heard for the first time of our Sovereign's illness, and his happy restoration to health. The French Revolution of 1789, with all the attendant circumstances of that wonderful and unexpected event, succeeded to amaze us. Now, too, the disaster which had befallen the *Guardian* ' (wrecked on her way out), 'and the liberal and enlarged plan on which she had been stored and fitted out by Government for our use, was promulged. It served also in some measure to account why we had not sooner heard from England.

'For had not the *Guardian* struck on an island of ice, she would probably have reached us three months before, and in this case have prevented the loss of the *Sirius*, although she' (the *Guardian*) 'had sailed from England three months after the *Lady Juliana*.'

The loss of this ship was a disaster great enough to merit a page of description here, but the name of her commander, of whom Nelson wrote as the 'gallant and good Captain Riou,' gives additional interest to the story of the wreck.

The *Guardian* was a forty-four gun ship, which had been selected for the service on account of her fast sailing qualities. Her guns were taken out, she was specially fitted, and had on board a great quantity of provisions and stores of all kinds for the settlement. She sailed from England in September 1789, and on the 23rd of December, after leaving the Cape of Good Hope, she struck some floating ice, receiving severe damage.

To prevent the vessel sinking, most of the live stock and other stores were thrown overboard. Riou, after doing what he could to save the ship, concluded that there was no chance of keeping her afloat, and so sent most of the people away in the boats, but himself with a few others remained on board, and after a wonderful and hazardous voyage lasting nine weeks, succeeded in getting back to the Cape.

After reaching Cape Town, although badly injured in the accident, Riou worked like a Trojan to get the ship repaired, but at last had to give it up. His great concern was for the people in the little colony, who were, as he fully understood, in sore need of the stores. Behind the *Guardian* the other vessels of the Second Fleet of transports were slowly arriving at the Cape, and Riou used every exertion to hasten on their departure, putting on board them what stores he had saved from the wreck.

In a despatch to the Admiralty sent by him on 20th May 1790, he writes :—

'By the *Lady Juliana*, transport, which sailed from this bay on the 30th of March, I sent seventy-five barrels of flour and one pipe of Teneriffe wine consigned to Governor Phillip. I had been so fortunate as to preserve the despatches which I had received from the hands of Vice-Admiral Roddam for Governor Phillip, and I delivered them to the care of Lieut. Thomas Edgar, superintendant of the *Lady Juliana*. In that ship I also sent the five surviving superintendants of convicts which were on board the *Guardian*.

'The *Neptune, Surprize,* and *Scarborough* arrived in False Bay the 14th of April, and in them I sent, under the care of Lt. John Shapcote, the agent, twenty convicts, which were all that remained alive of the twenty-five that were sent on board the *Guardian* at Spithead. I also put on board those ships four hundred tierces of beef and two hundred tierces of pork ; and had not a misunderstanding existed between Lieutenant Shapcote and myself, it is my opinion I could have sent many articles which would not have taken up much stowage in the ships under his direction that would have been very acceptable to His Majesty's colony in New South Wales. But as that officer waited my orders for his proceedings, and afterwards persisted in his own resolution of sailing from False Bay on a certain day which he determinately fixed upon, I lost no time to endeavour to acquiesce in his measures, resolving that nothing should be wanting on my part to give all possible assistance to the colony, fearing that it might severely experience the effects of the accident that has befel His Majesty's ship under my command. The *Neptune*, *Surprize*, and *Scarborough* sailed from False Bay on the 29th of April.

'Permit me now, sir, to address you on a subject which I hope their Lordships will not consider to be unworthy their notice. It is to recommend as much as is in my power to their Lordships' favour and interest the case of the twenty convicts which my duty compelled me to send to Port Jackson. But the recollection of past sufferings reminds me of that time when I found it necessary to make use of every possible method to encourage the minds of the people under my command, and at such a time, considering how great the difference might be between a free man struggling for life, and him who perhaps might consider death as not much superior to a life of ignominy and disgrace, I publicly declared that not one of them, so far as depended on myself, should ever be convicts.

And I may with undeniable truth say that had it not been for their assistance and support, the *Guardian* would never have arrived to where she is. Their conduct prior to the melancholy accident that happened on the 23rd of December last was always such as may be commended, and from their first entrance into the ship at Spithead, they ever assisted and did their duty in like manner as the crew. I have taken the liberty to recommend them to the notice of Governor Phillip; but I humbly hope, sir, their Lordships will consider the service done by these men as meriting their Lordships' favour and protection, and I make no doubt that should I have been so fortunate as to represent their cases in proper colours, that they will experience the benefit of their Lordships' interest.'

The twenty convicts were pardoned upon condition that they remained in the colony until their sentences expired.

The arrival of the *Lady Juliana* was not an unmixed blessing. Collins says that when the women were landed many of them appeared to be loaded with the infirmities incident to old age, and to be 'very improper subjects for any of the purposes of an infant colony. . . . Instead of being capable of labour, they seemed to require attendance themselves, and were never likely to be any other than a burden to the settlement, which must sensibly feel the hardship of having to support by the labour of those who could toil, and who at the best were but few, a description of people utterly incapable of using any exertion towards their own maintenance.'

This ship's arrival was followed a fortnight later by that of the *Justinian* with a cargo of provisions, but fortunately no prisoners to help eat them, and on the day following full rations were ordered to be issued; the drum for labour was beat as usual at one o'clock, and hope ran high that the worst was over, and that no further hardships would have to be endured.

In order to relieve the community on Norfolk Island, whose situation, says Collins, 'everyone was fearful might call loudly for relief,' it was decided to send the *Lady Juliana* there as quickly as possible, and as she was in a bad state of repair, some carpenters from the shore were sent to sheath her bends, which were in a very bad state.

Then in quick succession there came into port the remaining vessels which, with the *Guardian*, made up the Second Fleet. These were the *Surprize*, the *Scarborough* and the *Neptune*. These ships brought with them a detachment of the newly-formed New South Wales corps—a gang of gaol-birds and ruffians raised for the service by Lieutenant-Colonel Grose— and the three last-named vessels established for themselves an infamous notoriety. The three ships brought 1038 persons, of whom 273 died on the passage, 486 were landed sick at Port Jackson, and 124 died in the hospital at Sydney.

This is what Tench says about them :—'Seventeen

pounds, in full of all expence, was the sum paid . . . for the passage of each person. And this sum was certainly competent to afford fair profit to the merchant who contracted. But there is reason to believe that some of those who were employed to act for him violated every principle of justice, and rioted on the spoils of misery, for want of controlling power to check their enormities. No doubt can be entertained that a humane and liberal Government will interpose its authority to prevent the repetition of such flagitious conduct.

'Although the convicts had landed from these ships with every mark of meagre misery, yet it was soon seen that a want of room, in which more conveniences might have been stowed for their use, had not caused it. Several of the masters of the transports immediately opened stores and exposed large quantities of goods to sale, which, though at most extortionate prices, were eagerly bought up.'

Phillip felt deeply for the victims of this system. On 13th July 1790 he wrote to Lord Grenville :—

'I will not, Sir, dwell on the scene of misery which the hospitals and sick-tents exhibited when those people were landed, but it would be a want of duty not to say that it was occasioned by the contractors having crowded too many on board those ships, and from their being too much confined during the passage. The convicts having the liberty of the deck depended on the agent and on the masters of the ships; the agent died on the passage, and the masters say it was granted so far as was consistent with their own safety, and that many of the convicts were sick when sent from the hulks. I believe, Sir, while the masters of the transports think their own safety depends on admitting few convicts on deck at a time, and most of them with irons on, which prevent any kind of exercise, numbers must always perish on so long a voyage, and many of those now received are in such a situation from old complaints, and so emaciated from what they have suffered on the voyage, that they will never be capable of any labour. . . . By the surgeon's returns of this day there are 488 under medical treatment; when the ships arrived we had not fifty people sick in the colony.'

The crisis was now over, and the outlook for the little colony brighter. We can imagine Phillip sleeping sounder o' nights, forgetting for a time what for many years to come was to be the most anxious care of the Governor—the food supply— and turning his attention to the progress of 'our public buildings.' But, alas! the despatches sent by the Second Fleet brought news that ten more vessels were on their way with convicts. They arrived between the months of July and December 1791, and out of their complement of 2061 prisoners, 1863 were landed, the rest having died on the voyage, and 576 of those landed were ill and incapable of work for

many weeks after debarcation.   There is, however, no
need to tell the story of the 'Third Fleet'—the arrival
of the convict ships for years to come was to be the
regular and chief event in the colony's history.

CHAPTER XI

IT is, or was until a few years ago, the common belief in England that Australians were very easily offended by any reference to the convict times. This is quite a mistake, convict transportation ceased half a century ago, a man who is an 'old lag' is as much a curiosity to Australians nowadays as he would be to Englishmen, and it is quite safe to talk of the subject in any of the colonies.

The penal establishments undeniably earned for themselves a very evil reputation, and the novel *For the Term of His Natural Life* has done more than anything else to spread abroad and perpetuate an exaggerated notion of the 'horrors of the system.' The system was undoubtedly brutal and degrading, but no more brutal and degrading than

the prison administration of the time in England—
perhaps not so bad.

When Marcus Clarke published his book, naturally
enough scores of imitators followed, and the sufferings
of poor, unjustly-convicted prisoners done to death
by heartless gaolers has ever since formed stock
material for writers of 'short stories.'

Neither writers nor readers troubled themselves
about the amount of truth to be found in these
stories, or were concerned with such details as the
time or place of the alleged acts of injustice, and
so no inconsiderable number of otherwise sensible
people picture Governor Phillip as a man who
hanged half a dozen convicts every morning before
breakfast, and spent the rest of the day in flogging
prisoners to death.

It is also often asserted that the British Government had no higher motive in the despatch of the
First Fleet than that of clearing the English gaols,
sending shiploads of prisoners to the other side of
the world, depositing them on shore and leaving
them to starve or die, or anything else, so long
as the old country was rid of them.

There is ample evidence to the contrary of this,
and Phillip's instructions, without going any further
into the matter, are proof enough that the Government was really animated by a sincere desire to
convert criminals into colonists. Their mistake
was a too great confidence in the possibility of

reform, which gave some ground for the charge of exiling these people to a far-off country, and leaving them to starve. It was too much to expect from Phillip that he could turn a few hundred idle rascals, landed in a desert, into a self-supporting community in less than half a dozen years.

Some particulars of Phillip's methods of punishing the idle and vicious, and of rewarding the industrious, will best answer the charges against his administration, and this chapter of his work, notwithstanding its hanging and flogging details, provides, in its account of the state of society at Sydney Cove, some lighter touches of comedy to relieve the gloom.

Whether it is or ever was right to hang and flog men, although there are still plenty of people who believe in such punishments, is no concern of these writers—but (and this is the point to be remembered) neither was it any concern of Governor Phillip's.

There was law in the land then as now, and Phillip's sole duty was to administer it as he found it. Courts of justice tried prisoners and sentenced them in Sydney in 1788 to punishments which a hundred years ago were generally less severe than judges were at every session passing at the Old Bailey, for in the year of the colony's foundation about 160 crimes were punishable by the death penalty, women were whipped through London streets at the cart-tail, and 500 lashes was a not uncommon punishment for breaches of discipline in the Army and Navy. It is a fact that a woman, for the crime of coining, was strangled and afterwards burnt in public in front of Newgate gaol in the very year that Phillip landed in Sydney, and about a hundred executions was the annual average for England at this time. Of course, twelve 'good men and true' did not in Sydney try their fellow-citizens when they 'got into trouble,' but then the country was at this time a gaol, and the most sanguine philanthropist has scarcely ventured to argue that gaol discipline can be maintained by trial by jury.

It is asserted that Phillip was severe—that granted he *had* to flog, he flogged unmercifully. Phillip was a naval officer, and in the Navy of those days flogging was almost the only punishment. A century ago such men as Phillip punished with a few lashes, if sailors, would have either been hanged or flogged round the fleet, and the number of strokes with the cat would have been measured by the hundred. A naval officer thus educated in punishing could scarcely be expected to be gentle in his methods, and if he showed in the least degree that he had got the better of such a training, posterity might well deal kindly with his memory.

It is difficult for readers at this end of the century to realise the shocking character of the English prison system, or rather utter absence of system, that prevailed until comparatively recent times. Mrs Fry, the prison reformer, thirty years after the establishment of Phillip's penal settlement, described the women's ward in Newgate as such a scene of 'begging, swearing, gaming, fighting, singing, dancing, dressing up in men's clothes, and such an awful place as only to be described as hell above ground, and too dreadful for us to take young persons with us on our visits.'

Years after Phillip was in his grave, Buxton gave an account of the prison system in London. He said that after the commitment of a prisoner was made out, he was handcuffed to a file of perhaps a dozen wretched persons in a similar situation, and marched through the streets, sometimes a considerable distance, followed by a crowd of impudent and insulting gazers, exposed to ·the stare of every passenger; the moment he entered prison, irons were hammered on to him; then he was cast into the midst of a compound of all that was disgusting and depraved. At night he was locked up in a narrow cell, with perhaps half a dozen of the worst thieves in London, or as many vagrants, whose rags were alive, and in actual motion with filth. He might find himself in bed, and in bodily contact, between a robber and a murderer; or between a man with a foul disease on one side, and one with an infectious disorder on the other. He might spend his days deprived of free air and wholesome exercise. He might be prohibited from following the handicraft on which the subsistence of his family depended. He might be half starved for want of food and clothing and fuel. He might be compelled to mingle with the vilest of mankind, and, in self-defence, to adopt their habits, their language and their sentiments; he might become a villain by actual compulsion. His health might be impaired or ruined by filth and contagion; and as for his morals, purity itself could not continue pure, if exposed for any length of time to the society with which he must associate. His trial might be long protracted; he might be imprisoned on suspicion, and pine in jail while his family was starving out of it, without any opportunity of removing that suspicion, and this for a whole year; if acquitted, he might be dismissed from jail without a shilling in his pocket, and without the means of returning home; if convicted, beyond the sentence awarded by the law, he might be exposed to the most intolerable hardships, and these might amount to no less than the destruction of his life now, and his soul for ever.

Contrast this condition of prisoners in London— many of them accused persons only — with the life of convicted felons in the ' Botany Bay penal settlement,' where all that was asked from the criminal was that he should make a fresh start, work, and refrain from thieving.

Unfortunately, however, among the convicts were men so sadly ignorant, so hideously vicious, so brutally low, that only those who know the crimes of great cities can picture to themselves what these criminals were like.

When the lives of all depended on the security of the public stores, to judge the man who was responsible by the number of thieves he hanged, or the amount of flogging he ordered them, is absurd. The true test of the man's character is to be sought, not in his manner of dealing with the idle and vicious, but in his treatment of the few who were men enough to deserve sympathy and encouragement.

In an old churchyard at Campbelltown, about thirty-five miles from Sydney, there is a tombstone erected to the memory of James Ruse, who died in 1837. Collins describes him as 'the first settler in this country, who, when he had been upon his ground for fifteen months, having got in his crop of corn, declared himself as relinquishing his claim to any further provisions from the store, and said that he was able to support himself by the produce of his farm. He had shown himself an industrious man; and the Governor, being satisfied that he could do without any further aid from the stores, consented to his proposal, and informed him that he should be forthwith put in possession of an allotment of thirty acres of ground in the situation he then occupied.'

Tench tells us that Ruse, a convict, 'was cast for seven years at Bodmin assizes in August 1782; he lay five years in prison and on board the *Dunkirk* hulk at Plymouth, and then was sent to this country.

When his term of punishment expired in August 1789, he claimed his freedom, and was permitted by the Governor, on promising to settle in the country, to take, in December following, an uncleared piece of ground, with an assurance that if he would cultivate it, it should not be taken from him. Some assistance was given him to fell the timber, and he accordingly began.'

The labour of clearing his ground for cultivation was very arduous, but Ruse was fortunate in having an industrious woman for his wife ; he had married her in the colony. As time went on, the Governor granted him the labour of one man, but only for a short time, and then Ruse's wife was his only helper. His greatest check, he told Tench, was the persistent manner in which his garden was robbed almost nightly by convicts, in spite of all his vigilance.

This man was the first successful 'experiment' among the convicts, and Phillip, one can imagine, signed the first land grant of thirty acres with a great deal of satisfaction.

Against the industrious Ruse there was a set-off of many failures, and among the rascals were some whose rogueries were amusing. For example, Tench tells us of one Daly, who was hanged for breaking into the public stores, but previous to this crime he 'was the author of a discovery of a gold mine a few months before. He produced a composition resembling ore mingled with earth, which he pretended to have brought from it. After a number of attendant circumstances, too ludicrous and contemptible to relate, which befel a party who were sent under his guidance to explore this second Peru, he at last confessed that he had broken up an old pair of buckles and mixed the pieces with sand and stone; and on assaying the composition, the brass was detected. The fate of this fellow I should not deem worth recording did it not lead to the following observation: that the utmost circumspection is necessary to prevent imposition in those who give accounts of what they see in unknown countries. We found the convicts particularly happy in fertility of invention and exaggerated descriptions. Hence large fresh water rivers, valuable ores, and quarries of limestone, chalk and marble were daily proclaimed soon after we had landed. At first we hearkened with avidity to such accounts; but perpetual disappointments taught us to listen with caution, and to believe from demonstration only.'

Captain Tench testifies to the surprising ingenuity of one prisoner.

'Frazer was an iron manufacturer, bred at Sheffield, of whose abilities as a workman we have witnessed many proofs. The Governor had written to England for a set of locks to be sent out for the security of the public stores, which were to be so constructed as to be incapable of being picked. On their arrival His Excellency sent for Frazer, and bade him examine them, telling him at the same time that they could not be picked. Frazer laughed, and asked for a crooked nail only to open them all. A nail was brought, and in an instant he verified his assertion. Astonished at his dexterity, a gentleman present determined to put it to farther proof. He was sent for in a hurry, some days after, to the hospital, where a lock of still superior intricacy and expence to the others had been provided. He was told that the key was lost, and that the lock must be immediately picked. He examined it attentively, remarked that it was the production of a workman, and demanded ten minutes to make an instrument, and open flew the lock. But it was not only in this part of his business that he excelled; he executed every branch of it in superior style. Had not his villainy been still more notorious than his skill, he would have proved an invaluable possession to a new country. He had passed through innumerable scenes in life, and had played many parts. When too lazy to work at his trade, he had turned thief in fifty different shapes; was a receiver of stolen goods, a soldier, and a travelling conjurer. He once confessed to me that he had made a set of tools for a gang of coiners, every man of whom was hanged.'

Forgers, however, do not seem to have been so successful as the locksmith, for we learn that 'several convicts brought recommendatory letters from different friends. Of these some were genuine, and many owed their birth to the ingenuity of the bearers. But these last were all such bungling performances as to produce only instant detection and succeeding contempt. One of them addressed to the Governor, with the name of Baron Hotham affixed to it, began " Honored Sir."

Phillip's simple code of regulations for dealing with his people are worth reprinting, as the first police system in the colony :—

' 1. A night-watch, consisting of twelve persons, divided into four parties, is appointed, and fully authorised to patrol at all hours in the night, and to visit such places as may be deemed necessary for the discovery of any felony, trespass or misdemeanour ; and for the apprehending and securing for examination any person or persons that may appear to them concerned therein, either by entrance into any suspected hut or dwelling, or by such other manner as may appear expedient.

' 2. Those parts in which the convicts reside are to be divided, and numbered in the following manner : The convicts' huts and the public farm on the east side of the cove to be the first division. Those at the brick-kilns and the detached parties at the different farms in that district the second division. Those on the western side, as far as the line that separates the district of the women from the men, the third division. The huts occupied from that line to the hospital, and from thence to the Observatory, to be the fourth division.

' 3. These districts or divisions each to be of them under the particular inspection of one person, who shall be judged qualified to inform himself of the actual residence of each individual in his district ; as well as of his business connections and acquaintance.

' 4. Cognizance is to be taken of such convicts as may sell or barter their slops or provisions, and also of such as game for either of the aforesaid articles, and report is to be made of them to the Judge-Advocate.

' 5. Any soldier or seaman found stragling after the taptoo has beat, or who may be found in the convicts' huts, is to be detained, and information to be immediately given to the nearest guard-house.

' 6. On any person's being robbed during the night, he is to give immediate information thereof to the watch of his district, who, on the instant of application being made, shall use the most effectual means to trace out the offender or offenders, so that he or they may be brought to justice.

' 7. The watch of each district is to be under the direction of one person, who will be named for that purpose, and all the patrols to be immediately under the inspection of Herbert Keeling. They are never to receive any fee, gratuity or reward from any individual to engage their exertions in the execution of the above trust ; nor are they to receive any stipulated encouragement for the conviction of any offender; but their diligence and good behaviour will be rewarded by the Governor, and for which purpose their conduct will be strictly attended to by those who are in authority over them.

'8. The night-watch to go out as soon as the taptoo has done beating; to return to their huts when the working-drum beats in the morning; and reports to be made at twelve o'clock to the Judge-Advocate, of all robberies and misdemeanours, by Herbert Keeling. Any assistance the patrols may require will be given them on applying to the officer of the the nearest guard, and by the civil power if necessary; for which application is to be made to the provost-martial.

'9. Any negligence on the part of those who may be employed on this duty will be punished with the utmost rigor of the law.

'10. The night-watch is to consist of the following [twelve persons].'

Soon after the inauguration of the colony, the question of what to do with convicts whose time had expired became a problem. When Phillip sailed, the Home Office had neglected to supply him with particulars of the prisoners' sentences, and convicts were continually asserting that as they had served their time, the Governor had no further power over them. However, this problem was settled by the position of the settlement—its isolation kept all alike prisoners, and in due course the necessary papers arrived.

A much more serious difficulty arose out of the legal interpretation of Phillip's power to emancipate any of his subjects. He had, before leaving, asked for that power, and the Government, without passing a special Act of Parliament, could only grant him authority to pardon persons whose offences were committed within the colony. The fleet sailed before the Act could be passed, and it was not until the arrival of the *Gorgon* late in 1791 that Phillip received the power to emancipate convicts.

He was not, however, the man to shirk responsibility. The need of power to give men their freedom whose conduct was highly meritorious was apparent, and the Governor of his own motion emancipated two men, one of whom, says Collins, had done such service in the building line that 'there was not a house or building in the settlement that did not owe something to him.' The other man was Ascott, who behaved so well when the *Sirius* went ashore.

Phillip, in a despatch dated 5th November 1791, says :—

'Of those convicts whose sentences are expired, some who are seamen or carpenters will be carried away by the transports ; but by far the greatest part of those people must remain, discontented and desirous of seizing the first opportunity which offers of escaping. Amongst the many great advantages which would attend settlers coming out who had some property of their own, their finding employment for this class of people would be one, for such settlers would separate them from the convicts, which cannot well be done while they are employed by the Crown, and probably most of them would soon be reconciled to remain in the country.

'Of the convicts whose terms of transportation are expired, or who, from their very meritorious behaviour, have been emancipated, there is one whose time is expired, and whom, in consideration of his remaining here a few months longer, I have promised to send home by the next ships. He is the only carpenter at this place who is capable of acting as a master carpenter, and while he remains here I have promised to allow him one shilling per diem.

'The first convict who was emancipated had been bred to surgery, and merited from his exemplary conduct what has been done for him; he acts as an assistant to the surgeons, who find him a very useful man. He is inclined to remain in the country. For him some allowance will be necessary, and for which he was recommended when the inconveniences which the superintendents and others laboured under, from there not being any money in the colony, was represented to your Lordship.

'The second convict who was emancipated had well earned his emancipation by his good conduct, and the pains he had taken to teach others the business of a bricklayer; this man has likewise my promise to be sent home before I leave the country ; and as he continues to carry on the public works with great diligence, will expect some little allowance. The time for which he was sentenced will be expired before he returns to England.

' The third convict was emancipated on the recommendation of the Lieutenant-Governor, for extinguishing the fire on board the *Sirius* after that ship went on shore. This man went to Calcutta in the *Atlantic*, and it now appears that his term of transportation had expired prior to his emancipation.

'One woman has been emancipated on her marrying a superintendent. The distinction directed to be made with regard to those convicts who have behaved well before they became settlers has been attended to ; and I hope the necessity there has been of deviating from the royal instructions respecting settlers will appear to have been sufficient to justify what I have done on that head. My letter to Mr Nepean undoubtedly gave little reason to suppose that many of the marines would be inclined to remain when the relief took place, and the opinion I formed when that letter was written was drawn from the great anxiety so many expressed of quitting a country which was said to be incapable of furnishing even the common necessaries of life ; the people who were to become settlers were men who had not been in the habit of judging for themselves, and the fears and apprehensions of some to whom they had been accustomed to look up with respect, had their effect, and there was some difficulty in persuading any man on whose judgment some dependence might be placed to think for himself; but I have now the pleasure of informing your Lordship that most of those fears and apprehensions are done away, and that we have now eighty-six settlers here and at Norfolk Island—that is, thirty-one from the marines, eleven seamen, and forty-four from those convicts whose sentences have expired; there are, likewise, more marines who have desired to be received as settlers when the detachment is to be embarked. No man of bad character has been received as a settler.'

The additional instructions which enabled Phillip to grant these emancipations enforced the condition that prisoners should not return to England until the expiration of the time for which they were sentenced. This was natural enough, considering the anxiety of the Home Government to settle the new colony. But most of the time-expired prisoners desired to go back, and Grenville wrote to Phillip pointing out that such men could not legally be detained, but that every indulgence should be offered to induce them to remain. Numbers of them, however, did return, working their passages home in returning transports, for the Government did not recognise any obligation on its part to provide them with a return passage.

Another source of trouble with the prisoners, which,

however, brought with it its own punishment, was their constant attempts to escape across country. Those who did not get 'bushed' and starved to death were generally murdered by the natives. Some, after undergoing dreadful hardships, returned to the settlement. A party once tried to walk to China. Tench saw them after their experiences. He says :—

'When at the hospital I saw and conversed with some of the Chinese travellers; four of them lay here, wounded by the natives. I asked these men if they really supposed it possible to reach China; they answered, that they were certainly made to believe (they knew not how) that at a considerable distance to the northward existed a large river, which separated this country from the back part of China; and that when it should be crossed (which was practicable) they would find themselves among a copper-coloured people, who would receive and treat them kindly. They added, that on the third day of their elopement one of the party died of fatigue; another they saw butchered by the natives, who, finding them unarmed, attacked them and put them to flight. This happened near Broken Bay, which harbour stopped their progress to the northward, and forced them to turn to the right hand, by which means they soon after found themselves on the sea shore, where they wandered about, in a destitute condition, picking up shell-fish to allay hunger. Deeming the farther prosecution of their scheme impracticable, several of them agreed to return to Rose Hill, which with difficulty they accomplished, arriving almost famished. On their road back they met six fresh adventurers sallying forth to join them, to whom they related what had passed, and persuaded them to relinquish their intention. There are at this time not less than thirty-eight convict men missing, who live in the woods by day, and at night enter the different farms and plunder for subsistence.'

There were several attempts to get away by sea, but as there were nothing but ship's boats to be stolen for the purpose, these endeavours generally ended in the same way as the China expedition. There was one noteworthy exception—that of the escape of William Bryant and ten others, including his wife and her two young children, who, in a small boat, succeeded in reaching the island of Timor, where those who survived were recaptured. This attempt was no doubt suggested to its daring projectors by the success of Bligh's boat voyage, the news of which had by this time reached the settlement, and the voyage of the convicts was not less remarkable than that of Bligh and his companions.

Tench relates how, in March 1789, sixteen convicts left their work at the brick-kilns without leave, and marched to Botany Bay with a design to attack the natives, and to plunder them of their fishing-tackle and spears. They had armed themselves with their working tools and large clubs. When they arrived near the bay, 'a body of Indians,' who had probably seen them set out, and had penetrated their intention from experience, suddenly fell upon them. 'Our heroes were immediately routed, and separately endeavoured to effect their escape by any means which were left. In their flight one was killed, and seven were wounded, for the most part very severely. Those who had the good fortune to outstrip their comrades and arrive in camp, first gave the alarm; and a detachment of marines, under an officer, was ordered to march to their relief. The officer arrived too late to repel the Indians; but he brought in the body of the man that was killed, and put an end to the pursuit. The Governor was justly incensed at what had happened, and instituted a most rigorous scrutiny into the cause which had produced it. At first the convicts were unanimous in affirming that they were quietly picking sweet-tea, when they were, without provocation, assaulted by the natives, with whom they had no wish to quarrel. Some of them, however, more irresolute than the rest, at last disclosed the purpose for which the expedition had been undertaken; and the whole were ordered to be severely flogged. Arabanoo was present at the infliction of the punishment, and was made to comprehend the cause and the necessity of it; but he displayed on the occasion symptoms of disgust and terror only.'

The blacks looked upon the spectacle of a man being flogged with feelings which does them honour, for on another occasion Tench says :—

'But toil cannot be long supported without adequate refreshment. The first step in every community, which wishes to preserve honesty, should be to set the people above want. The throes of hunger will ever prove too powerful for integrity to withstand. Hence arose a repetition of petty delinquencies, which no vigilance could detect, and no justice reach. Gardens were plundered; provisions pilfered; and the Indian corn stolen from the fields, where it grew for public use. Various were the measures adopted to check this depredatory spirit. Criminal courts, either from the tediousness of their process, or from the frequent escape of culprits from their decision, were seldomer convened than formerly. The Governor ordered convict-offenders either to be chained together, or to wear singly a large iron collar, with two spikes projecting from it, which effectually hindered the party from concealing it under his shirt; and thus shackled, they were compelled to perform their quota of work.

'Had their marauding career terminated here, humanity would have been anxious to plead in their defence; but the natives continued to complain of being robbed of spears and fishing-tackle. A convict was at length taken in the act of stealing fishing-tackle from Daringa, the wife of Colbee (Coleby). The Governor ordered that he should be severely flogged, in the presence of as many natives as could be assembled, to whom the cause of punishment should be explained. Many of them, of both sexes, accordingly attended. Arabanoo's aversion to a similar sight has been noticed; and if the behaviour of those now collected be found to correspond with it, it is, I think, fair to conclude that these people are not of a sanguinary and implacable temper. Quick indeed of resentment, but not unforgiving of injury. There was not one of them that did not testify strong abhorrence of the punishment, and equal sympathy with the sufferer. The women were particularly affected; Daringa shed tears; and Barangaroo, kindling into anger, snatched a stick and menaced the executioner. The conduct of these women on this occasion was exactly descriptive of their characters. The former was meek and feminine; the latter fierce and unsubmissive.'

Phillip, before leaving England, wrote a memorandum to the Home Office in which he outlined his views on the treatment of prisoners. This document certainly of itself shows that he was no ardent believer in hanging.

For instance, he says :—

'Rewarding and punishing the convicts must be left to the Governor; he will be answerable for his conduct, and death, I should think, will never be necessary—in fact, I doubt if the fear of death ever prevented a man of no principle from committing a bad action. There are two crimes that would merit death — murder and another. For either of these crimes I would wish to confine the criminal till the opportunity offered of delivering him as a prisoner to the natives of New Zealand, and let them eat him. The dread of this will operate much stronger than the fear of death.'

The alternative of landing men in New Zealand to be eaten by the natives is certainly not a very amiable suggestion, but it ought not to be judged too harshly. A hundred years ago, sailors who had committed awful crimes which put them outside the pale of nautical society, were often punished by the masters of their ships marooning them on some desert island or place supposed to be inhabited by savages, and Phillip no doubt meant something of this kind by his proposal.

Collins describes how a desperate rascal was dealt with, and Phillip's humanity on this occasion is stated by the historian :—

'Caesar, being closely attended to, was at length apprehended and secured. This man was always reputed the hardest working convict in the country ; his frame was muscular and well calculated for hard labor ; but in his intellects he did not very widely differ from a brute ; his appetite was ravenous, for he could in any one day devour the full ration for two days. To gratify his appetite he was compelled to steal from others, and all his thefts were directed to that purpose. He was such a wretch, and so indifferent about meeting death, that he declared while in confinement that if he should be hanged he would create a laugh before he was sent off by playing off some trick upon the executioner. Holding up such a mere animal as an example was not expected to have the proper or intended effect; the Governor, therefore, with the humanity that was always conspicuous in the exercise of the authority vested in him, directed that he should be sent to Garden Island, there to work in fetters; and in addition to his ration of provisions he was to be supplied with vegetables from the garden.'

Phillip, writing to Grenville in July 1790, says, in illustration of the class of men he had to deal with :—

'Experience, Sir, has taught me how difficult it is to make men industrious who have passed their lives in habits of vice and indolence. In some cases it has been found impossible; neither kindness nor severity have had any effect; and tho' I can say that the convicts in general behave well, there are many who dread punishment less than they fear labour; and those who have not been brought up to hard work, which are by far the greatest part, bear it badly. They shrink from it the moment the eye of the overseer is turned from them.'

With such men in such a situation it was not wonderful that recourse was frequently had to what were practically the only punishments of that time— the gallows and the triangles.

CHAPTER XII

PHILLIP'S governorship is drawing to a close. How,
after four years of his rule, is the little community
progressing? Besides finding food for the people,
has anything else been done? Are the felons yet
showing signs of becoming industrious colonists?

Tench, in December 1791, went to the settlement
at Rose Hill with the intention of answering for himself these very important questions. This is what he
says :—

' Public buildings here have not greatly multiplied
since my last survey. The storehouse and barrack
have been long completed ; also apartments for the
chaplain of the regiment and for the Judge-Advocate,
in which last criminal courts, when necessary, are
held ; but these are petty erections. In a colony

which contains only a few hundred hovels, built of twigs and mud, we feel consequential enough already to talk of a treasury, an admiralty, a public library, and many other similar edifices, which are to form part of a magnificent square. The great road from near the landing-place to the Governor's house is finished, and a very noble one it is, being of great breadth, and a mile long, in a strait line. In many places it is carried over gullies of considerable depth, which have been filled up with trunks of trees, covered with earth. All the sawyers, carpenters and black-smiths will be soon concentred under the direction of a very adequate person of the Governor's household. This plan is already so far advanced as to contain nine covered sawpits, which change of weather cannot dis-turb the operations of, an excellent work-shed for the carpenters, and a large new shop for the blacksmiths ; it certainly promises to be of great public benefit. A new hospital has been talked of for the last two years, but is not yet begun.'

There were, however, temporary quarters for the sick—two long wooden sheds, with accommodation for 200 patients; at the time of Tench's visit the sick list contained 382 names; dysentery was very prevalent, and many cases terminated fatally. The appearance of the land about Rose Hill did not impress Tench very favourably.

'The corn,' he says, 'looks miserably. . . . At the bottom of the garden, which certainly in beauty of form and situation is unrivalled in New South Wales, are 8000 vines planted, all of which in another season are expected to bear grapes. Besides the vines are several small fruit trees, which were brought in the *Gorgon* from the Cape, and look lively; on one of them are half a dozen apples as big as nutmegs.

'. . . My next visit was to the cattle, which consists of two stallions, six mares and two colts; besides sixteen cows, two cow-calfs, and one bull-calf, which were brought out by the *Gorgon*. Two bulls which were on board died on the passage; so that on the young gentleman just mentioned depends the stocking of the colony. The period of the inhabitants of New South Wales being supplied with animal food of their own raising is too remote for a prudent man to calculate. The cattle look in good condition, and I was surprized to hear that neither corn nor fodder is given to them. . . .

' Divine service is now performed here every Sunday, either by the chaplain of the settlement, or the chaplain of the regiment. I went to church to-day. Several hundred convicts were present, the majority of whom, I thought, looked the most miserable beings in the shape of humanity I ever beheld; they appeared to be worn down with fatigue.'

The farming operations at Rose Hill and around it were conducted by 500 convicts under the supervision of a man of experience. These men were housed in huts, to every one of which two men were appointed as watchmen, to prevent them from being robbed of the rations stored therein. Work began in the summer months at 5 o'clock in the morning, at 10 a.m. four hours' rest was given, at 2 p.m. work was continued till sunset. After finishing his inspection of the farms about Rose Hill, Tench crossed the country to Prospect Hill, and visited those belonging to thirteen convicts who had been given allotments of land by the Governor.

'The terms of which these allotments have been granted are: That the estates shall be fully ceded for ever to all who shall continue to cultivate for five years, or more. That they shall be free of all taxes for the first ten years; but after that period, to pay an annual quit-rent of one shilling. The penalty on non-performance of any of these articles is forfeiture of the estate, and all the labour which may have been bestowed upon it. These people are to receive provisions (the same quantity as the working convicts), clothes and medicinal assistance for eighteen months from the day on which they settled. To clear and cultivate the land, a hatchet, a tomahawk, two hoes, a spade and a shovel are given to each person, whether man or woman; and a certain number of cross-cut saws among the whole. To stock their farms, two sow pigs were promised to each settler; but they almost all say they have not yet received any, of which they complain loudly. They all received grain to sow and plant for the first year. They settled here in July and August last. Most of them were obliged to build their own houses; and wretched hovels three-fourths of them are. Should any of them fall sick, the rest are bound to assist the sick person two days in a month, provided the sickness lasts not longer than two months; four days' labour in each year from every person being all that he is entitled to. To give protection to this settlement, a corporal and two soldiers are encamped in the centre of the farms, as the natives once attacked the settlers, and burnt one of their houses. These guards are, however, inevitably at such a distance from some of the farms as to be unable to afford them any assistance in case of another attack.

'With all these people I conversed, and inspected their labours; some I found tranquil and determined to persevere, provided encouragement should be given; others were in a state of despondency, and predicted that they should starve unless the period of 18 months during which they are to be clothed and fed should be extended to three years. Their cultivation is yet in its infancy, and therefore opinions should not be hastily formed of what it may arrive at with moderate skill and industry. They have at present little in the ground besides maize, and that looks not very promising. Some small patches of wheat which I saw are miserable indeed. The greatest part of the land I think but indifferent, being light and stony. Of the 13 farms 10 are unprovided with water; and at some of them they are obliged to fetch this necessary article from the distance of a mile and a half. All the settlers complain sadly of being frequently robbed by the runaway convicts, who plunder them incessantly.'

Tench says that Ruse's farm was given to him by the Governor on these conditions: 'The place was to be called Experiment Farm; the said lot to be holden free of all taxes, quit-rents, etc., for ten years, provided that the occupier, his heirs or assigns shall reside within the same, and proceed to the improvement thereof; reserving, however, for the use of the Crown all timber now growing, or which hereafter shall grow, fit for naval purposes; at the expiration of ten years, an annual quit-rent of one shilling shall be paid by the occupier in acknowledgment. Ruse now lives in a comfortable brick house built for him by the Governor. He has eleven acres and a half in cultivation, and several more which have been cleared by convicts in their leisure hours, on condition of receiving the first year's crop. He means to cultivate little besides maize; wheat is so much less productive. Of the culture of vineyards and tobacco he is ignorant; and with great good sense he declared that he would not quit the path he knew for an uncertainty. His live stock consists of four breeding sows, and thirty fowls.'

'Of my Sydney journal, I find no part sufficiently interesting to be worth extraction. This place had long been considered only as a depot for stores; it exhibited nothing but a few old scattered huts and some sterile gardens; cultivation of the ground was abandoned, and all our strength transferred to Rose Hill. Sydney, nevertheless, continued to be the place of the Governor's residence, and consequently the headquarters of the colony. No public building of note, except a storehouse, had been erected since my last statement. The barracks, so long talked of, so long promised, for the accommodation and discipline of the troops were not even begun when I left the country; and instead of a new hospital, the old one was patched up, and with the assistance of one brought ready framed from England, served to contain the sick... The employment of the male convicts here, as at Rose Hill, was the public labour. Of the women, the majority were compelled to make shirts, trowsers and other necessary parts of dress, for the men, from materials delivered to them from the stores, into which they returned every Saturday night the produce of their labour, a stipulated weekly task being assigned to them. In a more early stage, Government sent out all articles of cloathing ready made; but by adopting the present judicious plan not only a public saving is effected, but employment of a suitable nature created for those who would otherwise consume leisure in idle pursuits only.'

The total number of persons of all descriptions in New South Wales and its dependency, Norfolk Island, on the 26th of November 1791, was, adds Tench, 4059.   They were distributed as follows : at Sydney, 1259 ; at Rose Hill, 1628 ; at Norfolk Island, 1172.

By the ships of the Second and Third Fleets there arrived 'The New South Wales Corps,' a regiment of infantry raised in England to do duty in the settlement in place of the marines, whose commanding officer, Major Ross, it will be remembered, was left at Norfolk Island by the *Sirius*.

The Major shall, in the following letter to Grenville, dated 29th August 1790, himself tell us how he fared at the island :—

'I think I may venture to say that if Providence had not worked a miracle in our favour, there would have been but few of us found alive when those ships [the *Justinian* and the *Surprize*] arrived to our relief.   And further, I think I may venture to assure you, and the rest of His Majesty's ministers, that, with respect to clearing and cultivating land on this island, I have established such a plan which, if pursued, will render it unnecessary ever to send any flour here.   On the contrary, in one year from the first of next January, the island will be able to spare grain for exportation, provided there is not more than seven hundred people kept upon the island.

'On the 8th instant, a man arrived from Port Jackson for the purpose of dressing and managing the flax-plant; he has began to clear ground and prepare the plant for the purpose of dressing. I am likewise, by the Governor's directions, cutting down some of the pine-tree spars, in order to be put on board the *Gorgon*, in order to their being brought to Europe for the purpose of experiments. And as I understand that we are to be embarked for a passage to England on board the *Gorgon*, I shall wait until I have the honour of explaining many matters which very much concern the territory at large, and this island in particular, all which matters, together with the whole of my conduct since my appointment as Lieutenant - Governor, I trust will be honored with approval of His majesty's ministers. And until that happy and much-to-be-wished period arrives, I have to request that whatever (perhaps false) representations with respect to my conduct may have appear'd before the ministers, that you and them may do me the justice and the honour to suspend passing any judgment upon it until it is investigated.'

The *Supply* meanwhile returned from Batavia after an absence of six months, and was then sent to Norfolk Island to fetch back Hunter and the crew of the *Sirius*. A Dutch snow had been engaged by the *Supply* at Batavia to bring provisions for the colony, and on her arrival (at Sydney) she was fitted as a transport to convey the people of the *Sirius* to England. She was miserably small for the purpose—less than 300 tons—and occupied thirteen months on the voyage, calling at Batavia and the Cape on the way. Those who sailed in her were much annoyed with Phillip for employing this vessel for such a purpose, and they had reason to be, for the voyage home was one of terrible hardship, but the Governor at the time had no other ship available. Hunter, on his return, wrote to the Admiralty pointing out what shipmasters know well enough nowadays, viz., that the proper route home from Australia is not round the Cape of Good Hope, or northward *via* Batavia, but round Cape Horn. The passenger of to-day has to thank his stars for the Suez Canal, if he is unable to fully appreciate the wisdom of Hunter's opinion.

The people of the *Sirius* had been on Norfolk Island for eleven months when they were thus relieved. Mrs Macarthur, in a private letter home, thus describes how the little settlement fared during this time :—

'On the 21st of January the *Supply* was sent to Norfolk Island to bring hither the *Sirius* ship's company, and learn the state of affairs at that place. She returned on the 25th of February with the officers and men in health, and brought a good account of the health of every individual left behind. This circumstance removed some considerable anxiety from our minds, but it proved our fears had been but too well grounded, and when the *Supply* arrived they had not more than ten days' provisions in the store at full allowance, and from the 14th of last May till the 18th of July they were reduced to the scanty pittance of three pounds of flour and one pound and a half of beef per week.

'At this time a most merciful relief came to their assistance. It had been observed on a high hill in the island (which they have named Mount Pitt) that many sea-birds frequented it. An endeavour was made to take some of them, which was successful; and by attending more particularly to the time of their appearance, and their favourite haunts, they were discovered in the greatest abundance. It was the season in which they laid their eggs, and both birds and eggs were taken in such incredible quantities as occasioned the small allowance of meat they had issued before to be stopped; and, however wonderful it may appear to you, yet true it is, that those birds for many weeks were the chief subsistence of seven hundred men, and they were so easily taken that after sunset it was impossible to walk on the mount without treading on them, and sometimes towards evening they have been observed hovering in the air in such innumerable flocks as considerably to exclude the light from the admiring spectators; but now the melancholy truth of their visible decrease became more and more apparent. Their flights were directed to other quarters, and at length few remained ; but before hope was quite extinguished, a ship appeared and brought them a long-expected supply.'

Lieutenant King, it will be remembered, had been sent home with despatches in April 1790. His voyage of eight months from Batavia to England, like Hunter's, was one of such danger and distress as can scarcely be realised nowadays. The little Dutch vessel in which he sailed had not been five days at sea before her captain and most of the crew were taken ill with fever. King took charge, and with the only four able-bodied men navigated the snow to the Mauritius. Here he embarked a fresh crew and continued his voyage, calling at the Cape of Good Hope, where he met Riou trying to patch up the wreck of the *Guardian*. He sailed again for England, arrived there in December, and had interviews with Lord Chatham and Lord Grenville.

Phillip's letters home had acquainted the Government with King's value, and a commission was already waiting for him as Lieutenant-Governor of the settlement at Norfolk Island. While at home he married, embarking with his wife on the *Gorgon*, and, reaching New South Wales in September 1791, he returned in a few weeks to his island command, where certain of his acts gave great offence to Grose, Phillip's successor. King in these disputes always shows to advantage, and his superiors in England approved of most of what Grose censured. The best proof of their confidence in King is that in 1800 he was appointed Governor of New South Wales.

Phillip's last long despatch, in which he gave details of the settlement's progress, was dated 2d October 1792, and was addressed to Dundas. Some extracts from this will prove that the food supply was still his chief anxiety :—

'With respect to those articles of which the colony stands so much in need, I beg leave to observe that all those wants that have been pointed out in my different letters from time to time still exist, or with very few exceptions; and for iron pots in particular, however trifling the article, we have been nearly as much distressed as for provisions; cross-cut saws, axes, and the various tools for husbandry are also much wanted. Many of those articles are now made here, but the demand for them is greater than can be supplied, as most of what have been received from England are worn out.'

The clothing recently sent out by the *Britannia* he complains of as being unsuited for men working in the woods; much of it, too, was so much injured by damp that it would not well stand a second washing. He proceeds as follows :—

'You will, Sir, naturally suppose that I anxiously look for the arrival of those ships by which we expect a further supply of provisions, and I am very sorry to be under the necessity of adverting to the observation I have so often made, that the colony, having been almost constantly on a reduced ration, is a great check on the public labour, as well as the cause of many very unpleasant circumstances. . . . When the *Atlantic* arrived from Bengal, this settlement had only thirteen days' flour and forty-five days' maize in store at the ration then issued, which was one pound and a half of flour and four pounds of maize per man for seven days. And when the *Britannia* arrived, we had only salt provisions for fifty-three days at the then ration, which was only two pounds of pork per man for seven days.

'The arrival of the above ships put it in my power to increase the ration, and which, though at present little inferior to the full ration, is, from the nature of some articles and the deficiency of others, very far from being satisfactory; nor can the present ration be continued many days longer if the *Kitty* does not arrive. . . . My letters by the *Supply*, *Gorgon* and *Pitt* will have shown that I look to England for the necessary supplies of which we still stand in great need, and which I doubt not are now on their passage; but the great length of time in which this colony has remained in its present state takes away hope from many, and the consequences must be obvious. It has, Sir, been my fate to point out wants from year to year; it has been a duty the severest I have ever experienced. Did those wants only respect myself or a few individuals I should be silent; but here are numbers who bear them badly; nor has the colony suffered more from wanting what we have not received than from the supplies we have received not arriving in time.'

In this letter, too, he says :—

'You have, Sir, observed in your letter that "the Admiralty had not determined on replacing the *Sirius*, but that that circumstance would not occasion any decrease of the pecuniary emoluments with which I understood my situation was to be attended." I beg leave to say that the opinion I gave as to the necessity of employing King's ships on this station—that is, as I explained in my letters, ships having the officers requisite for keeping a proper discipline on board, and deterring the convicts from making any attempt to escape by seizing on the ship—did not proceed from any view of pecuniary advantage to myself, and to which I never adverted. That object never drew my attention, and the advantages I derived from the *Sirius—a captain's pay for a sixth rate*—being by the royal instructions of the twenty-fifth day of April, 1787, directed to be continued, although there should not be any of His Majesty's ships employed on this station, rendered it totally unnecessary for me to wish for a King's ship under any other idea but the one pointed out in my letters. As that proposition does not appear to meet their Lordships' ideas, I have prepared for the safety of such ships as may be employed here, as far as depends on me, by sending to Norfolk Island those whom it might be presumed would be the ringleaders, should the seizing of any transport be ever determined on.'

At the conclusion of this letter he tells Dundas that the commander of the *Pitt* transport had sold four thousand pounds' worth of stores brought out as a private venture to the settlement. Much of this sum was for articles bought by the Commissary for the use of the convicts. This fact, said Phillip, would serve to indicate 'what might be brought by a ship loaded wholly on the account of Government.' He did not, he added, wish to reflect on the master of the *Pitt*, but felt obliged to point out this circumstance in order that a similar evil might not occur again.

CHAPTER XIII

IN the early days of the settlement, contemporary chroniclers relate a few incidents showing that all was not dull routine. There were occasionally little social entertainments which helped to make the hideous prison atmosphere more endurable, and in spite of the peculiar character of most of the first colonists, and the ever-present dread of starvation, the officials and even the prisoners sometimes kept holiday.

For example, on the King's birthday, 1789, the first play acted in the colony was staged. Tench reports the performance in these words :—

'The anniversary of His Majesty's birthday was celebrated, as heretofore, at the Government House with loyal festivity. In the evening, the play of *The Recruiting Officer* was performed by a party of convicts, and honoured by the presence of His Excellency and the officers of the garrison. That every opportunity of escape from the dreariness and dejection of our situation should be eagerly embraced, will not be wondered at. The exhilarating effect of a splendid theatre is well known ; and I am not ashamed to confess that the proper distribution of three or four yards of stained paper, and a dozen farthing candles stuck around the mud walls of a convict hut, failed not to diffuse general complacency on the countenances of sixty persons, of various descriptions, who were assembled to applaud the representation. Some of the actors acquitted themselves with great spirit, and received the praises of the audience ; a prologue and an epilogue, written by one of the performers, were also spoken on the occasion ; which, although not worth inserting here, contained some tolerable allusions to the situation of the parties, and the novelty of a stage-representation in New South Wales.'

The same writer, when describing his first sight of the French vessels under La Pérouse, conveys to the reader's mind in a few words how remote was the new country from civilisation. The announcement of a ship in sight was one that required him who made it to be a man of 'great veracity.' Writes Tench :—

'But judge of my surprise on hearing from a sergeant, who ran down almost breathless to the cabin where I was dressing, that a ship was seen off the Harbour's mouth. At first I only laughed, but knowing the man who spoke to me to be of great veracity, and hearing him repeat his information, I flew on deck, on which I had barely set my feet when the cry of "another sail" struck on my astonished ears. Confounded by a thousand ideas which arose in my mind in an instant, I sprang upon the barricado, and plainly descried two ships of considerable size standing in for the mouth of the bay. By this time the alarm had become general, and everyone appeared lost in conjecture. Now they were Dutchmen sent to dispossess us, and, the moment after, storeships from England with supplies for the settlement. It was by Governor Phillip that this mystery was at length unravelled, and the cause of the alarm pronounced to be two French ships, which, it was now recollected, were on a voyage of discovery in the Southern Hemisphere.'

There is now probably no hour in the twenty-four when a vessel is not passing over the same spot as that where the Frenchmen were sighted.

Among the notorious prisoners who arrived in Phillip's time was Barrington, the pickpocket—a sort of Brummel in his profession. Tench writes of him thus :—

'But before I bade adieu to Rose Hill, in all probability for the last time of my life, it struck me that there yet remained one object of consideration not to be slighted. Barrington had been in the settlement between two and three months, and I had not seen him. I saw him with curiosity. He is tall, approaching to six feet, slender, and his gait and manner bespeak liveliness and activity. Of that elegance and fashion, with which my imagination had decked him (I know not why), I could distinguish no trace. Great allowance should, however, be made for depression, and unavoidable deficiency of dress. His face is thoughtful and intelligent; to a strong cast of countenance, he adds a penetrating eye and a prominent forehead; his whole demeanour is humble, not servile. Both on his passage from England and since his arrival here, his conduct has been irreproachable. He is appointed high-constable of the settlement of Rose Hill, a post of some respectability, and certainly one of importance to those who live here. His knowledge of men, particularly of that part of them into whose morals, manners and behaviour he is ordered especially to inspect, eminently fit him for the office. I cannot quit him without bearing my testimony, that his talents promise to be directed, in future, to make reparation to society for the offences he has heretofore committed against it.'

And King, in one of his letters, says that 'the convicts on board the different ships behaved extremely well, and Mr Barrington is now a religious convert. He performs service, and gives a sermon twice on Sundays.'

Religion was not altogether absent from the settlement, although the British Government did not trouble itself to provide a very elaborate clerical establishment. The only provision of this kind was the appointment, at the last moment before the fleet sailed, of the Rev. Richard Johnson, who according to one authority was 'one of the people called Methodists.'

Phillip, King and Hunter all speak well of the disinterestedness of the man, and the good done by him in the face of the greatest difficulties, and Johnson testifies to the help and encouragement always given him by Phillip, who made him a magistrate of the colony. Grose, Phillip's immediate successor, quarrelled with the parson, and there was afterwards much friction between the two. He was not paid handsomely—£182 was allowed him by the Government—and for five years after landing he was without a church. Early in 1791 Phillip began the erection of a place of worship, but before it was finished the exigencies of the colony, as we shall hear, required its conversion into a jail, and subsequently into a granary, so that the services were generally performed in the open air, or in 'an old boathouse close by the waterside, not fit for a stable.'

Poor Johnson thus wrote to Phillip, in March 1792, detailing his grievances :—

'As to my habitation I am very well satisfied ; it is pretty commodious and convenient—few better provided for in this respect in the colony than myself. My principal family complaint is, that I cannot better

provide for them. We are now eight in number. . . .
Our allowance . . . is scanty, and is likely to be
still less. 'Tis seldom we get a fresh meal, and then
in general it is at a dear rate. Fresh pork, one
shilling per pound ; a moderate size fowl, three, four
or five shillings, and sometimes more. Indian corn,
ten shillings per bushel. Everything else, whether
from on ship or on shore, in the same proportion.
Have frequently asked to have the privilege of a man
to shoot for me now and then ; this favour I never
have been granted.'

Phillip did his best to help him, but that best was
not much. When the *Lady Juliana* storeship arrived
in June 1790, the Governor told Johnson that 400
acres were to be surveyed as Church ground, and this
promise was fulfilled, but he could spare no labour
even to clear the ground. Surely, writes the unfortunate Methodist, the Government did not mean him
to use axe and spade himself? Nevertheless, being
a man of energy he did make the attempt, and by
continuous toil managed to better his position somewhat. 'The sound of four hundred acres,' he says
plaintively, 'will appear great. But what, Sir, are
four hundred or four thousand acres full of large green
trees, unless some convicts be allowed to cultivate it ?

'I did not come out here as an overseer or as a
farmer. I have other things more, much more important, to attend to. My duty as a clergyman fully
takes up all my time. Neither will my constitution

admit of it—this is much impaired since I came into this country, and at this very time I feel such rheumatic pains and weakness that I can scarcely go through the duties of my office. This brings me to mention another circumstance. I have to perform divine service at three different places, vizt., at Sydney, Parramatta, and at a settlement about three miles to the westward of Parramatta, and at never a one of these three places is there to this day any place of worship erected, nor so much as talked of. The last time I preached at Sydney was in the open air. On the 11th instant we could not have service at all, because of the rain. . . . By the grace of God, however, I am resolved to go on in the discharge of my duty till I can hold out no longer, and then I must give up and leave this miserable people to spend their Sabbaths in a manner wholly like heathens.

' Last spring there was a foundation of a church laid at Parramatta ; before it was finished it was converted into a jail or a lock-up house, and now it is converted into a granary. Have had this place to perform divine service in for several Sundays ; but now am again turned out, and must again turn field-preacher there also. I go up to Parramatta as usual once a fortnight —the distance by water about fourteen miles. Generally go up on the Saturday—sometimes four, five, six hours upon the water. On Sunday morning early I now ride up to the new settlement ; preach in the open air about seven o'clock to about 600 convicts ;

at ten and at four in the afternoon I preach at Parramatta. I fear, however, I shall not be able to continue this much longer, especially as the winter is now approaching, unless some places be erected for the purpose. Besides my public duty I have to visit the sick, which at present both at Sydney and Parramatta are a great many; numbers dying every day. Last month above sixty died, and I fear before this expires there will be again near the same number.'

It was no wonder that in such circumstances Phillip was compelled to issue an order that convicts who neglected to attend public worship without good reason would be punished by having part of their flour ration stopped. When the first church was built, Johnson himself worked upon it, and its cost was paid by him.

The chaplain wrote asking to be reimbursed for his outlay, and Grose not only refused to support the application, but did all he could to obstruct the clergyman. To such an extent was this carried that King, in a letter to the Home Department, written when Johnson resigned, said he (Johnson) 'had met with much persecution from Grose when he commanded here.'

William Wilberforce had a high opinion of the chaplain at Botany Bay. In 1794 he wrote to Dundas, who was then at the head of the Home Office, a letter which not only concerns Johnson, but, as the following extract proves, shows there were people in the old country then who were beginning to take an interest in the young colonials:—

'As it may be longer than I expected before I have the pleasure of seeing you, and in the interim Captain Hunter may have sailed, I take up my pen, meaning to detain you as little as I can on the subject of New South Wales. Mr Johnson, the chaplain, has transmitted to me the copy of a letter you must have received from him, wishing me to mediate with you for its favourable reception. However, when I tell you he is one of the worthiest men breathing, the most active, the most humble, and at the same time very little acquainted with the world, I have said enough to excuse the steps he has taken, and to obtain his reimbursement. In truth, £67 for a church is rather a more moderate charge than Government, I believe, is used to, and I know from his private letters that he worked very hard with his own hands, and often by night as well as day. In my last letter, I mentioned to you that I had been informed a sufficient number of tolerably qualified instructors for the children, both of the convicts and the natives, might be found on the spot; but it occurred to me that it would be highly desirable to send over some person to act as a general superintendent of all the schools which should be instituted. . . . I must add, and will then have done, that the expense of settling schools, Governor Hunter being directed accordingly, both for natives and Europeans, and of establishing a superintendent, will, if you approve of it, be very trifling, compared with the advantages which may follow—even the pecuniary advantages : for the more decently and orderly the colony will be maintained.'

According to Joseph Holt, the Irish rebel who arrived in the colony, a prisoner, in 1800, Johnson's position was then greatly improved. Holt, in his *Memoirs*, says that in the same year as he arrived, the worthy clergyman returned to England, having acquired a large fortune before leaving by selling his stock and his farm of 600 acres.

We are told that Phillip entertained the officers after the inauguration ceremony, and on royal birthdays, with 'a cold collation,' and Collins relates how, on the arrival of the Second Fleet of transports, 'we learned that our beloved Sovereign had been attacked and for some months afflicted with a dangerous and alarming illness, though now happily recovered. Our distance from his person had not lessened our attachment, and the day following the receipt of this information, being the anniversary of His Majesty's birth, it was kept with every mark of distinction that was in our power. The Governor pardoned all offenders who were under confinement, or under sentence of corporal punishment ; the ration was increased for that day that everyone might rejoice ; at the Governor's table, where all the officers of the settlement and garrison were met, many prosperous and happy years were fervently wished to be added to His Majesty's life.' . . . 'On the 9th, being the day appointed for returning thanks . . . the attendance on divine service was very full. A sermon on the occasion was preached by the Rev. Mr Johnson' . . . and 'the officers were afterwards entertained at the Governor's, when an address on the occasion of the meeting was resolved to be sent to His Majesty.'

The address as a whole may be 'taken as read,' but the following paragraphs are perhaps of sufficient interest to be placed on record here :—

'The little community which has now the honour of addressing your Excellency for the first time, cannot pass it by without anticipating in idea the many and memorable occasions which will be represented hereafter to His Majesty's faithful subjects of this distant settlement, to congratulate him and his illustrious descendants—whether extending the arts and blessings of peace, or covered with the trophies of necessary and glorious war.

'Although from remoteness of situation, and want of intercourse with the seat of government, we are the last in His Majesty's far extended empire to testify our joy on this occasion, we trust that our zeal and fidelity to his royal person will for ever remain unquestioned, as we know them to be pure and unalterable.'

Phillip sent it to Grenville with the following short

and dignified letter, dated June 14th, 1790, with which this chapter may fitly conclude :—

'Sir, — The approbation which His Majesty has been pleased to express of my conduct can only be merited by an earnest desire of faithfully and successfully discharging the charge reposed in me.

'It is, Sir, through you that I am honoured with this mark of attention from my Royal Master, and through you, Sir, I hope that my grateful sense of His Majesty's bounty will be made known.

'The address I received on His Majesty's being happily restored to health I have the honour to enclose ; and faithfully attached to His Royal Person, by every tie of duty, gratitude and affection, I rejoice in the happy event.'

CHAPTER XIV

IN the famine time, Collins says, the little society that
was in the place was broken up, and every man seemed
left to brood in solitary silence over the dreary prospect
before him.

With the exception of the Johnsons, the only free
women and children in the settlement were the
families of the marines, and it was not until the
arrival of the New South Wales Corps, in the ships
of the Second and Third Fleets, that a 'Government
House set' began to loom on the social horizon.

Many of the officers of the regiment were men of
good family. Major Grose, who brought with him a
Commission as Lieutenant-Governor, and was accompanied by his wife, was a man who had seen much
active service, and it was at his suggestion, and by
him, that the corps was raised. The senior captain
was a brother of Nepean, the Under-Secretary to the
Home Department, and Macarthur, the senior lieutenant (whose name will be remembered when all

the others are forgotten, since he founded the wool industry of the colony), took pains to prove himself, on the passage out, 'an officer and a gentleman.' Says the *Morning Post* of 2d December 1789 :—

'In consequence of a private dispute on board the *Neptune*, Captain Gilbert, the commander of that ship, attended by his second, Mr Nelson of Plymouth Dock, met by appointment Lieutenant Macarthur of the Botany Bay Rangers, with his second, the surgeon's mate of the *Neptune*, at the Old Gun Wharf, near the lines. The distance of ten paces being measured, both gentlemen fired their pistols together. Lieutenant Macarthur's ball passed through Captain Gilbert's coat. They then fired a second pistol, each without effect, when the seconds interposed, and the business was settled by Lieutenant Macarthur declaring Captain Gilbert's conduct was in every respect that of a gentleman and a man of honour. In the evening, Lieutenant Macarthur declared the same on the quarter-deck of the *Neptune*, to the satisfaction of all parties. It is said that the quarrel originated on a refusal of Captain Gilbert to admit Lieutenant Macarthur into his own private mess ; at the same time he offered him every accommodation for himself and his family that the ship would allow. This brought on some dispute, which occasioned very high words, but we are happy to say the duel ended without bloodshed.'

Mrs Macarthur, in letters to England written soon

after her arrival at Sydney in 1791, gives us a not altogether gloomy picture of the colony. Some weeks were passed cheerfully, if not gaily. 'On my first landing everything was new to me—every bird, every insect, every flower, etc.—in short, all was novelty around me, and was noticed with a degree of eager curiosity and pertubation that, after a while, subsided into that calmness I have already described. In my former letters I gave you the character of Mr Dawes, and also of Captain Tench. Those gentlemen and a few others are the chief among whom we visit; indeed, we are in that habit of intimacy with Captain Tench that there are few days pass that we do not spend some part of together. Mr Dawes we do not see so frequently. He is so much engaged with the stars that, to mortal eyes, he is not always visible. I had the presumption to become his pupil, and meant to learn a little astronomy. It is true that I have had many a pleasant walk to his house (something less than half a mile from Sydney), have given him much trouble in making orrerys, and explaining to me the general principle of the heavenly bodies; but I soon found I had mistaken my abilities, and blush at my error.

'Still, I wanted something to fill up a certain vacancy in my time, which could neither be done by writing, reading or conversation. To the two first I did not feel myself always inclined, and the latter was not in my power, having no female friends to unbend my mind to, nor a single woman with whom I could converse with any satisfaction to myself.

'I shall now tell you of another recourse I had to fill up some of my vacant hours. Our new house is ornamented with a pianoforte of Mr Worgan's. He kindly means to leave it with me, and now, under his direction, I have begun a new study ; but I fear, without my master, I shall not make any great proficiency. I am told, however, I have done wonders in being able to play off *God Save the King*, and Foot's *Minuet*, besides that of reading the notes with great facility.'

The Governor gave a dinner during the stay of the *Gorgon*, when, according to Collins, upwards of fifty persons were at table, and such a gathering had not before been witnessed in the colony.

We have a picture of Phillip's entertaining the new arrivals from England in the *Gorgon*, drawn by Mrs Parker, wife of the captain of the ship, which is worth reproducing here :—

'When we went on shore, we were all admiration at the natural beauties raised by the hand of Providence without expense or toil. The gentle ascents, the valleys, and the abundance of flowering shrubs, render the face of the country very delightful. The shrub which most attracted my attention was one which bears a white flower, very much resembling our English hawthorn ; the smell of it is both sweet and fragrant, and perfumes the air around to a considerable distance.

'In Botany Bay there are not many land-fowls; of the larger sort, only eagles are seen; of the smaller kind, though not numerous, there is a variety, from the size of a wren to that of a lark; all of which are remarkable for fine loud notes and beautiful plumage, particularly those of the paroquet kind. Crows are also found here, exactly the same as those in England.

'Our amusements, although neither numerous or expensive, were to me perfectly novel and agreeable; the fatherly attention of the good Governor upon all occasions, with the friendly politeness of the officers, rendered our *séjour* perfectly happy and comfortable.

'After our arrival here, Governor King and his lady resided on shore at Governor Phillip's, to whose house I generally repaired after breakfasting on board; indeed it has always proved a home for me : under this hospitable roof I have often ate part of a kangaroo with as much glee as if I had been a partaker of some of the greatest delicacies of this metropolis, although latterly I was cloyed with them, and found them very disagreeable.

'We made several pleasant excursions up the cove to the settlement called Parramatta. The numerous branches, creeks and inlets that are formed in the harbour of Port Jackson, and the wood that covers all their shores down to the very edge of the water, make the scenery beautiful; the north branch is particularly so, from the sloping of its shores, the interspersion of tufted woods, verdant lawns, and the small islands, which are covered with trees, scattered up and down.

'Upon our first arrival at Parramatta, I was surprised to find that so great a progress has been made in this new settlement, which contains above one thousand convicts, besides the military. There is a very good level road, of great breadth, that runs nearly a mile in a straight direction from the landing-place to the Governor's house, which is a small, convenient building, placed upon a gentle ascent, and surrounded by about a couple of acres of garden ground : this spot is called Rose Hill. On both sides of the road are small thatched huts, at an equal distance from each other. After spending the day very agreeably at the Governor's, we repaired to the lodging which had been provided for us, where we had the comfort of a large wood fire, and found everything perfectly quiet, although surrounded by more than one thousand convicts.

'This little excursion afforded us the opportunity of noticing the beautiful plumage of the birds in general, and of the emu in particular, two of which we discovered in the woods. Their plumage is remarkably fine, and rendered particularly curious, as each hen has two feathers generally of a light brown ; the wings are so small as hardly to deserve the name. They can run with such swiftness that a greyhound

can with difficulty keep pace with them. The flesh
tastes somewhat like beef.'[1]

Before the first Governor left, the traffic in rum
was already growing into an evil, and Phillip,
foreseeing the consequences, wrote home more than
once on the subject. Grose, Phillip's successor, as
soon as he took charge, relaxed the wise restrictions
put upon the sale of spirits by Phillip.

Mr Johnson, in a letter to Hunter on the state
of the colony during the administration of Phillip's
successor, shows the effect of the liquor traffic :—

' Yourself, sir, being a kind of resident amongst us
at the first formation of the colony, and for some time
afterwards, I need not state to you the plans adopted
and the measures pursued by Governor Phillip for
the proper regulation and good order of the colony,
as well as in a moral as in a civil point of view.

'Little or no alterations were made from those
plans or measures, from the time you then left us
to that when Governor Phillip himself returned to
England, in December 1792.

'Some time previous to his going I was at his
request sworn in to act as a civil magistrate in your
place, which duty I continued to perform until the
time he left us, at which time the colony was as
peaceable, orderly and moral as could be expected

[1] 'A Voyage Round the World in the *Gorgon*, man-of-war. Captain
John Parker ; performed and written by his widow for the advantage of a
numerous family. Dedicated by permission to Her Royal Highness the
Princess of Wales.' London : John Nichols, Fleet Street.

from such a description of people as the colony was formed of.

'But no sooner had Governor Phillip left the colony than I was convinced that the plan or measures of Government were about to undergo an entire change. The civil magistrates, within two days, received an order that their duty would in future be dispensed with, and from that time till your Excellency's arrival again in the colony, everything was conducted in a kind of military manner.

'This, I believe, was the first step toward overturning all those attempts and endeavours that had hitherto been planned and pursued for the establishment of good order to be kept up amongst the different ranks and orders of the inhabitants of the colony.

'Every order that had been given tending to promote morality and religion seemed to be laid aside, and fresh orders issued tending to banish whatever (in the opinion of a good and virtuous mind) is or ought to be the first considered and promoted (and particularly in a colony like this, where by far the major part of the inhabitants are lost to all sense of virtue, and abandoned to every species of wickedness), viz., a reverence for the Supreme Being, and a strict observance of all His just and righteous precepts.'

Surgeon Arndell in a letter on the same subject says :—

'Nothing more painful or distressing can be imagined than our situation during the last-mentioned period. The departure of Governor Phillip from the colony was soon followed by a surprising change in the management of civil affairs : for the security of good order and public peace were in a moment almost annihilated, and a torrent of licentiousness bore everything civil and sacred before it. Whatever was injurious or disgraceful to human nature might have been reasonably expected from general drunkenness ; yet general and habitual drunkenness absolutely became the unfortunate fashion of the times : the consequence was that crimes of every sort increased to an alarming degree : thefts and robberies became so numerous that they were spoken of as mere matters of course, and even rapes and murders were not infrequent. The respect due to superiors, and the subordination so essential to the welfare of civil society, seemed banished from the minds of the unthinking multitude, and that to such a degree that no one could think himself safe in passing from one part of the town to another. Among several insults I have myself met with, a soldier accosted me one evening in the road at Parramatta and insisted on my spending a bottle with him. Upon saying that I would see him home to his barracks he told me he would spare me that trouble by knocking me down, which he would certainly have done at the moment if he had not been prevented by a person who joined us at the time.'

Six years before this time Phillip had written thus to Nepean :—

'The impossibility of preventing the convicts' cloathing and necessaries from passing into the hands of those for whom those articles are not intended, makes me wish that every article intended for the convicts should be marked. Their linens and woollens might, I think, without any additional expense, have stripes of a different colour wove in them. The iron pots and every other article should likewise be marked : and this is absolutely necessary, for a convict will sell for a pint of spirits the necessaries which should serve him for months, and there always will be those who will purchase them. . . .

'The landing of spirits without having a permit has been prohibited in the Port Orders, in order to prevent the convicts procuring any ; but if some duty was laid on all spirits landed in the settlement it would more effectually answer the purpose. The duties so collected would, of course, be applied for the benefit of the Crown. You will, Sir, favour me with your opinion on that head.'

The Government informed him that an allowance of rum for the troops was on the way out, and to this Phillip replied, in 1792, that 'the permitting of spirits amongst the civil and military may be necessary, but it will certainly be a great evil.'

A similar, but less serious, scandal was promptly put a stop to by Phillip. This was the bringing out of contraband cargo.   The Governor wrote home in reference to this in November 1791, to the Commissioners of the Navy, as follows :—

'Having been informed that there were great quantities of cordage, copper, lead and iron on board the *Albemarle*, *Active*, *Admiral Barrington* and *Queen* transports, the masters of those ships were sent for, and from the master of the *Albemarle* an account was received of what they admitted to have been put on board by the owners, which they say was done after Government had sent all the stores and provisions which were intended for the colony, and that they had never declared their ships full. A copy of the account received from the master of the *Albemarle* is enclosed, but which can be but a very small part of what those ships have brought out : a copy of the masters' declaration as to their having never declared their ships full is likewise enclosed.

'The great inconvenience attending the want of limestone has been pointed out : and if it was necessary for those ships to bring ballast, limestone might have been put on board, and would have been easily changed for the stone of this country, and which I hope the Board will order to be done on any future occasion.'

It must be admitted that Phillip's time was pretty well occupied in the serious duties of his office, and that in a colony where the Governor had to devise means to feed his people, to see that ships arriving in his territory brought limestone for general use, instead of lead for private purposes, and to take care that the rum traffic was kept within bounds, it is scarcely to be wondered at that the 'social functions,' which nowadays are among the chief duties of Australian Governors, in Phillip's time took the form of an occasional 'cold collation,' or an invitation to dinner with a request to 'bring your bread in your pocket.'

CHAPTER XV

'WHENEVER I want a thing well done in a distant part of the world, when I want a man with a good head, a good heart, lots of pluck and plenty of common sense, I always send for a captain of the Navy.'

Lord Palmerston, when Minister for Foreign Affairs, is alleged to have more than once used these words in the Council Chamber, and English ministers were apparently of this opinion long before his time, for during the first dozen years of Australian colonisation three naval commanders—Phillip, Hunter and King—were at different periods appointed to govern the distant colony.

If, in Palmerston's day, the shade of Lord Sydney ever lingered near his old chair at the council-table, one can imagine an approving whisper, 'Hear, hear ! my appointment of Phillip proved that long ago.'

Before coming to the date when Phillip began to pack up what few worldly goods his four years' service in New South Wales had left him, there is one act of his administration which cannot be overlooked—that is the manner in which he regulated the disposal of Crown lands.

The Land Laws of New South Wales are now in such a condition that an eminent Queen's Counsel has said, with truth, that no man living can safely undertake to interpret their meaning.

That 'good head' with 'plenty of common sense,' which Palmerston extols as qualifications found in sea-captains, enabled Phillip, in dealing with the land, to form a sound theory and to put it into practice ; and from Phillip's time to the present the theory has been much the same, but in its practical application common sense has long since departed, and a confused jungle of land legislation has grown up in its place.

Phillip's 'Instructions' when he left England empowered him to issue land grants to emancipated convicts. He very soon found that the country would never be settled without free colonists of the farming class, and his despatches continually urged upon the Home Government the necessity of offering some inducement to such people to come out. No notice was taken of these representations, but he was, by an additional set of 'Instructions' sent out in the Second Fleet, empowered to offer Crown lands as an inducement to the non-commissioned officers and men of the military force to remain in the colony after their term of service had expired.

Phillip knew very well how land should be granted, for, six months after his arrival, he wrote to Lord Sydney as follows :—

'Farmers and people used to the cultivation of lands, if sent out (and without which agriculture will make but very slow progress), must be supported by Government for two or three years, and have the labour of a certain number of convicts to assist them for that time, after which they may be able to support themselves, and to take the convicts sent out at the expense which Government is put to for their transportation ; but then, I presume, none should be sent whose sentence is for a less term than fourteen years. A yearly fine is to be paid for the lands granted, after the fifth year ; the fine to be in grain, and in proportion to the crop : and this, I hope, would be the only tax laid on the crops : giving the church lands in the room of tythes. The sending out settlers who will be interested in the labour of the convicts, and in the cultivation of the country, appears to me to be absolutely necessary. Lands granted to officers or settlers will, I presume, be on condition of a certain proportion of the lands so granted being cultivated or cleared within a certain time, and which time and quantity can only be deter- mined by the nature of the ground and situation of the lands : and, in that case, when lands are granted to officers, the garrison must be sufficient for the service of the place, and to permit such officers occasionally to be absent at the lands they are to cultivate, and for a certain time : they likewise must be allowed convicts, who must be maintained at the expence of the Crown. Your Lordship will be pleased to consider this opinion as given in obedience to orders, on a subject which requires more consideration than I can give at present, and at a time when I have only a very superficial knowledge of the country for a few miles around.'

Here, then, was outlined the assignment system, and the plan of granting land on condition that it was turned to a good use. Of course it is not pretended that Phillip originated these ideas, but that he had studied the subject sufficiently to be able to make the suggestions is remarkable enough in a man whose life had been spent on board ship—and on board ship over a hundred years ago !

The conditions on which he was empowered to grant land were, as Phillip saw, impossible of fulfilment, and he gave settlers inducements in the way of provisions and labour in excess of his instructions, a step on his part which his superiors never questioned. The Government, curiously enough, at first made no provision for granting land to commissioned officers, and as a result the land lent them by Phillip to cultivate brought in only small returns, since those to whom it was lent could take but a languid interest in such temporary ownership. When the case was represented to the Home Office, permission was granted, but the despatch reached the colony after Phillip left it. With the granting of authority to assign land to officers began the growth of the abuses of the privilege, for in the case of commissioned officers no limit was assigned in the 'Instructions' as to the maximum grant which the Governor might make. Yet Phillip foresaw the necessity for restriction, and a few months before he left the colony he wrote :—

'Experience has also pointed out many inconveniences attending the receiving men as settlers who only look to the convenience of the present moment. With some the sole object in becoming settlers is that of being their own masters, and with others the object is to raise as much money as will pay their passage to England, and then assign their lands to those who take them with the same view. There are many of this description at Norfolk Island ; . . . but, as they have not received their grants, the necessary steps will be taken to prevent this imposition by removing some from the island, and by granting leases of only five or seven years to others, for one or two of these people have attempted to dispose of their grounds as soon as their huts were built, and they had received that assistance which had been promised them.'

With regard to free settlers there is on record a quaint correspondence between a Quaker named John

Sutton and the Home Department. Sutton thus wrote to Under-Secretary King :—

'Friend King,—Thou being so busy, it is not likely I can see thee to-day. Have inclos'd a paper similar to that given to Evan Nepean, only it is more specific. I hope thou will give it a proper sanction, and it will obveate any future disapointments. And if it be agreable to let me have any terms to carry persons, or provisions live or dead, I believe I can do it as low and more beneficial to the colony than it has hitherto been done. I will call in two or three days for thy opinion.'

Nothing came of Sutton's proposal, which was that he should be given land-grants, free passages, tools, and all the rest of it, for a party of Quaker emigrants ; but in February 1793, the *Bellona* arrived in the colony with five men who were given a grant of land near Parramatta, which was appropriately named Liberty Plains. .These five men were the first batch of *bona-fide* emigrants—the advance guard of that great army of colonists who have made Australia what it is.

Previously to 1791—although Dampier saw whales in Australian waters—no one appears to have thought that a whale or seal fishery could be founded there. But Phillip in a despatch, written in November 1791 to Secretary Stephens, commented upon the great number of 'spermaceti whales' that had been observed upon the coast, which gave him reason to hope that a whale fishery might be established at some port in the colony. Melville, the master of the transport *Britannia*, before alluded to in these pages, had seen such vast numbers of whales after doubling the south-west cape of Van Diemen's Land, that after disembarking his cargo of convicts he asked Phillip to expedite his ship's departure in order that he might cruise in search of them. Phillip gave him every assistance, and Melville, who was a shrewd man, got away as quietly as possible, but the object of his haste soon leaked out, and the *Britannia* was quickly followed by four other transports—the *Matilda, William and Ann, Salamander* and *Mary Ann.* Fifteen days later Melville returned to Sydney, and reported that although he had seen great numbers of whales the bad weather prevented his lowering his boats except upon rare occasions. However, the *Britannia* and the *William and Ann* between them had killed seven; but a heavy south-east gale coming on they saved but one fish each. The *Mary Ann* soon followed them back, her coppers having been 'washed down' in the gale. She, with the *Matilda*, had gone southward in search of seals and had seen no whales, and when they were returning to Sydney, the latter vessel put in to Jervis Bay to stop a leak. Phillip was pleased to learn from her master that it possessed 'an exceedingly good anchorage, and room for the largest ship to work in or out with great safety.'

From that time, Phillip, though disappointed at

the result of the transports' first cruise, took a deep interest in forwarding the whaling industry. He doubtless did not realise that one reason for the want of success that attended the first venture was the lack of knowledge on the part of the masters of the transports. None of them, probably, knew anything of the migratory habits of the cetacean tribe in the Southern Seas, nor the difference between the highly valuable 'sperm,' 'right' and 'humpback' whale, and the dangerous and unassailable 'finback.' But experience was soon to be gained, and, in March 1792, Phillip again wrote home, expressing this opinion :—

'The information given in my former letters respecting the prospect there was of establishing a spermacetic whale fishery on this coast was drawn from the accounts I received of the great number of fish which had been seen by two of the whalers. None of those ships remained out but for a very short time ; but when the *Britannia* sailed, the master of that vessel told me he intended to remain three months on the coast, in order to give it a fair trial, that he had no doubt of seeing fish, but feared the currents. From some information which I have received since that ship sailed, I fear that the fur trade on the north-west coast of America, and the trade amongst the islands, is too great an object to those who are employed in the fishery ever to admit their giving this coast a fair trial, and apprehend that all the

ships have left it.   Should a fishery ever be established
on this coast, and which I should suppose likely to
answer as well as the one which has been established
many years in the Brazil (at Sta Catharina and Rio de
Janeiro), I think it would be found to answer best
if carried on in small vessels, as it is from Rio de
Janeiro ; and with respect to the currents, I believe
they are neither more frequent nor stronger than
what they are on the Brazil coast.'

This was the beginning of South Pacific whaling,
which, now practically extinct, for the first half
century of Australian colonisation was only second
in importance to the wool trade in the commercial
history of the colonies.

In April 1790, King had carried home this modestly-
worded and characteristically unselfish request from
Phillip, in a private letter to Lord Sydney :—

'As the settlement is now fixed, whenever His
Majesty's service permits, I shall be glad to return
to England, where I have reason to suppose my
private affairs may make my presence necessary ; but
which I do not ask in any publick letters, nor should
I mention a desire of leaving this country at this
moment, but that more than a year must pass before
it can possibly take place, and I make no doubt but
that every inconvenience now felt in this colony will
be done away before this letter reaches your Lordship.
I am sorry to say that nine-tenths of us merit every
little inconveniency we now feel.'

And again in 1791 he wrote to Lord Grenville, in March and November :—

'It is not without concern that I find myself obliged to request His Majesty's permission to return to England. A complaint in the side, and from which, in more than two years, I have been seldom free, has impaired my health, and at times puts it out of my power to attend to the charge with which His Majesty has been pleased to honor me in the manner I wish and the state of the colony requires. The settlement is now so fully established that the great labour may be said to be past ; and it has, Sir, been attained under every possible disadvantage, though it is not in that situation in which I should wish to leave it, for it is not independent for the necessaries of life ; and, as I feel myself greatly interested in the good of a colony with the establishing of which I have been honored, and to which I should wish to return, if the cause which now obliges me to desire permission to leave it should be removed by the voyage, or by the assistance I may find in London, I therefore only request leave of absence from the government.' . . .

'I am honoured with your Lordship's letter of the 19th of February, in answer to mine to Lord Sydney, and beg leave to assure your Lordship that I should not hesitate a moment in giving up my private affairs to the public service ; but from a complaint which so very frequently puts it out of my power to use that exercise which my situation requires, and the present state of this colony, in which I believe every doubt respecting its future independency as to the necessaries of life is fully done away, I am induced to request permission to resign the government that I may return to England in hopes of finding that relief which this country does not afford.'

The only reply he received to these letters was the following paragraph of a despatch, dated May 1792, from Dundas, then at the head of the Home Office, who wrote :—

'I cannot conclude this letter without assuring you how much I lament that the ill state of your health deprives His Majesty of your further services in the government of New South Wales, and I have only to hope that, on quitting the settlement, you will have the satisfaction of leaving it in a thriving and prosperous situation.'

This was so obscure that Phillip cannot be blamed for not understanding it, as he writes in the following October :—

'You are, Sir, pleased to express your regret at my being obliged to return to England on account of my health, and I feel much satisfaction from the manner in which that circumstance is mentioned.

'How far that part of your letter to which the above alludes may have been intended to convey to me His Majesty's permission to return, I am doubtful, and although I am inclined to think it has been written with that intention, and feel how necessary it is for me to give up, at least for a time, the charge of this government, which is very far from what I wish to do at the moment the colony is approaching to that state in which I have so long and anxiously wished to see it; still, Sir, I fear there is a possibility of its being expected that I should remain until permission to quit the government is more fully and clearly expressed; and as there appears to be a wish that I should remain in this country some time longer, I shall wait the arrival of the next ships.'

And at the same time he wrote to Nepean :—

'The manner in which Mr Dundas speaks of my leaving this country is very handsome; but I do not well understand that part of his letter. I fear that it may have been supposed I would remain until His Majesty's permission was clearly expressed; and I should be sorry, after all my labours, to have it said on my return that I was not expected. The ship which was to follow the *Royal Admiral* will, I hope, clear up the doubt, and not only leave me at liberty to quit the government, but also put the means of doing it in my power, otherwise I do not see how I am to get home after the *Atlantic* has sailed, unless it is by the way of China or the north-west coast of America, neither of which would be very agreeable to a man going in search of health.'

And Collins tells us that in October 'The month closed with a circumstance that excited no small degree of concern in the settlement : Governor Phillip signified a determination of quitting his government and returning to England in the *Atlantic*. To this he was induced by perceiving that his health hourly grew worse, and hoping that a change of air might contribute to his recovery.'

On the 11th December 1792, Phillip embarked for England. Among his last acts before leaving was to increase the weekly ration at Sydney, and to send some stores to Norfolk Island. Says Collins :—

'His Excellency had always attended to this little colony with a parental care; often declaring that from the peculiarity of its situation he would rather that want should be felt in his own Government than in that dependency; and as they would be generally eight or ten weeks later than this colony in receiving their supplies, by reason of the time which the ships necessarily required to refit after coming in from sea, he purposed furnishing them with a proportion of provisions for three months longer than the provisions in store at this place would last : and His Excellency took leave of that settlement, by completing, as fully as he was able, this design.

'He was now about taking leave of his own Government. The accommodations for His Excellency and the officers who were going home in the *Atlantic* being completed, the detachment of marines under the command of Lieutenant Poulden embarked on the 5th, and at six o'clock in the evening of Monday the 10th, Governor Phillip quitted the charge with which he had been entrusted by his Sovereign, and in the execution of which he had manifested a zeal and perseverance that alone could have enabled him to surmount the natural and artificial obstacles which the country and its inhabitants had thrown in his way.'

CHAPTER XVI

THE story of the growth of Australia, after Phillip left it, need not be told here. Things did not, indeed, go smoothly under his immediate successors, and the officials in England soon found the despatches from 'Botany Bay' more worrying than the mild requests of Phillip for something to eat. In 1808 Governor Bligh, the hero of the *Bounty* mutiny, was forcibly deposed by the military, who took the government of the colony into their own hands. This revolt led to the appointment by the Home Office of Governor Macquarie, under whose rule the colony made rapid progress.

Other milestones in Australian history are the settlement of Van Diemen's Land (Tasmania), West Australia, South Australia, Port Phillip (Victoria), and Queensland, and their formation into independent colonies ; the stoppage of convict transportation ; the establishment of representative government; and the discovery of gold. With all these things we have nothing here to do, for they all happened long after Phillip's day. It only remains to tell what little is known of the after life of the first Governor.

Phillip arrived in England in May 1793, and a couple of months later, in this letter to the Home Secretary, he formally resigned his office :—

'London, 23d *July* 1793.

'Sir,—Being convinced by those I have consulted that the complaint I labour under may in time require assistance which cannot be found in a distant part of the world, and that the time in which such assistance may become necessary is very uncertain, I find myself obliged to request that you will, Sir, represent my case to His Majesty, and that I may be permitted to resign the Government of New South Wales.

'It is, Sir, with the greatest regret that I ask to resign a charge which, after six years' care and anxiety, is brought to the state in which I left it; but I have the consolation of believing that I have discharged the trust reposed in me to the satisfaction of His Majesty's Ministry, and hope that I may still be of service to a colony in which I feel myself so greatly interested.

'As I remain in town in consequence of the message I received from Mr King that you would speak to Mr Pitt respecting my enjoying the moiety of the salary for my life, I shall, Sir, take it as a favor if you will inform me if my continuing in town is still necessary, or whether that matter, to me of such consequence, is or will be settled, and that I am at liberty to leave town; for, although I have given up all hopes of the Bath waters being of any service in my complaint, they may in other respects be beneficial.—I have, etc.,   A. PHILLIP.'

For his colonial service the Government granted him a pension of £500 a year, which reward he acknowledged in the following letter :—

'I should long since have done myself the honor of writing to acknowledge the obligation I am under for the pension which His Majesty has been pleased to grant me, but that I flattered myself I should have an opportunity of doing it in person, as I was so frequently at the office on matters relative to the colony. I now, sir, beg leave to assure you that I shall ever retain a due sense of the obligation, and trust that my hope of having the pension fixed, so as not to cease on my attaining any one of those places to which officers look up as rewards of past services, or to which in the course of service a commanding officer might find it expedient to appoint me, will meet with your approbation. I allude to a seat at either of the Naval Boards, Colonel of Marines, or Greenwich Hospital, places to which I may hope hereafter to lay a just claim, independent of my services in New South Wales.'

Many letters are in existence showing that, despite his failing health, he never lost interest in the colony. For example, in November 1793, remembering what delay in the despatch of store ships meant to the exiles, he wrote privately to the Home Office :—

' By a letter I have just received, I am informed that the *Mangoff George* has been examined and approved of ; but that the captors' demands are something more than what the surveyors have valued her at, though the difference is very small. If that ship is calculated to answer the purpose, and I understand she is, do, for God's sake, point out to the Naval Board that every day lost is attended with a very considerable expence to this country. It is exactly the value of the animal food consumed by 4000 people when the freight is added. The state of the colony, probably without any vessel on the station, is still of more consequence.'

His old officers often wrote to him to confirm their statements of their services, and he frequently interceded on their behalf at the Home Office. King he was especially anxious to see promoted for his good work, and he strongly recommended his appointment as Governor of New South Wales, a recommendation which, after Hunter had been consulted, was acted upon.

When King was at Portsmouth in 1799, preparing

to leave England to take command at New South Wales, we find Phillip still his warm friend and among the last to wish him good-bye. Writing to Sir Joseph Banks in reference to the matter of conveying plants across the sea, King says :—

'Captain Phillip, who is now standing by me, says that he has no doubt, if the *Atlantic* had been able to furnish a tarred or painted canvas to cover the plants, but that the most part of those he brought from New South Wales would have arrived home. The precautions they took, and those he would have taken if he had the means, he has communicated to me, and I shall be happy to give my assistance in making that alteration.'

Just before King sailed, Phillip wrote to him this letter, which shows both his generosity and the esteem in which he always held his comrade :—

'As two of the cows lost' (in the bush) 'soon after our landing in New South Wales were my property, I have an undoubted claim to a share in the cattle, since found to have increased in so extraordinary a manner, and as Government puts the care of such part of their cattle, to which they have a claim, under the protection of the Governor for the time being, I now give you all my interest therein, to dispose of as you may judge proper ; and in doing this I may, and certainly shall, render a very essential service to that country, as no cattle can be killed without the consent of the Governor and yourself, or whoever you vest your property in when you leave the country.

'When the cows were lost, they were five in number; three were the property of the Crown, and two were mine. The bull and heifer belonged to the Crown also.'

And in a subsequent letter, he says :—

'You will not forget that before you left England I gave you a full power to take possession of, and dispose of, as your property, my claim on and share in the cattle running wild in the woods, and two cows belonging to me, having strayed with the cows belonging to the Crown.'

Long after he left the colony he was being continually quoted by his successors as an example of a 'good Governor.' Hunter, on his arrival in 1795, for instance, wrote thus :—

'Had the original regulations of Governor Phillip, as they stood when I left the colony in 1791, remained, with such alterations or amendments as the various existing circumstances might have rendered necessary, I should have known at once what I had to do ; but to find upon my arrival in 1795 that the whole had been abolished as soon as he departed, I own, surprised me. There surely were some good rules amongst those he had established ; and I can venture to say from my own knowledge that there was order and discipline in the colony then, and not near so many robberies. But by this rather too sudden and indeli-

cate abolition of these regulations, which certainly had
the appearance of a reflection on the conduct and
measures of that gentleman, we would suppose there
had not been one fit to be continued.'

And again in a reply to a petition from some
settlers, enclosed in a despatch written in 1800,
Hunter uses these words :—

' The settlers should recollect that there is a wide
difference in ;the situation of the colony from the
years 1791 and 1792 to 1800. At the former period
there was no commerce, and but little farming.
Governor Phillip . . . gave every encouragement to
agriculture in his power. The number of farmers
was few, and the little stock that was brought into
the country in 1788, after an interval of four years,
enabled him to issue the increase to such people his
goodness led him to consider as deserving. Whether
they were does not admit of a doubt. It is notorious
they (almost to a man) approved themselves un-
deserving of this indulgence. The Governor, therefore, wishes to contrast that time with the present.
At Governor Phillip's departure in 1792 there were
not above sixty settlers throughout the whole territory
—Port Jackson and Norfolk Island. Of these a few
received sheep ; some goats ; but several had neither
the one nor the other. Now, there are upwards of
a thousand settlers.'

A year later King wrote to the Home Office, describing the state of the colony, and he tells us how :—

' Previous to Governor Phillip's departure, he gave each settler two ewes belonging to the Crown ; to some officers he had been equally liberal. As these sheep were given with an expectation and an injunction not to be parted with, it was hoped that each settler might raise a good stock ; but on his departure, every ewe, except those belonging to one settler, was purchased from those unthinking people at five gallons of spirits a head. This accounts for so great a proportion of sheep being in the hands of officers, and those which do not now belong to officers have been sold by them to the present possessors.'

Even Margarot, most contumacious of men, one of the 'Scotch martyrs' transported just after Phillip reached England, seems to have found something to admire in the first Governor. In a letter written by the 'Martyr' expressing his views upon the way in which the colony should be governed, he says : 'When you recalled one gentleman you ought to have given us another. The first error of the Ministry was the suffering Major Grose to succeed to that worthy man, Governor Phillip.'

After leaving the colony, Phillip saw very little further sea service, the only recorded appointment of his that we can find being the command of the *Alexander* from March to October 1796. He was promoted, in 1801, Rear-Admiral of the Blue ; in April 1804, Rear-Admiral of the White ; in November 1805, Rear-Admiral of the Red ; in October 1809, Vice-

Admiral of the White; in July 1810, Vice-Admiral of the Red; and on the 4th June 1814, Admiral of the Blue.[1]

Phillip's old friend wrote to his son in 1808 two letters which give us a last glimpse of the old admiral. The first letter is from Tooting in Surrey, written in July, 1808, and in it King says :—

'I was with Admiral Phillip a week; he is very much altered, having lost the entire use of his whole right side, arm, and leg; his intellect and spirits are as good as ever. He may linger on some years under his present infirmity, but, from his age, a great reprieve cannot be expected.'

Seven days before his death in September 1808, King wrote another letter from Bath, in which he says :—

'As this letter may probably reach you before you sail, I just write to say that I came here on Tuesday with Mr Lethbridge, on his return to London, merely to see Admiral Phillip, whom I found much better than I possibly could expect from the reports I had heard, although he is quite a cripple, having lost the entire use of his right side; but his intellects are very good, and his spirits are what they always were.'

Phillip lingered on until the 31st of August 1814, when he died at Bath at his residence, No. 19 Bennett Street, on the lower slopes of Lansdown

---

[1] For the verification of these particulars the Authors have to thank Mr Ferdinand Brand, Librarian to the Admiralty.

Hill.   For eighty-three years his burial-place remained unknown, until, through inquiries instituted by the New South Wales Government nine years ago, his tomb[1] was finally discovered in St Nicholas's Church, Bathampton—a short distance from Bath —by the present vicar, the Rev. Lancelot John Fish.   It is a quiet and beautiful spot, in spite of its proximity to the Great Western Railway, and has been chosen as the last resting-place of many distinguished servants of the State.

The first Australian newspaper, the *Sydney Gazette*, which had then been in existence about ten years, thus briefly records the death of the first Australian Governor :—

'A London paper of a recent date announces the death of Vice-Admiral Arthur Phillip, at an advanced age.   This event took place at Bath on 31st August last.   To this gentleman the colony of New South Wales owes its original establishment in 1788 ; and in

---

[1] It is a plain flat slab in the passage leading from the door into the aisle, and the inscription upon it is as follows :—' Underneath lie the remains of ARTHUR PHILLIP, Admiral of the Blue, who died 31st August 1814, in his 76th year.   Also of ISABELLA, relict of the above ADMIRAL PHILLIP, who died 7th March 1823, in the 71st year of her age.'   There is also a small and unobtrusive monument, high up on the north wall of the tower, on which is stated that ' Near this Tablet are the Remains of *Arthur Phillip*, Esq., Admiral of the Blue, First Governor and Founder of the Colony of *New South Wales*.'   It would certainly seem fitting that some more worthy memorial of so good and great a man should be placed in the church, and the vicar has suggested that one of the windows in the aisle facing the tomb might be filled with stained glass.—[ED.]

taking a retrospect of the arduous duties of such an undertaking, the many difficulties he had to struggle with, and the perils to which he was exposed, it will be only rendering a just tribute to him to remark that Governor Phillip manifested, during the period of his administration, much fortitude, zeal and integrity; and that to the wisdom of his early regulations and indefatigable exertions, the present flourishing state of the settlement bears most honourable and ample testimony. Governor Phillip died in the 77th (*sic*) year of his age.'

Phillip's contemporaries have left little enough material from which biographers can to-day create a personal interest in the man, and the writers feel that in their attempt to describe the first Governor of New South Wales and .the manner of his governing, Phillip never stands out distinctly from the picture of his work. His quiet, self - contained nature gave. Collins, Tench, and the others no chance to write of what the Governor said or how he behaved on this or that occasion. They can only tell us what the Governor did. His own letters speak for themselves, but all they reveal is that he invariably knew how to go about the work in hand, and that he had every confidence in himself to carry it through successfully. With a mind large enough to write in 1787 that 'I would not wish convicts to lay the foundations of an empire,' with the statesmanlike foresight that could in the next year add, ' I do not doubt that this country will prove the most valuable acquisition Great Britain ever made,' Phillip was still so thorough, so possessed of that capacity for detail, of that thoughtfulness in little things which counts for so much in the management of all great concerns, that he could in the very despatch which contained these memorable sentiments ask for iron pots for cooking, and remember that the women were short of gowns.

His perfect self-reliance and belief in his ability to pull the colony through its worst misfortunes, led him sometimes, perhaps, to write too cheerfully for his own and his charges' comfort. Even in the dismal time of famine, a month after the wreck of the *Sirius,* when the settlement was on the brink of starvation, he sent to the Home Secretary such moderately worded letters that Lord Sydney either affected to think or actually believed that the colony was almost flourishing ; for in April 1790, Sydney stated that he had received two letters containing three requests from ' our friend Phillip, who represents the new settlement as having nearly overcome its difficulties. . . .   The last (letter) refers to his request for leave to return home for the regulation of his private affairs. . . .   He makes his last request with much the least earnestness. . . .'

And this was the nature of the man. Is it not the nature of most true Englishmen ? Does not this habit of working silently, 'putting a good face on it,' doing the thing given them to do, and not talking of it—does not this, above all, characterise the best of the men who have gone out from home to the uttermost parts of the earth, and there so wrought that to-day we know them as 'Builders of a Greater Britain ?'

[APPENDIX

APPENDIX I

THE information obtainable with regard to Admiral Phillip's family is of the most meagre description. His father, Jacob Phillip, as has been said, was a native of Frankfort, who settled in London as a teacher of languages, and his mother was an Englishwoman, Elizabeth Breach, whose first husband was Captain Herbert, R.N.   He had at least one sister, whose Christian name is unknown. She married a Mr Dove, and left a daughter, Mary Ann Dove, from whom, by her marriage in 1811 with Mr Thomas Lancefield, the present representatives of the family are descended.

The writer of the *Anecdotes of Governor Phillip*, prefixed to his '*Voyage*' (Stockdale, 1789), after an allusion to the restoration of Peace[1] in 1763, says that '*Phillip now* found leisure to marry'; but the surname of his wife is not stated. On the tombstone in Bathampton church her Christian name (Isabella) is given, and she is described as being 'in the 71st year of her age' in 1823, so that she must have been born in or about 1752, and could consequently only have been 11 years old at the date mentioned by the writer of the '*Anecdotes*.'   As Phillip did

---

[1] The words 'Peace, with its blessings, was restored in 1763,' are omitted from the official transcript of these *Anecdotes* in Vol. I. of the *History of New South Wales from the Records*, p. 496.

not enter the Portuguese Service until 1774-5 (*see* Appendix II.), and is supposed to have been living at Lyndhurst,[1] in Hampshire, during the interval, it is probable that the marriage took place at a later date ; but further uncertainty is caused by a statement to be found in the *Adventures and Recollections of Captain Landman, late of the Corps of Royal Engineers* (1852), who mentions a meeting that he had in 1796 with the Admiral and 'Mrs Phillip, a lady he had *recently* married.' On the whole, one is driven to the conclusion, that either the date given by the writer of the *Anecdotes* is incorrect, or that Phillip was[2] twice married. There is no doubt that he left a wife behind him when he went to Australia. I am indebted to the Rev. Arthur Phillip Lancefield, of Over Tabley, Knutsford, for the subjoined letter, in which the history of the Admiral's collateral descendants is traced :—

'OVER TABLEY,
'KNUTSFORD, 8 *March* 1899.

'DEAR SIR,—My father (Thomas William Lancefield) died in my infancy, having given my mother hardly any information as to his connection with Admiral Phillip. I think you have a copy of Phillip's will, and as legacies are left by it (after his wife's decease) to persons not bearing his

---

[1] A careful examination of the Lyndhurst and Minstead registers, kindly undertaken by the Rector, has so far failed to produce any evidence of this.

[2] This is distinctly stated in Vol. LXXXV. (1815) of the *Gentleman's Magazine*, as also the fact that he died without issue.

surname, the presumption is that he left no children, and that no direct descendants of his are living.

'I believe the connection to be this. Phillip's sister, of whose Christian name I am ignorant, was my great-grandmother and married a Mr Dove; his Christian name is also unknown, as well as the time and place of marriage. Their daughter, Mary Ann Dove, was married on August 1, 1811, to my grandfather, Thomas Lancefield. You will see that my grandmother, Mary Ann Lancefield, was one of Phillip's legatees, she being his niece, but all her share of the property was lost in the costs of a Chancery suit of the type of "*Jarndyce* v. *Jarndyce*." My grandparents had a family of nine children, but only two sons reached manhood, my father, Thomas William Lancefield, born 1814, died 1869, and my uncle, Arthur Phillip Lancefield, born 1823, died 1871. A daughter, Anne, was married to Charles Widgeon Haywood, M.D., and died in 1864, leaving one son, James.

'To the best of my knowledge, my elder brother and I are the only two individuals named after the Admiral. My brother, Victor Phillip Lancefield, has one daughter, Maud Vernon Lancefield.

'Regretting much that I can give you so little information.—I am, Sir, yours very truly,

'ARTHUR PHILLIP LANCEFIELD.'

With Mr Lancefield's assistance the following pedigree has been compiled :—

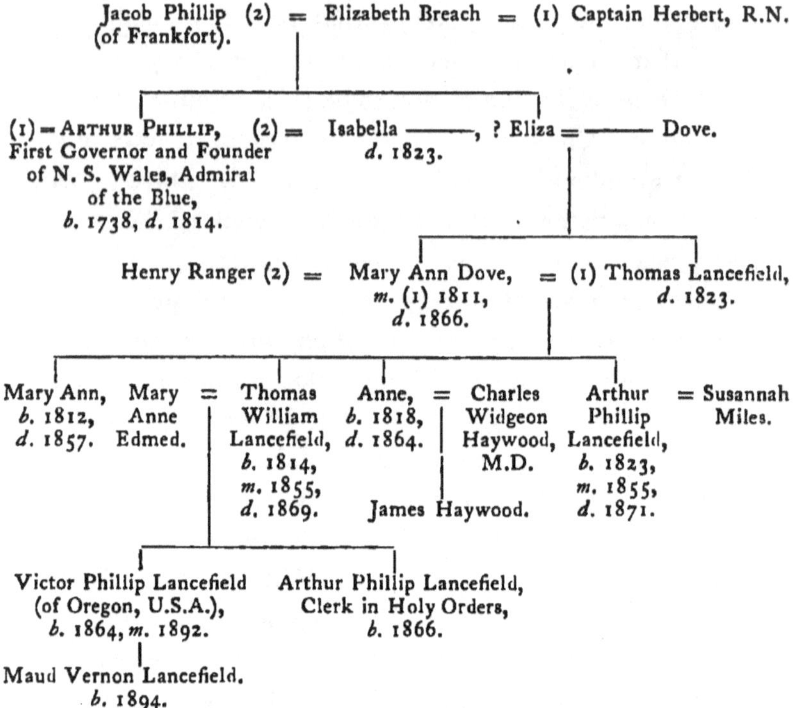

The other children of Thomas and Mary Ann Lancefield were Thomas (*b.* 1813, *d.* 1814), Isabella and Eliza (twins) (*b.* 1815, *d.* 1816 and 1822), Isabella Phillip (*b.* 1817, *d.* ? 1818), and Matilda Eliza (twin with Arthur Phillip) (*b.* 1825, *d.* 1825). It seems possible (says Mr Lancefield) that the Christian name of the Admiral's sister was Eliza; and he draws attention to the attempts to perpetuate the names 'Isabella' and 'Eliza,' as well as to the combination 'Isabella Phillip.'   H. F. WILSON.

APPENDIX II

THE following documents, which it has been thought best to print *in extenso*, and partly in the original Portuguese as well as in translations, have been discovered in the National Archives at Lisbon by General de Brito Rebello, who is the Principal Librarian and Keeper of the Records, and translated by Mr G. J. Henriques. Nos. 1-10 give a connected account of the introduction of Phillip by one of his official superiors at the Admiralty (Rear-Admiral the Hon. Augustus John Hervey, afterwards Earl of Bristol) to the Portuguese Minister in London, as a candidate for employment in the Portuguese Navy. Admiral Hervey's first letter (No. 2) is dated 25th August 1774, and the royal warrant of appointment (No. 10) the 14th January 1775. As Mr Henriques, in his letter to myself communicating the discovery, puts it, 'you now have a complete narrative of the circumstances under which Phillip entered the Portuguese Service; the name of the gentleman (apparently connected with the Admiralty in London) who introduced him; nearly the exact dates of his leaving London and arriving in Lisbon; the terms of his engagement; and last, but not least, the unbiassed testimony to his worth and capacity given by his contemporaries when he was still of subordinate rank.' Nos. 11-34 afford a number of interesting glimpses into the life the young Englishman led while serving abroad in the Portuguese Navy, and show how much appreciated he was by his foreign employers.

I have to thank the Portuguese Minister in London (M. de Soveral) and the British Minister in Lisbon (Sir Hugh Macdonell) for the kind interest they have taken in this quest, nor must I forget my friend Mr Eric Barrington of the Foreign Office, who first gave me the clue which I have followed up. To General de Brito Rebello, for his painstaking researches in the Archives, and to Mr G. J. Henriques for the excellent translations of the Portuguese documents I must also express my sincere acknowledgments. The letters, etc., only came to light last March, when this book was already in print; so that they could not be inserted in their natural place in the biography. The notes are due to General de Brito Rebello.

H. F. Wilson.

No. 1.

(From Senhor Luiz Pinto de Souza[1] to Senhor Martinho de Mello e Castro).[2]

Illm⁰ e Exm⁰ Senhor,—Ponho na prezença de V.

[1] Portuguese Minister in London.
[2] Minister for the Marine and Colonies at Lisbon.

Exa a carta original que ultimamente recebi de Mr Hervey, sobre o official que pretende entrar no serviço de Sua Magestade.

O mesmo official me procurou depois em direitura ; e me expoz, de viva voz, o detalhe das suas condições, que consistem nos pontos seguintes :—

1.—Que em attenção ao que aqui deixa, e ás maiores vantagens que costumam ter os officiaes inglezes no estado de reforma, se lhe concede, no serviço de Portugal, a mesma paga que tem os officiaes estrangeiros quando se acham em actual exercicio sobre o mar.

2.—Que no estado de reforma, se lhe concederá ametade do referido soldo.

3.—Que se lhe fará promessa de se lhe expedir a patente de Capitão de Mar e Guerra immediamente que chegar a Portugal.

O dito official me não fallou palavra a respeito de ajuda de custo ; porem como é provavel que me possa tocar n'essa materia, desejarei ser instruido positivamente sobre o que devo responder-lhe. Emtanto me limitei a assegurar, assim a Mr Hervey como ao seu recommendado, que poria a mesma carta, com as tres proposições, na presença da minha Corte ; e que lhe communicaria a resposta que tivesse a esse respeito.

Deos Guarde a V. Exa. Londres, 30 de Agosto de 1774. (Signed) Luiz Pinto de Souza.

Illm⁰ e Exm⁰ Senhor Martinho de Mello e Castro.

No. 1 (*Translation*).

Your Excellency,—I place before Your Excellency the original letter which I lately received from Mr Hervey about the officer who desires to enter His Majesty's service.

The said officer, since then, came direct to me, and verbally stated the details of his conditions, which consist in the following points :—

1.—That, in consideration of what he gives up here, and the superior advantages which it is the custom for English officers to enjoy when they are on the Retired List, he be allowed, in the Portuguese Service, the same pay as foreign officers receive when on active service at sea.

2.—That when on the Retired List he be allowed half of that pay.

3.—That a promise be made to him that, immediately upon his arrival in Portugal, a Commission of Captain of the Fleet will be issued to him.

The officer in question said not a word to me about an allowance for travelling expenses ; but, as it is probable that he will broach the subject, I should like to be positively informed as to what I ought to reply. Meanwhile, I limited myself to assuring both Mr Hervey and the person recommended by him that I would place the said letter and proposals before my Court, and would communicate to him the reply which I might receive thereon.

God preserve Your Excellency. London, on the 30th August 1774.

(Signed) Luiz Pinto de Souza.

To His Excellency Senhor Martinho de Mello e Castro.

No. 2.

(From Rear-Admiral the Hon. Augustus John Hervey [1] to Senhor Luiz Pinto de Souza.)

A l'Amirauté ce 25me d'Aôut, 1774.

Monsieur,—Je suis très mortifié de n'avoir pas eu l'honneur de vous trouver chez vous, d'autant plus que je suis obligé d'aller prendre les eaux d'Aix-la-Chappelle pour une mois, mais j'espére être plus heureux à mon retour.

Mons⁾ de Mello m'en a parlé quelque temps passé pour me prier de recommander quelque officier de merite de la Marine pour entrer dans votre service ; je lui ai repondu alors la dessus (comme a mon ami Mons⁾ Martine de Mello en Portugal) que vraiment je ne pouvait prendre sur moy un telle commission, puisque ceux que je voudrai recommander ne serez pas dans le cas de quitter l'Angleterre ; et ceux que voudront entrer dans votre service peut être seront ceux que je ne voudrait pas recommander au Roi

---

[1] Afterwards Earl of Bristol, one of the Lords Commissioners of the Admiralty from 1771 to the end of 1774.

votre Mâitre, à qui je doit tant d'obligations et que j'honnore tant ; mais hereusement j'ai l'offre d'un officier que aura l'honneur de vous presenter cette lettre ; qui je peut très bien à toutes égards hazarder' de me commetre pour lui un très bon officier de Marine, un en qui se rencontre le Theorie avec beaucoup de Pratique ; et qui a toujours très bien servi :—il parle fort bien[1] françois et joint plusieurs qualités d'un officier ensemble. Il desire servir votre Auguste Mâitre, et je lui ai promis la permission (si du rétour de vos lettres le Roy de Portugal l'accept) pour commander un vaisseau de haut bord. Il est Lieutenant ici, mais il mérite bien d'avoir un commande si vos usages et la Paix permettoit une promotion. Il s'appelle Lieut. Phillips (*sic*).

Je serai charmé qu'il ira en Portugal parceque je connais son mérite, et je vous serai bien obligé Monsr si vous aurai la bonté d'écrire a Monsr de Pombal et a Monsr de Mello la dessûs, pour lesquelles je lui donneroit des lettres, si en cas il est assez heureux d'y aller.

J'ai l'honneur d'être avec tout le respect et l'estime possible, Monsieur, Votre très humble et très obeissant serviteur,   A. HERVEY.

Je n'aurait pas pris la liberté de vous écrire sur ce

---

[1] The writer was not a particularly good judge of this, as his own letter, printed *verbatim et litcratim*, will show. [Ed.]

sujet, sans votre permission, si j'avoit eu le moindre esperance d'avoir l'honneur de vous voir avant mon depart.

No. 3.

(From Senhor LUIZ PINTO DE SOUZA to Senhor MARTINHO DE MELLO E CASTRO.)

ILLM° E EXM° SENHOR,—Polo Officio de 30 de Agosto tive a honra de dirigir a V. Exa uma carta de Mr Hervey sobre a proposição de entrar no serviço da marinha de S. Mag^{de} o Tenente de Mar e Guerra Phillips ; como tambemas propozições que vocalmente me fez o mesmo official, como preliminares do seu ajuste ; porem, como athé o presente, não tenho recebido resposta de V. Exa desejo certificar-me se acaso o referido Officio foi entregue, e a resposta que devo dar a Mr Hervey, que hoje mesmo mandou saber aqui se tinha vindo.

Deos Guarde a V. Exa. Londres, o primeiro de Novembro de 1774.

LUIZ PINTO DE SOUZA.

Illm° e Exm° Senhor MARTINHO DE MELLO E CASTRO.

No. 3 (*Translation*).

YOUR EXCELLENCY,—With my Despatch of August 30th, I had the honour of addressing to Your Excellency a letter from Mr Hervey upon the offer of Lieutenant Phillips of the Royal Navy, to enter His Majesty's service in the Navy, together with the proposals which that officer made verbally to me as a preliminary to his engagement. As, however, I have not, down to the present time, received any reply from Your Excellency, I wish to know if the said Despatch was delivered, and what reply I ought to give to Mr Hervey, who this very day sent here to enquire if any had arrived.

God preserve Your Excellency. London, the 1st of November 1774. .

(Signed) Luiz Pinto de Souza.

To His Excellency Senhor Martinho de Mello e Castro.

No. 4.

(From Senhor Martinho de Mello e Castro to Senhor Luiz Pinto de Souza.)

Illm° Senhor,—Levei á presença de Sua Magestade a carta de V. Sa, e, juntamente, a que lhe escreveu Monsieur Hervey, sobre o Tenente de Mar Phillips, que pertende entrar ao serviço de Portugal, debaixo das condições apontadas na referida carta de V. Sa, sobre as quaes deve V. Sa responder e segurar a ambos o seguinte :—

Que El Rey Nosso Senhor está bem certo que as

informações dadas por Mons' Hervey na carta que escreveu a V. Sa não podem deixar de ser muito conformes ao prestimo, experiencia e capacidade de um official digno da sua recommendação.

Que, n'esta intelligencia, logo que o Tenente Phillips chegar a este Reino, se lhe expedirá a patente de Capitão de Mar e Guerra das Armadas de Sua Magestade.

Que os officiaes estrangeiros que são admittidos ao Real Serviço, e com as circumstancias d'elle Tenente Phillips, vencem em terra e no mar soldo dobrado dos que vencem os officiaes Portugueses em uma e outra parte.

Que este soldo dobrado he de quarenta mil reis por mez em terra, e de oitenta mil reis no mar; tendo, além d'isto, em quanto andam embarcados em Fragatas de Guerra, quatro mil e oitocentos, e em Naus de Linha, seis mil e quatrocentos por dia para a sua mesa, á qual devem admittir os officiaes de patente e capelães da sua guarnição, percebendo igualmente para a mesma mesa, tantas rações do porão quantos fôrem as pessoas da qualidade acima indicadas que comerem a ella.

Que não se pratica em Portugal convencionar soldos em caso de reforma; que os officiaes benemeritos não se costumam reformar em quanto podem servir, e que quando isto acontece por impossibilidade dos mesmos officiaes ou por qualquer outro motivo que não seja desagradavel á Corte, os manda Sua

Magestade gratificar, accordando-lhes não só meios soldos, mas soldos inteiros e outras graças proporcionadas aos postos, prestimo, capacidade e comportamento de cada um d'elles.

Deos Guarde a V. Sa. Palacio de Nossa Senhora da Ajuda em 15 de Outubro de 1774.

MARTINHO DE MELLO E CASTRO.

Illm° Senhor LUIZ PINTO DE SOUZA.

No. 4 (*Translation*).

SIR,—I placed before His Majesty your letter together with the one written to you by Monsieur Hervey relating to Lieutenant Phillips, of the Navy, who desires to enter the Portuguese service upon the conditions set forth in your said letter, with regard to which you should reply to and assure both of them as follows :—

That the King Our Master is quite convinced that the information given by Monsieur Hervey in the letter which he wrote to you cannot be otherwise than in accordance with the worth, experience, and capacity of an officer who merits his recommendation.

That, such being the case, as soon as Lieutenant Phillips reaches this kingdom, a Commission of Captain of His Majesty's Fleets shall be issued to him.

That foreign officers who are admitted to the Royal service under such circumstances as Lieutenant Phillips, receive, both afloat and ashore, double the pay which is given to Portuguese officers in either case.

That this double pay is forty mil reis [1] per month on land, and eighty mil reis [2] at sea; and they have, in addition, when on board of frigates of war, four thousand eight hundred reis,[3] or, on board of ships of the line, six thousand four hundred reis [4] per day for their table, to which they ought to admit the Commissioned Officers and the Chaplains of their crews, they receiving, in addition, for their said table, as many rations from the hold as there are persons of the aforesaid rank who eat at it.

That it is not customary in Portugal to fix the amount of pay in case of retirement; that it is not usual for deserving officers to retire so long as they are able to serve; and that when it so happens, from incapacity of those officers, or other motive which may not be displeasing to the Court, His Majesty orders them to be rewarded, granting them not only half-pay, but full pay, and other favours, in proportion to the post, worth, capacity and behaviour of each.

God preserve you. Palace of our lady of Ajuda, on the 15th of October 1774.

(Signed) MARTINHO DE MELLO E CASTRO.

To Senhor LUIZ PINTO DE SOUZA.

[1] Say £8, 18s. at par.
[2] Say £17, 16s. at par.
[3] Say £1, 1s. 6d. at par
[4] Say £1, 8s. 6d. at par.

No. 5.

(From Senhor Luiz Pinto de Souza to Senhor Martinho de Mello e Castro.)

Illm° e Exm° Senhor,—Acabo de receber o Officio que V. Exa me dirigio em data de 15 de Outubro, sobre a resposta que devia dar ao Capitão Phillips, a quem logo a communiquei, assim como a Mr Hervey.

Este cavalheiro me segurou que aquelle official não podia desejar mais ; porem que não concluisse eu este negocio sem que primeiro se recolhesse do campo, para onde partia por seis dias.

Disse-me, unicamente, que prezumia que na Marinha Portugueza os Capitães de Mar e Guerra se embarcavam tambem sobre Fragatas ; em cuja pratica podia haver alguma difficuldade da parte de Mr Phillips, por quanto a sua pretenção era ser capitão de navio de alto bordo, como aqui se explicam ; o que em Inglaterra fazia grande differença.

Confessei a Mr Hervey em como me não achava instrudo na pratica da Marinha Portugueza : Que podia talvez dar-se o caso em que a precisão assim o pedisse ; porem que os capitães de mar e guerra da Corôa eram Commandantes de Navios, e que esta ere a sua graduação em Portugal.

Fico esperando a sua volta do campo afim de avizar V. Exa sobre a concluzão d'este negocio.

Deos Guarde a V. Exa. Londres, 8 de Novembro de 1774. Luiz Pinto de Souza.

Illm° e Exm° Senhor Martinho de Mello e Castro.*

No 5 (*Translation*).

Your Excellency,—I have just received the Despatch which Your Excellency addressed to me, dated 15th of October, regarding the reply which I should give to Captain Phillips, to whom, as well as to Mr Hervey, I at once communicated it.

The latter gentleman assured me that the officer in question could not desire anything more; but that he wished me not to conclude the affair until he had returned from the country, where he was going for six days.

He only said to me that he presumed that, in the Portuguese Service, Captains of the Fleet sailed also in Frigates; a practice which might give rise to some difficulty on the part of Mr Phillips, because his pretension was to be captain of a ship of the line as it is understood here; which, in England, makes a great difference.

I confessed to Mr Hervey that I was not informed as to the practice in the Portuguese Navy; that it was possible that a case might occur in which necessity would require it; but that the Captains of the Fleet of the Crown were Commanders of ships and ranked as such in Portugal.

I am awaiting his return from the country to inform Your Excellency as to the conclusion of this affair.

God preserve Your Excellency. London, the 8th of November 1774.

(Signed) Luiz Pinto de Souza.

To His Excellency Senhor Martinho de Mello e Castro.

No 6.

(From Senhor Luiz Pinto de Souza to Senhor Martinho de Mello·e Castro.)

Illm⁰ e Exm⁰ Senhor,—Recebi com o maior reconhecimento as Provas de benevolencia com que V. Exa se dignou honrar-me na sua carta familiar de 15 de Outubro, e aproveito esta occasião para render a V. Exa as devidas graças.

Porei, immediatemente, em pratica todas as ordens de V. Exa relativas assim ás machinas como ao Capitão Phillips ; . . .

Deos Guarde a V. Exa. Londres, em 9 de Novembro de 1774. Luiz Pinto de Souza.

Illm⁰ e Exm⁰ Senhor Martinho de Mello e Castro.

No. 6 (*Translation*).

Your Excellency,—With the greatest gratitude I received the proofs of your consideration with which Your Excellency was pleased to honour me in your private letter of 15th October, and I profit by this opportunity to render to Your Excellency my sincere thanks.

I will immediately set about carrying out all Your Excellency's orders, both with regard to the machines and to Captain Phillips. . . .

God preserve Your Excellency. London, the 9th of November 1774.

(Signed) Luiz Pinto de Souza.

To His Excellency Senhor Martino de Mello e Castro.

(The rest of this letter is solely about certain machines.)

No. 7.

(From Senhor Martinho de Mello e Castro to Senhor Luiz Pinto de Souza.)

Illm° Senhor,—Em 25 de Novembro de 1774 recebi a carta de V. Sa com data de 8 de Novembro, em resposta da que lhe dirigi em 15 de Outubro: E para V. Sa puder informar Monsr Hervey e Mr Phillips sobre a pergunta que lhe fizeram, é preciso dizer-lhe que na Marinha de Portugal não ha a differença de Capitão de Fragata e Capitão de Nau de Linha, ou de alto bordo. Todos os capitães de mar e guerra tem a mesma graduação, e só preferem uns aos outros pela antiguidade das patentes. O soldo é o mesmo ou andem em nau ou em fragata; e só os que commandam Nau de Linha tem para mesa $6400 reis por dia, em razão de ser maior o numero de officiaes a quem dão de comer; os que andam em Fragata tem $4800 reis em razão de ser menor o dito numero; e além d'isto cada official dos que comem á mesa, tem ração do porão que recebe o capitão de mar e guerra.

Todo o capitão de mar e guerra deve embarcar em nau de linha ou em fragata, como lhe fôr determinado, sem lhe ser permittido fazer sobre estã materia, nem outra alguma que respeite ao Real serviço, a menor duvida ou difficuldade.

É preciso que V. Sa informe igualmente a Mr Hervey e Mr Phillips que no serviço de Portugal muito frequentemente embarcam na mesma nau primeiro e segundo capitão de mar e guerra, e quando isto succede, o mais antigo é sempre o que commanda : de sorte que um capitão de mar e guerra deve sempre estar prompto a embarcar ou seja em nau de linha ou em fragata, e em qualquer d'ellas ou por primeiro ou por segundo, conforme a antiguidade da sua patente.

Pode haver outros usos e costumes que presentemente me não lembram; mas a todos elles se deve sujeitar o official que entra n'este Serviço; sem que de alguma sorte pretenda que se altere com elle o que se não pratica com os outros.

Deos Guarde a V. Sa. Em 25 de Novembro de 1774.　Martinho de Mello e Castro.

No. 7 (*Translation*).

SIR,—On the 25th of November 1774, I received your letter of the 8th of November, in reply to the one which I wrote to you on the 15th of October. And to enable you to reply to Monsieur Hervey and Mr Phillips, upon the question put by them to you, it is necessary to inform you that, in the Portuguese Navy, there is no distinction between the captain of a frigate and the captain of a ship of the line. All Captains of the Fleet rank alike, and only take precedence of each other according to the age of their Commissions. The pay is the same whether they sail in a ship of the line or in a frigate; only those who command a ship of the line have for their table six thousand four hundred reis per day on account of the number of officers whom they have to feed being larger, and those who sail in frigates have four thousand eight hundred reis, because the said number is smaller; and, in addition thereto, each of the officers who eats at the table has a ration from the hold, which is received by the Captain of the Fleet.

All Captains of the Fleet have to sail in ships of the line or in frigates, as they may be ordered; and it is not permissible for them to raise, upon this subject, or upon any other relating to the Royal Service, the slightest question or difficulty.

It is necessary that you should also inform Mr Hervey and Mr Phillips that in the Portuguese

Service very frequently a first and second Captain of the Fleet sail in the same ship, and that when this occurs it is always the senior in rank who commands; consequently a Captain of the Fleet should be always prepared to sail, whether it be in a ship of the line or in a frigate, and, in either case, to be first or second in command, according to the age of his Commission.

There may be other usages and customs which do not occur to me at this moment; but an officer who enters this service must subject himself to them all, without in any way presuming that alterations will be made for him which are not practised with the others.

God preserve you. Lisbon, on the 25th of November 1774.

(Signed) Martinho de Mello e Castro.

To Senhor Luiz Pinto de Souza.

No. 8.

(From Senhor Luiz Pinto de Souza to Senhor Martinho de Mello e Castro.)

Illm⁰ e Exm⁰ Senhor,—Accuso recebido o ultimo despacho de V. Exa que trouxe a data de 25 de Novembro, o qual chegou a tempo que o Capitão Phillips se achava em vesperas de partir.

Logo que o recebi, communiquei tanto a Mr Hervey, como ao referido official a sua materia, e lh'a expuz na sua verdadeira luz, para que em nenhum tempo se queixasse ; elle nada achou duro mais que a pratica de servirem dois capitães muitas vezes no mesmo navio ou fragata ; porem a tudo se sugeitou e n'esta disposição lhe disse que podia partir quando quizesse.

Todas me dão boas informações da sua intelligencia e prestimo ; desejarei agora que corresponda a ellas e á opinião que Mr Hervey deu do seu caracter.

Deos Guarde a V. Exa. Londres, 22 de Dezembro de 1774. Luiz Pinto de Souza.

Illm⁰ e Exm⁰ Senhor Martinho de Mello e Castro.

No. 8 (*Translation*).

Your Excellency,—I beg to acknowledge the receipt of Your Excellency's Despatch, dated the 25th of November, which arrived at the moment when Captain Phillips was on the eve of starting.

As soon as I received it, I communicated the contents of it both to Mr Hervey and to the officer in question, to whom I put it in its true light, so that he might never have cause for a grievance. The only thing in it which he thought hard was the practice of two captains very often serving in the same ship or frigate ; but he subjected himself to everything, and, in view of this, I informed him that he could start whenever he liked.

Everybody reports highly of his intelligence and worth ; I will now hope that he will bear them out, and also the opinion given by Mr Hervey of his character.

God preserve Your Excellency.   London, the 22nd of December 1774.

(Signed) Luiz Pinto de Souza.

To his Excellency Senhor Martinho de Mello e Castro.

No. 9.

(From Rear-Admiral the Hon. Augustus John Hervey to Senhor Martinho de Mello e Castro.)

A Londres, ce 22 me de Xbre 1774.

Mon cher Monsieur,—Je ne sçaurai résister les prières de Monsieur Phillips en lui recomandant au Protection de V. Exce : il part dans l'instant pour Lisbonne, et quoique je suis très enrhumé, je ne pouvoit refuser cette témoinage à son mérite, ni cette justice à votre désire de le protéger par toute ou vous le trouverait.   V. Exce peut être assurée que je ne lui auroit pas procurer l'agreement qu'il vient d'obtenir, sans être convaincu que je n'aurait pas a rougir pour son égard.

Il y a bien long tems que je n'ai eu des nouvelles

de V. Exce; mais il n'y a point de temps que m'empêchera d'être, avec le plus grand respect et estime. — De V. Exce, le très humble et très obeissant sr.,

A. HERVEY.

Son Ex^ce Mon^r De Mello, Sécretaire d'Etât, etc., etc.

No. 10.

(Royal Appointment of ARTHUR PHILLIP to be Captain in the Portuguese Fleet.

Hey por bem fazer mercê a ARTHUR PHILIPE do posto de Capitão de Mar e Guerra das Naus da minha Armada Real, em cujo posto vencerá soldo dobrado. O Conselho de Guerra o tenha assim entendido e lhe mande passar os Despachos necessarios. Salvaterra de Magos em 14 de Janeiro de 1775.

(Rubrica de Sua Magestade.)

[Archivo Nacional da Torre do Tombo Livro XXVII, 2a serie do Conselho de Guerra F27.]

No. 10 (*Translation*).

It is my pleasure to grant to ARTHUR PHILIPE the post of Captain of the Ships of War of my Royal Fleet, in which post he will draw double pay. The Council of War will take cognizance of this, and will cause the necessary documents to be issued to him. Salvaterra de Magos, on the 14th of January 1775. (His Majesty's Sign Manual.)

No. 11.

January Tuesday, 17 1775.

The Report was brought from the Ship of War *Belem*, now fitting, by Sergeant Ricardo José.

Password.	*Countersign.*
São Gonçalo.	Amarante.

ORDERS.

. . . . . .

OCCURRENCES.

Arthur Philipe made Captain of the Fleet, and named to the war-ship *Belem*.

By His Majesty's Decree, dated . . ., Arthur Philips was made a Captain, and was this day informed that he is to embark as second captain of the war-ship *Belem*.

[Marine Archives. Book IV. of the Registers of Orders of the Day, fol. 83.]

No. 12.

January Wednesday, 25. 1775.

The Report was brought from the said ship of war, now fitting, by Sergeant Luiz Antonio.

<table>
<tr><td align="center">Password.</td><td align="center">Countersign.</td></tr>
<tr><td align="center">São Jorge.</td><td align="center">Irlanda.</td></tr>
</table>

ORDERS.

.   .   .   .   .   .

OCCURRENCES.

Leave granted to Captain Arthur Philips to go to Salvaterra.	Captain Arthur Philips, just appointed, announced that H.E. the Marquis de Pombal had granted him leave to go to Salvaterra.
Leave granted to Captain Antonio de Salles.	Captain Antonio de Salles e Noronha announced that he had leave to go to Salvaterra.

[Ibid., fol. 83, reverse side.]

No. 13.

February   Monday, 6   1775.

Report brought from the war-ship *Belem* by Lieutenant Joaquim d'Almeida.

<table>
<tr><td align="center">Password.</td><td align="center">Countersign.</td></tr>
<tr><td align="center">São João Baptista.</td><td align="center">Campo-maior.</td></tr>
</table>

ORDERS.

OCCURRENCES.

The war - ship *Belem* set sail, and the reason why she cast anchor in front of Junqueira.	At about half-past seven the war-ship *Belem* set sail, the day being clear and the wind somewhat fresh from the N.N.E. In front of Junqueira a calm came on, and as the sea was running strongly south, there was no remedy but to cast anchor, which was done at half-past one p.m., and she was brought to in front of Junqueira.
The Captain reported that one of the top - gallant masts was rotten. Measures taken in consequence.	On the same day the Captain of the said vessel reported that one of the top-gallant masts was rotten, and His Excellency the Marquis de Pombal ordered the Master of the Dock-yard to examine the said mast. He condemned it, and was ordered to immediately replace it, which he did.

[Ibid., fol 85 (reverse side).]

No. 14.

February   Thursday, 9   1775.

The war - ship *N. S. de Belem* sailed.	At ten o'clock in the morning the war-ship *Nossa Senhora de Belem* set sail with a fresh breeze from the N., and at a quarter to 12 she crossed the Bar.
etc.	etc. etc.

[Ibid., fol. 86 (reverse side).]

No. 15.

A list of the Ships of the Line and Frigates sent in by the Chief of the Fleet R. MacDonell,[1] on 31st January 1776, shews that the Frigate *Pilar* had a crew, officers, infantry, artillery-men and sailors included, of 208 men ; and an armament of 26 guns, 24 of which were calibre 9, and 2 calibre 4. It further states that she had sailed on the 27th, to endeavour to make captures at the mouth of the Rio Grande, and was provisioned for three months. Phillip was at this time in command of her.

No. 16.

Extract from a Letter of Captain MacDonell to the Marquis[2] do Lavradio.

Your Excellency,—In spite of the orders which I gave to Captain Antonio Jacintho, and of the orders given to him by Captain José dos Santos Ferreira, when he ordered him to leave, and of still another order which I directed to be delivered to him by Captain Arthur Filips (*sic*), who left this port on the 27th of January and only met with the frigate *Principe do Brazil* on the 27th of February, when he delivered to him the said order, a copy of which I send herewith. . . . On board of His Majesty's

---

[1] An able Scotsman and a thorough disciplinarian ; but undecided, and a constant raiser of objections to the carrying out of orders, or to the combination of operations with the Generals.

[2] Viceroy in the Brazils.

ship *Santo Antonio*, lying in the port of Saint Catherine's, 19th March 1776.—Your Excellency's most obedient and most humble servant,

(Signed) ROBERT MACDONELL.

To His Excellency The Marquis Viceroy.

No. 17.

Extracts from a Letter of Captain MACDONELL to the MARQUIS DO LAVRADIO.

YOUR EXCELLENCY,—I had the honour of addressing Your Excellency on the 20th, and since then have further to inform Your Excellency that, on the afternoon of the 28th, the frigate *Pilar* came in after sixty-two days of prize-hunting, having nothing to report, short of water, because her casks were in a very bad condition. I am now having them repaired. This frigate requires that a great deal be done to her to enable her to continue, as she ought, in the Royal Service ; and, if it is not done, she will, in a short time, be completely disabled ; but as, in the state in which she is, she can still serve if we can manage to repair the pintles of the helm, I am provisioning her for a period of three months, which will be until the end of June, so as to be ready for whatever may be required of her ; and I am going to repair that which is most urgent, as far as time will allow.

.   .   .   .

The result of the survey by the carpenters and caulkers of the Fleet is that the pintles of the frigate *Pilar's* helm can still serve for some time.

.   .   .   .

On board of His Majesty's ship of the Line *Santa Antonio*, lying in the port of Saint Catherine's, 31st March 1776.   (Signed) ROBERT MACDONELL.

To His Excellency The Marquis Viceroy.

No. 18.

Extracts from a Letter of the MARQUIS DO LAVRADIO to Captain MACDONELL.

SIR,—Having received your Despatches, dated 21st of February and the 5th, 6th, 11th, 19th and 31st of March of this year, together with the papers which accompanied them, I have placed them before the King, my Master, through the Office of His Secretary of State, just as I have done with all those of most importance which you have addressed to me. However, until our Court sends me its orders as to what I am to do with regard to the contents of the said Despatches, I consider it my duty to reply to you upon that which I think is more extraordinary in the said Despatches, and which requires a prompt and positive answer.

In the first place, as regards the bad condition of the vessels, etc., etc. .   .   .   .   .

In the second place, you tell me that all that has

taken place from the time you left until now is the result of none of your proposals having been attended to, and, from the context of the paragraph, the conclusion to be drawn is that there has been a want of attention, and that I did not send vessels of the kind that you asked for in the expedition to Rio Grande; which is true. I did not send any of the kind that you asked for, because there were none in this port, as I told you, but the others which I sent, although inferior to those you wanted, were much superior to the greater part of those which the Spaniards had, with the exception of the three which they have at the entrance, and for which the frigate *Graça Divina*, the frigate *Pilar*, the frigate from Pernambuco, and the corvette *Nossa Senhora da Victoria* would have been more than a match. All of these, with the exception of the corvette, were much stronger than the Spanish vessels; and our other and smaller vessels could not only have helped the large ones, but would have been ample in number and strength for attacking the five insignificant vessels which the Spaniards have got at Fort Mosquito. Such being my orders, and such the fleet which I had appointed for the operation, I believe that no one will fail to confess that, if those orders had been carried out to the letter, the result would have been vastly different to what it was, owing to your having altered everything, as you have always been in the habit of doing, from the moment that you know that an order is mine. You commenced by not allowing the frigate *Pilar* to be one of those appointed to enter the river, alleging that it was impossible for it to do so; whereas, when the vessels entered, it was evident that the river was quite deep enough for her to have entered just as the others did.

It is a fact that the river has not always the same depth of water, and that there are many and many occasions on which neither that vessel, nor others of lesser draught than her, could enter; but those who were well acquainted with the river assured me repeatedly that there were times when the river contained such a depth of water that the vessel in question could go in without any danger whatever.

I gave no order that she should enter whether there was sufficient water or not; so why could you not have taken her with you upon the chance that if the water was deep enough she should profit by the opportunity, and thus have availed yourself of the extraordinary addition to your strength which would result from the co-operation of that frigate? Nothing of this you chose to do; but you sent her prize-hunting, instead of letting her accompany the expedition, which was the chief object I had in view when I commissioned her, and thus she was rendered useless, although the want of her was felt when the time came.

Further on you say that the vessels I sent were not seaworthy, at the same time that you tell me that the sloop [1] which you built in this port was an excellent vessel, and so good that you sailed in her and found her competent to lead the way before the others. If you could find her to be seaworthy, built as she was of green wood, with her seams wide open, leaking like a sieve, and, moreover, smaller than the others, which were not in like circumstances, surely they were as good as she was.

But more, I ordered you to select for that service the officers and crews which you considered most competent. I would not appoint a single person. I trusted everything to your zeal, honour and intelligence; because, as you would be answerable to me for the undertaking, I did not wish to hinder you in any way from acting with every freedom, and entirely as you thought fit. What was the result of my mode of proceeding? The vessels were manned by the worst sailors of the Fleet. With the exception of two, the officers appointed to command them were either people who had been taken from the forecastle to be trained as officers, or volunteers, without experience, to whom rank was at once given; and some subalterns from the infantry, without any experience of these parts. These were the commanding officers who were to carry out so important an enterprise; while the officers of the Navy who had been in battle, and under fire, such as Arthur Phillips, Lieutenant-Captain Gaula (Gal-

[1] The *Santa Catharina*.

way ?), and other officers of great value on account of their honour and energy, were left out, and sent to do that which the others could have done equally well.

. . . . . .

Rio de Janeiro, 17th April 1776.

(Signed) Marquez do Lavradio.

To Senhor Robert MacDonell.

No. 19

From the Marquis do Lavradio to Senhor Martinho de Mello e Castro.

Your Excellency,—Since I last had the honour of writing to Your Excellency, there has been nothing fresh as regards the South, as Your Excellency will see by Lieut.-General João Henrique de Böhm's letter, a copy of which I have the honour to forward to you, together with a copy of my reply and the other papers which bear upon the said letter. I further forward to Your Excellency a copy of the reply which I wrote to the Lieut.-General with regard to the letter which I had already received, and of which I have already sent a first copy to Your Excellency, and now send you a second.

By the letter last received Your Excellency will see that the Spaniards are doing all that they can, and it is my belief that if they were not afraid of the forces which I have on that continent, and the

T

quality of the troops, they would not have remained so quiet, but would have continued to be as insulting as ever.

In compliance with the Royal Orders, I ordered the two frigates which were in this Colony to withdraw. They were the *Nazareth*, commanded by Captain Thomas Stives, and the *Nossa Senhora da Gloria*, commanded by Captain Tristão da Cunha e Menezes. I allowed the frigate *Nossa Senhora do Pilar*, commanded by Captain Arthur Phillips, to remain, because I consider that, so soon as we have no war-ship there, it will not be possible to prevent the insolent acts which the Spanish Corsairs are continually perpetrating in that river.

The presence of the said three vessels had effectually put a stop to all the acts of daring which they had practised upon our merchant vessels and upon the fishermen, overhauling all and even capturing some of them, as I have already informed Your Excellency. The moment they discovered on board of them any hides or other merchandise which they could allege had been obtained by contraband, and, as regards the fishermen, even without that excuse, they captured them and seized the slaves which they found on board of them.

My intention is to order the said frigate to be relieved by the *Graça Divina*, which was at Rio Grande, they being the two of those which I have most appropriated for navigation in the River Plate.

If three frigates are kept constantly in this district, one to remain in the Colony, another in the port of St Catherine's, and the third in the port of this the capital city, in order to go to the assistance of either of the others when necessary, and to guard the coast, not only of that island, but of Rio Grande, as well as to exchange every now and again with the one which is at the Colony, that will, I think, be the only way to make ourselves respected and ensure quiet.

The two frigates, the *Assumpção* and the *Gloria* are utterly unseaworthy. Out of the two a very handsome frigate might be built, to be the third to be stationed at the River Plate, if Your Excellency will send the drawings for that purpose.

Should the King, my Master, be pleased to decide to have these frigates in this port and that the third one be built, it will be most desirable that an officer, prudent, active and intelligent, be sent to command this Division and superintend the building of the frigate.

The most competent, in my opinion, of those who are here is Captain Antonio Januario do Valle,[1] who is a most intelligent, active, prudent and disinterested officer. There may be many others equal to him in merit; but of those I know of I prefer him.

[1] It was in his vessel and under him that Captain Phillips sailed to the Brazils as Second Captain.

The war-ship *Belem* which that officer commanded is almost finished repairing. She was in a very bad state and has been thoroughly overhauled. I might almost say that she has been rebuilt. Every one assures me that she will be in first-rate condition and will require nothing to be done to her for the next seven or eight years. At the same time, I am having the *Principe do Brazil* repaired, and, one after another, all the vessels of the Fleet shall be gone over. They suffered terribly this year on the Southern Coast and Rio Grande. The Commanding Officers tell me that the roughness of the sea in those parts is indescribable, and bears no comparison with that met with in the worst parts of the European seas.

The two frigates which I have the honour to mention to Your Excellency are utterly unseaworthy, so I have determined to lay them up. I intend, however, to have them gone over, roughly, to prevent their getting into a worse condition while I am awaiting Your Excellency's answer.

As the frigate *Gloria* has not yet reached here, I cannot send the report of the state in which she is, as I did with regard to the two frigates, the *Assumpção* and the *Princeza do Brazil;* but I will do so as soon as she arrives.

I am informed that the Chief of the Fleet has sent to Your Excellency a report with regard to me, a copy of which I forward herewith, and I also send a sailor whom he had selected to be the bearer of these despatches, because he would not entrust them to me, thinking that I would try to prevent his laying before the King, my Master, his account of my imprudences.

The General at St Catherine's would not allow this sailor to proceed without a passport from me ; but as I cannot tell but what he may be charged with some more private matter of which Your Excellencies ought to be informed, I send him on so that he may execute his commission.

I must say that I am not in the least surprised at the force of that Officer's language in the said letter. It is a common saying with him before all the Fleet, that His Majesty ought to cut off the heads of all the Generals who have the honour to serve him ; that they are all ignorant and traitors ; and other expressions of a similar nature. Your Excellency may imagine how constant has been my pain, and that of all the officers who have the honour to serve the King, my Master, and the misfortune to have to deal with this man. But I have had the satisfaction of observing that from me myself, the General in the South and the General at St Catherine's, down to the lowest sailor, all, out of obedience and respect for the Royal Orders of the King, my Master, have made the sacrifice of putting up with him, and letting him see as little as possible what our sentiments are.

I ask nothing of the King, my Master, upon this

head. It will be sufficient that His Majesty should see the extent to which my respect and my obedience have guided me.

I have nothing more to lay before Your Excellency, whom God preserve. Rio de Janeiro, 18th August 1776. (Signed) MARQUEZ DO LAVRADIO.

To H.E. Senhor MARTINHO DE MELLO E CASTRO.

[From the Archives of the Conselho Ultramarino.]

No. 20.

Extract from a Letter from the MARQUIS DO LAVRADIO to the MARQUIS DE POMBAL.

YOUR EXCELLENCY,— . . . .
The Spaniards who, as regards Rio Grande, are reported to be quiet, the Governor of the Colony continues to inform me are, in those parts, more in evidence, not only as regards their squabbling and their arrogant and defiant language, but because they have got ready the three frigates and the ship of the line which they have in the port, are sending more troops to Montevideo, are working with great activity upon the barracks for fresh troops, and are, at the same time, adding to the works of defence of their ports.

In spite of this the Governor, as he had received

my order withdrawing two of the frigates, caused them to leave for this port, retaining only the frigate *Pilar*, commanded by Captain Arthur Phillips.

.   .   .   .

Rio de Janeiro, 16th October 1776.

(Signed) Marquez do Lavradio.

To H.E. The Marquis de Pombal.

No. 21.

Extract from a Letter of the Marquis do Lavradio to Senhor Martinho de Mello e Castro.

Your Excellency,—   .   .   .   .
The merchant vessel *Nossa Senhora do Pilar*, which also serves as a frigate, has been staying at the Colony, for the purpose of restraining the continual attacks which the Spanish corsairs have been making upon the inhabitants of that place, and which have only been prevented by the presence of that small vessel.

.   .   .   .   .   .

Rio de Janeiro, 20th November 1776.

(Signed) Marquez do Lavradio.

To His Excellency Senhor Martinho de Mello e Castro.

No. 22.

A LIST of the Officers and the Vessels of War serving in the Fleet which the King, My Master, ordered to be formed at Amoreira, under my orders, of which Naval-Colonel Robert MacDonell is Commander-in-Chief.

(Part relating to Arthur Phillip.)

Rio de Janeiro, 27th November 1776.

Names of the Vessels.	CAPTAINS.				LIEUTENANT-CAPTAINS.			NAVAL LIEUTENANTS.	
	By Commission.	By Warrant.	Nature of the Service.	Condition of the Vessels.	Commission.	Warrant.	Nature of the Service.	By Commission.	Nature of the Service.
Nossa Senhora do Pilar.	Arthur Phillips.		This Officer is intelligent and active, and shews that he has been reared as a soldier; he is a little head-strong, but can easily be brought to reason.	Requires to be repaired and careened.	Joaquim de Almeida.		This Officer is very intelligent and has always served with much honour.	Ignacio José Peres, Lieutenant of Infantry, and Estanislau de Almeida.	The first is an old Lieutenant of the Regiment of Marines. He is fairly intelligent, and I have always seen him serve very honourably and obediently. My opinion is that he is deserving of promotion. The second was a volunteer; he does his duty.

(Signed) Marquez do Lavradio.

No. 23.

Extract from a Letter of Francisco José da Rocha to the Marquis do Lavradio.

Your Excellency,—To-morrow, which will be the 30th inst., the *Pilar* will sail, and I think also that Antonio João's corvette will proceed, to Saint Catherine's to fetch wood.

.   .   .   .

Colony, 29th December 1776.

(Signed) Francisco José da Rocha.

To His Excellency The Marquis Viceroy.

No. 24.

From the Marquis do Lavradio to the Marquis de Pombal.

Your Excellency,—1st. With the greatest sorrow, as Your Excellency may imagine, I now have to announce the arrival of the Spanish Fleet at the port of St Catherine's.

I forward to Your Excellency the first letter which I received from the General of that Division. The second announcement which the said General has made to me, and which it is my duty to repeat to Your Excellency, was brought by the Captain of a small vessel, who assures me that, down to the 25th of last month, the Spaniards had not taken any action of importance, and it was only known that they had landed some troops at Canavieiras Point, which is the port by which they entered.

2nd. Although the General and the Governor of that island inform me that the troops and the people who are there are very unconcerned, and that they hope to offer a vigorous defence, I do not consider that the island is strong enough to support itself and resist; and this chiefly because the Enemy has no fear of our Fleet, since the Chief, the moment he saw the Spaniards entering, gave orders to all the ships to go as speedily as they could to Rio de Janeiro. Any stroke of good fortune which may befall us will be, to my mind, miraculous.

3rd. Shortly before receiving the news sent to me by the General of the forces at St Catherine's, I was informed by the scouts which I had upon the coast that seven vessels were in sight, coming from the south and steering for this port. This information was confirmed, so I at once proceeded to arm.

4th. After having been under arms during the greater part of the following day, I received a letter from Captain Arthur Fillips, informing me that he was accompanying the Fleet in obedience to orders which he had received from the Chief, and that as he was the one nearest to the land he acquainted me with the fact.

5th. Later on I received, through the First Officer of the Chief's vessel, the letter which I forward to

Your Excellency, and which was followed, almost immediately, by the Chief himself.

6th. When he appeared before me, his countenance betrayed the anguish which every man ought to feel under circumstances such as those in which he was placed.

7th. I requested him to give me his reasons for leaving unprotected the ports which were most exposed, and coming to put in at Rio de Janeiro, which is the most defensible.

8th. He replied that the orders of the King, my Master, and mine had forced him to do so. I shewed him that the contrary was the fact; because, although the orders of the 31st July of last year, a copy of §§ 29, 30 and 31 of which, being those referring to the Fleet, had been communicated to him by letter, I had personally read to him the last orders but one, and the last which I received in Your Excellency's letters of the 9th and 29th of September, and the 8th and 9th of October, both of last year, and upon his saying that he could not carry them out, and would not take the responsibility of their execution, I placed them actually in his hands, requesting him to take them, turn the matter over in his mind, and give me his opinion and reply in writing, as I have already informed Your Excellency in my Despatch of the 20th of November of last year, when I sent you a copy of the said Chief's reply. In consequence of that reply, I issued the Letter of Orders, of which I have also already sent you a copy, making him responsible for all his actions, leaving him free to do whatever he might consider to be most useful and honourable for the State, and although I made some suggestions in the said letter, telling him not to carry any of them into execution if he did not find that by doing so the glorious results which we ought all to desire for the State would not be attained. My said suggestions in no way hindered him from doing whatever he might think to be most advisable for the success of his movements, because, as he would be responsible to me for the results, he ought to be entirely at liberty to act as his intelligence and experience might lead him to believe was most prudent.

9th. After that letter I wrote to him the other of which I enclose a copy, which he asserts that he did not receive.

10th. He further told me that he had taken the opinions of the other Captains of the vessels, which they had given in writing, all being to the effect that they ought to come to Rio de Janeiro. The only dissident was Captain José de Mello, who, in my opinion, was the only one who voted as he ought to have done.[1]

11th. The Chief further said that the Spanish Fleet came in such good order that it was impracticable to

---

[1] Further on (§ 12) and in the postscript we are told when, and under what circumstances, the Captains were consulted.

attack it, because its forces were united, without there being a single point at which any attempt could be made to throw them into disorder.

12th. The Chief sailed from the port of St Catherine's on the 16th of last month, upon receiving the first news of the Fleet being in sight. On the 18th, when the Spaniards caught sight of us, some of the Officers have informed me that we could have attacked them to great advantage ; because, not expecting us, they drew all their force to the front, leaving their convoys to the rear, in which direction we might have attacked them, if we had navigated that night in a different way to that which we did. The Chief kept our Fleet at so great a distance from the enemy that they were unable to ascertain, with any certainty the number of vessels we had. They paid no attention whatever to our Fleet, but improved their line and steered straight for the port, *which they entered on the 20th of last month, and when they were already entering, and consequently were masters of the port, then it was that the Chief called for the opinions of the Captains,* and, after receiving them, issued the order for all of them to steer for this port.

13th. During this retreat, they twice sighted the two frigates from Montevideo, which were looking out for their Fleet. Some of our vessels gave chase to the said frigates, but with no results ; and although the chase ought to have been kept up in order to prevent their entering the port with the pilots which they had on board, this was not considered worth attention, and they came to take refuge at Rio de Janeiro, where there are still to enter the war-ship *Belem*, the *Principe do Brazil*, and two of the smaller vessels, fitted as fighting ships, and called the *Sacramento*, and the yacht *São Francisco Xavier*.

14th. Finding myself in these circumstances, I wrote immediately to the Governor of St Paul's for him to come to the assistance of the island with all the forces of his district, by land ; and, as soon as the missing vessels arrive, I intend to send off a body of 800 or 900 men selected from the very few regulars which I have here, for the purpose of seeing if it is possible to relieve the island, either by the river St Francisco, or by crossing the range of mountains at the base of which lies the lake, or by availing myself of the route along the coast which leads to the mainland.

15th. The place at which our forces may be and the intentions of the Spaniards must decide which will be the best starting-point. I ordered the Chief to immediately commence cruising with our Fleet between Port St Catherine's and the River Plate, in order to impede, as much as possible, the Spaniards at the island from communicating with the other ports which they hold on the banks of that river. He stated that the greater part of the vessels composing his Fleet are incapable for that service, or for anything else that could be useful ; that the best ones for the purpose would be the three war-ships, the

Santo Antonio, the *Prazeres,* and the *Belem,* and the three frigates *Principe do Brazil, Princeza do Brazil,* and *Nossa Senhora do Pilar,* [1] as the *Graça Divina* is absolutely fit for nothing, and the war-ship *Ajuda* is almost entirely rotten. Of the small vessels only two can be made use of for the different orders which it may be necessary to convey.

.   .   .   .

GOD preserve Your Excellency. Rio de Janeiro, 10th March 1777.

(Signed) Marquez do Lavradio.

To the Marquis de Pombal.

P.S.—Among the papers I am forwarding to Your Excellency I send a copy of the letter which I wrote to the Chief requesting him to state whether or not I had read over to him, and handed to him for his private perusal, the last orders which I received as to what the Fleet was to do at the island of St Catherine's. His reply you will see by the copy of his letter, which I also send, in which he denies those orders, but mixes up things in such a way that he confesses some and denies others. At the same time, the reply which he gave with regard to the carrying out of those orders, a copy of which I have already sent to Your Excellency, and now forward another, shows that he examined them with sufficient minuteness to be able to make

---

[1] The vessel which Captain Arthur Phillip commanded.

the reflections thereon contained in his letter ; and this *lack of sincerity is the spirit in which this Officer has always sought, sometimes to deny, and at others to mis-interpret the orders given to him, to avoid the carrying out of which he refrained from mentioning them when he called the Council of the Captains.* All of these documents I forward to Your Excellency for your full knowledge and my justification ; and it is my duty to repeat to you, that when I have erred it has simply been from lack of ability, which I have always insisted was wanting in me for such important matters.

(Signed) MARQUEZ DO LAVRADIO.

No. 25.

OPINIONS of the different COMMANDING OFFICERS of the Vessels composing the Fleet.

We, the Captains and Commanding Officers, José dos Santos Ferreira, Thomas Stevens, Antonio Januario do Valle, José da Silva Pimentel and D. Francisco Xavier Telles, giving our votes upon the question as to what our Fleet ought to do under its present circumstances, are of opinion that :—

As all the movements which we can, for the present, execute, whether attacking the Spanish Fleet, which is superior to ours, or cruising in sight of it, imply a risk of our inferior Fleet being destroyed, in spite of all our efforts, desires and diligence, *which is contrary to His Majesty's positive orders which were read to us*, we, consequently, ought to go and receive fresh orders from H.E. Marquez do Lavradio, such as our present position requires, whether risk should be incurred or not. On board of the war-ship *Santo Antonio*, under sail, 20th February 1777.

(Signed) ANTONIO JANUARIO DO VALLE, *Captain;* JOSÉ DOS SANTOS FERREIRA PINTO, *Captain;* THOMAS STEVENS, *Captain;* D. FRANCISCO XAVIER TELLES, *Captain;* JOSÉ DA SILVA PIMENTEL, *Captain.*

With regard to His Majesty's orders, nothing can be done without risk, not only because of the weakened state in which our Fleet is, but also on account of the enemy's great strength. Every movement implies risk ; more especially when the forces are unequal.

Should our Fleet be destroyed, there will remain nothing to prevent the enemy from carrying out hostilities in America.

They will endeavour to sack the ports at which they can do so ; and, under these circumstances, we ought, in any case, to fulfil His Majesty's commands, confronting them with those of H.E. Marquez do Lavradio.

All the movements of this Fleet ought to be executed in harmony with His Majesty's orders, whether they be risky or not.

On board of His Majesty's war-ship *Santo Antonio e São José*, 20th February 1777.

(Signed) ANTONIO JACINTHO DA COSTA FREIRE,
Captain.

On the twentieth day of February 1777, at a Council of War called by the Commander-in-Chief of the Southern Fleet, Robert MacDonell, His Most Faithful Majesty's, my Master's, orders to the said Commander having been read, which orders say that he ought to leave St Catherine's to avoid an encounter with the Spanish Fleet, which (so the orders say) is much superior to the Portuguese Fleet, and the said orders stating that he ought to take every precaution possible to prevent our Fleet being either lost or ruined by the enemy ; and stating further that should the enemy attack any part of His Most Faithful Majesty's dominions in the Brazil, he ought to attack Maldonado, Montevideo and Buenos Ayres, circumstances permitting him to do so ; I, finding myself obliged to give my opinion as to what we can do of service to His Majesty, say :—

That *my opinion always has been that our Fleet ought to remain at St Catherine's to assist the fortresses in defending this island; or, if we left it, that we ought to attack the Spanish Fleet at all risks ; but the Commander of the Fleet does not believe that His Majesty's orders permit of his doing either of these things. Now that the enemy is free from the encumbrance of its transports, because they are anchored in the harbour of St Catherine's,* their strength being, according to the general opinion of the Commanding Officers of this Fleet, far superior to ours, and they not being in want of men, because they can draw as many artillery-men and infantry as they like from the ten thousand men which they have to disembark, and, considering *the great advantage that a strong fleet at anchor has over a weaker one which goes to attack it, I see, at this moment, no advantage to be gained by disobeying His Majesty's orders, or reason to warrant us in doing so, and I therefore decide that we ought not to attack.*

Maldonado cannot be taken without troops to be disembarked, neither can Montevideo; and I do not think that it would be prudent to risk our Fleet for the purpose of burning one ship of the line and a few merchantmen, which may or may not be met with in the harbour at Montevideo.

To be able to take Buenos Ayres with the few men that this Fleet could land, it must be taken by surprise; and this cannot be done with ships of the line, on account of the difficulty of navigating the River Plate.

Off the island of St Catherine's.

(Signed) ARTHUR PHILLIPS,

Commanding His Majesty's frigate 'Nossa Senhora do Pilar e São João Baptista.'

Having been asked about the resolution which we ought to take with regard to the Spanish Fleet commanded by the Marquis de Cara-Tilli (*sic*), which has arrived at this coast for the purpose of conquering the Brazils, and in conformity with the orders which this Fleet has received both from the Court at Lisbon and from the Viceroy of the State, I reply :—

1st. That the orders received from Rio de Janeiro leave it open to us to attempt every species of action against the Spanish Fleet, let the order in which it comes be what it may, seeing that in two places the order is to attack, and in one place to rather await the attack of the Fleet, even although ours be inferior to it. In the same orders the preservation of the Portuguese Fleet is recommended, which does not agree with that which precedes it.

2nd. The River Plate and Buenos Ayres scheme cannot be carried out because of the absence of a combination with the Governor of the Colony and the General of the South. For this reason it must be held to be non-existent, and I therefore say no more about it.

3rd. The orders of the Court of Lisbon are very clear in prohibiting that the forces of this Fleet be risked, ordering that it retire to the safer ports ; and as the combination of these orders forms the ground upon which my vote is based, I say :—

That, at this present time, we have no course to pursue other than to attack the Fleet, let its condition be what it may; for, if the Court of Portugal knew the country as we know it, they would have given the clearest and most precise orders upon this subject. If the Spanish Fleet is not attacked it will effect the disembarkation unimpeded, and afterwards turn upon us with greater strength when it is free of its convoy. Although the Portuguese Fleet be small it can do a great deal of damage to the Spanish Fleet, and, should the latter be destroyed, they can undertake nothing that can affect this State without reinforcements, before the arrival of which fresh measures can be taken. This is the vote I give in Council.

On board of the war-ship *Santo Antonio*, 20th February 1777.

(Signed) José DE MELLO,
Commanding the war-ship ' Prazeres.'

No. 26.

The MARQUIS DO LAVRADIO to Senhor MARTINHO DE MELLO E CASTRO.

On the 26th of April there entered the harbour of this city our Fleet which I had ordered to leave it on the 1st of that month, as I informed Your Excellency direct, and also did so at greater length through the Home Office, in a Despatch dated the 3rd of the said month of April.

When the said Fleet was sailing towards the port

and coast of the island of St Catherine's, in obedience
to my orders, they sighted two vessels which appeared
to be small, and the Chief at once signalled the Fleet
to give chase. The one who pressed most to the
front was Captain José de Mello, and, as one of the
Spanish vessels thought, at first, that our Fleet was
theirs, she made no great effort to get away. The
result of this piece of carelessness was that when they
found out who we were it was too late to escape our
man-of-war, and the Spanish vessel was forced to
strike. The other, however, got away.

An examination of the papers found on board of the
captured vessel, which was a *setia*, commanded by
Lieut. Don José Justo Salcedo, shewed that the
said officer had been charged by the Marquis de Casa
Tely to collect at Assumption Island[1] the rest of the
vessels of the Fleet which were wanting, and to
conduct them to Montevideo, which he did. A
short time after his arrival there came to that port
two ships of the line, one called the *Santo Agostinho*
and the other the *Serio*, which had sailed from
Ferrol one month after the Fleet had left Cadiz.
These vessels carried despatches, with special instructions as to their delivery to the two Generals, and
these despatches were entrusted to Don Bernardo
Bonavia, Captain of the Regiment of Infantry of
Gallicia, who came in the Expedition, and was thus
already at Montevideo, and who, it is said, had been

---

[1] It ought to be *Ascension Island*.

sent out appointed to a higher post in which he was to be employed in the island.

To ensure a more rapid delivery of the said despatches, the *setia*, just mentioned, was ordered to set sail with the officer in charge of them on board. As soon as they saw the risk they ran of being captured, they threw the despatches overboard.

At the same time it was discovered that the two ships which had arrived from Europe were to have sailed with the first tide. Captain José de Mello went to inform the Chief of all this, and he ordered them to remain off the coast a few days in the hope of encountering them. This was done ; and, on the 19th of that month, the Chief signalled to all the Fleet to give chase, which they did in the direction indicated by the signals. Captain José de Mello was the foremost in the chase, his vessel being the fastest, and he was followed, but at a good distance, by Captain Arthur Phillips.

These two vessels continued the chase, and, as soon as Captain José de Mello saw that they were within the range, he fired, and his vessel it was that did the first damage. Captain Arthur Phillips came up with his frigate, and was allowed by the enemy to get closer, because they thought this vessel was one of their own, as they were unable to convince themselves that a vessel so small and so weak in artillery would venture to attack a 70-gun ship. It was only when Captain Phillips poured a broadside into them that they became aware that it was a frigate of ours.

The said Officer did this with a view to retarding the ship sufficiently to allow José de Mello to get closer ; but the Spanish Captain did nothing but crowd on sail to get away. All through the night the two vessels chased the other, but they were becalmed, and so the enemy managed, during the night, to get clear of them. This, however, did not avail them much, for, when the morning broke, the ship found herself near to the Chief of the Fleet, who at once gave chase with the other vessels, and, in a short time, got so close as to be able to open the fight. The battle lasted only one hour and a quarter ; and during that time José de Mello was able to attack with the rest of the Fleet.

The Spanish Captain struck without losing more than four men, and when his vessel had received no damage that he could not have repaired while the fight was going on.

The disorderly way in which the Spaniards fought, the state of confusion in which their vessel was, and the fright they were in, appears to have been incredible. I think myself that they were in as abject fear of our Fleet as were the wretches of the Island of St Catherine. I hear that the men of our Fleet behaved in a most praiseworthy manner. Of our people only one ordinary seaman received a wound of any importance. His leg was shot off. The other wounds were of so little importance that the men continued to fight in spite of them.

The prize is a valuable one, for she is a new vessel, built of excellent wood. She has first-rate artillery, and is completely supplied with all munitions and accessories of the first class. As the only damage she suffered was in the sails and the rigging, and some splinters knocked out of the masts by the cannon balls, she can be got ready at once to sail with the Fleet.

This encounter prevented our Fleet carrying out my orders. Had they been executed, we should, by this time, have again been masters of the port of the Island of St Catherine, and should have destroyed the vessels at anchor in that port, which were of small import-ance. We should also have captured the convoy which was arriving from Montevideo with provisions for the Island; and the want of food which the garrison, all over the Island, was already beginning to feel, would have, undoubtedly, assisted the success of the operation. But the Chief, fearing to meet with the entire Fleet in that port, refusing to believe the information which was given to him, as well as that which he derived from the sailing orders which he seized, shewing that the Fleet had already set sail for Rio Grande, in which latitudes it was sighted by the ships of war, who counted more than forty vessels, as the log-books proved to him; nothing of this sufficing, because that Officer's want of courage can only be appreciated by those who, like myself, have had a large experience of him on occasions of this kind, his fears, I say, had more effect upon him than my orders and the information which he had received, and he put into this port, bringing to me the two prizes and reporting what had occurred.

The consequence of the failure to carry out my orders was that the Spaniards received assistance and supplies, with which their wants will be relieved for some time ; and, if the Spanish Fleet had not encountered, on the coast of Rio Grande, the violent storms which have kept it in check from the 7th of April, when they were met with some forty leagues to seaward of the mouth of that river, down to the 3rd of May, when I had a letter from the General of our army stating that they had not yet appeared, our enemy's run of luck would have continued, and we should have been, each moment, less in a position to obtain any victory over them. However, as the private information which I have received from the Island of St Catherine assures me of the inferiority of the naval force left there, the fear which the Spaniards are in that they will again suffer a want of provisions, the want of unity among the officers, and the tendency of the men to desert, I feel bound to profit by the opportunity, while our enemy's forces are divided, to destroy them, little by little, until we remain the stronger, or, at least, are in a position to fight them on equal terms.

With this view I have taken the following measures :—Availing myself of some of the officers who had served in that Island, men of recognised fidelity, liked by the troops and by the people of the Island, and sufficiently robust for work of any kind, I sent them, disguised, with instructions to enter the Island, to find out the state in which the Spaniards were, and the feeling of the people towards them, and to secretly furnish the former with the means for throwing off the yoke the moment I attacked the Spaniards. I further ordered them to make overtures to the Spanish soldiers, inviting them to desert, facilitating their desertion, and assisting them in every way. I sent another officer, also trustworthy, to collect, upon the mainland, with the greatest precaution, as many as he could of the Portuguese soldiers who had withdrawn themselves in order to avoid being given up, and to hide with them in the most eligible point of the forest which he could find, so as to be ready, when the right moment arrived, to assist in the attack or surprise which would have to be made upon the Island.

These arrangements having been made, and the officers having sent me word that everything was ready for the time when I might order the vessels lying in the port of the Island to be attacked by sea, I got the Fleet ready, increasing it by two more ships of the line and a frigate. When it set sail it was composed of the five line of battle ships—*Santo Antonio*, which is the Flag-ship; *Nossa Senhora dos Prazeres*, Captain José de Mello; *Nossa Senhora de Ajuda*, now commanded by D. Francisco Xavier

Telles, because José dos Santos Ferreira, who was commanding it, remained dangerously ill in this city; *Nossa Senhora de Belem*, commanded by Antonio Januario; the prize, the *Santo Agostinho*, commanded by Arthur Phillips; and the four (*sic*) frigates—*Principe do Brazil*, Captain Thomas Stevens; *Graça Divina*, Captain George Hardcastle; and *Nossa Senhora do Pilar*, Captain Francisco Bettencourt. All of these I supplied with everything that was requisite to the entire satisfaction of the Commanding Officers, and according to their wishes, and I caused them to set sail from this port on the 29th of May, on which day, later on, the frigate *São João Baptista*, Captain William Roberts, came in.

I ordered the Chief to go to the Island of S. Catherine, reconnoitre the naval forces which the Spaniards had there, and, should he find that, without its being too rash a proceeding, our forces were sufficient for the purpose, attack them and destroy the vessels, but not to engage the fortresses, in order to avoid endangering our Fleet, before we had destroyed some part of our enemies, and also because, when once we were masters of the port, we could prevent them from receiving supplies, without which they would be forced to capitulate, as they have no other means of obtaining food. GOD preserve Your Excellency. Rio de Janeiro, 2nd June 1777.

(Signed) MARQUEZ DO LAVRADIO.

To H.E. Senhor MARTINHO DE MELLO E CASTRO.

LIST of the Officers of the Fleet, setting forth the merits of each, and the services upon which they are employed, and also whether they are serving under the Royal Letters or Order of the Queen, or by Warrant from me, issued in consequence of the want of Officers alleged by the Chief, and whom I appointed in conformity with the Royal Orders which have been sent to me.

RIO DE JANEIRO, 22nd October 1777.

(Part referring to Captain Phillips.)

VESSELS.	CAPTAINS.			LIEUTENANT CAPTAINS.			LIEUTENANTS.		
	By Royal Letters.	By Warrant.	Remarks.	By Royal Letters.	By Warrant.	Remarks.	By Royal Letters.	By Warrant.	Remarks.
Santo Agostinho.	Arthur Phillips.		This Officer is most honorable and meritorious. When at the Colony [1] he, with only his own frigate,[2] made the Spaniards respect that fortress as they ought to. When the Fleet sailed from St Catherine's upon receiving news of the Spanish Fleet he made every effort to induce the Chief to attack the enemy; and, finding that he did not do so, he wrote a private letter to him imploring him, for the sake of his own honour and that of the Nation, not to refrain from attacking them. The Chief replied that his orders were positive, and were to the contrary; and when he called upon all of them to give their votes, which was when the Spaniards were already commencing to enter the port, in order to make Phillips change his opinion he read to him the orders which he had previously received, informing him that he had received no others since them, and that it was those which they were all bound to obey. This he did, but only out of the great deference he renders to the orders of his superiors. *His health is very delicate, but he never complains, excepting when he has nothing special to do for the Royal Service.*	José Caetano de Lima.	Agostinho da Rosa.	The first-mentioned was named in the orders which I received from the Court, and I wrote a letter to him to that effect to serve as his Warrant, as I had been charged to do. He has served very well. The second came out here as a Lieutenant. He has served with much distinction, and was appointed to serve as Lieutenant-Captain upon the application of the Chief.		Jeronimo Pereira. Antonio da Rosa.	The first-mentioned passed from ordinary mariner to volunteer, and, as such, sailed in one of the vessels which entered Rio Grande on the 19th February last year. He bore himself with great valour and promptness. He is not wanting in intelligence, but, as he was not brought up to be an officer, it is difficult for him to adapt himself to that particular mode of life. The second was a coasting Captain of Rio da Prata and all the southern ports. He is a very intelligent and brave officer. They were appointed by Warrant, upon the application of the Chief. They have fulfilled their duties most perfectly.

[1] *Sacramento*, which the Portuguese Crown was at that time most anxious to retain.
[2] The *Nossa Senhora do Pilar.*

(Signed) MARQUEZ DO LAVRADIO.

No. 28.

A list of the rigging, spars and other stores applied for by Captain Arthur Phillips, from March 6th to the 25th of that month during this present year, 1777, for Her Majesty's frigate *Nossa Senhora do Pilar e S. João*.

[This list is only interesting on account of the dates. It refers to the Arsenal at Rio de Janeiro.]

No. 29.

Another list, caused to be drawn up by the Marquis Viceroy on the 23rd October 1777, shews that the Ship of the Line *Santo Agostinho* (which had been captured from the Spaniards), commanded by Arthur Phillips, had a crew of 462 men, officers, sailors, artillery-men and infantry included; and that it carried 70 guns, 28 of which were calibre 24, 30 calibre 18, and 12 calibre 9; thus being the most powerful vessel of the Fleet.

No. 30.

Extract from a Letter of the Marquis do Lavradio to Senhor Martinho de Mello e Castro.

Your Excellency,—   .   .   .   .

The vessels of war which sail with this convoy are the Ship of the Line *Prazeres* and the *Santo Antonio*. The former is commanded by José de Mello; the latter by Arthur Phillips. José de Mello commands the convoy. This Officer has always conducted himself with great precision in all his duties, and shewn the greatest activity and intelligence in his profession, coupled with a large amount of zeal for the Royal Service. I might say something more about him if our relationship and the intimacy which I have enjoyed with him for many years did not render me suspect.

The other Officers of that vessel have correctly done their duty.

The commander of the *Santo Antonio* is Captain Arthur Phillips, whom I consider to be one of the officers of the most distinct merit that the Queen, my Mistress, has in her service in the Navy, and I think that it will be a most important acquisition to secure that he should remain in the Royal Service. This Officer not only has a large theoretical knowledge of his profession, but is well up in fortification and every other branch of the military profession, and, moreover, has had practical experience from the age of nine, when he commenced to serve as 'Guard to the Standard' (midshipman ?) on the war-ships of his country, up to Naval Lieutenant. He took part in all of the more important engagements which the English Fleets have had since he entered the service. As regards his disposition, he is somewhat self-distrustful ; but, as he is an Officer of education and principle, he gives way to reason, and does not, before doing so, fall into those exaggerated and unbearable excesses of temper which the majority of his fellow-countrymen do, more especially those who have been brought up at sea. He is very clean-handed; is an Officer of great truth and very brave; and is no flatterer, saying what he thinks, but without temper or want of respect.

The length of my Report upon this Officer implies that I regret him very much, and I confess that I do. *It is the consequence of my having noted the great difference in the way he served, as compared with the greater part of the others.* This which I write to Your Excellency you will not only find to be corroborated by such officers of merit as Your Excellency may consult; but you yourself, with your great talent, when you have formed his acquaintance, will render the same justice to his worth that I do.

.   .   .   .

Rio de Janeiro, 10th May 1778.

(Signed) Marquez do Lavradio.

To His Excellency Senhor Martinho de Mello e Castro.

No. 31.

August	Thursday, 20	1778.

OCCURRENCES.

	1st. .	.	.	.
	2nd.	.	.	.
	3rd.	.	.	.

Entrance of the war-ship *Santo Antonio e São José.*

4th. At about three o'clock in the afternoon His Majesty's ship of war, the *Santo Antonio e São José,* which has come from Rio de Janeiro under the command of Captain Arthur Filipps, crossed the Bar, and cast anchor at six o'clock.

[Marine Archives. Book IV. of the Registers of Orders of the Day, fol. 207.]

No. 32.

August   Sunday, 23   1778.

ORDERS.

1st. .   .   .   .

To the Capt. of the *S. Antonio.*

2nd. That the Captain of the war-ship *Santo Antonio e São José* retain his sails on board until further orders.

OCCURRENCES.

1st. A communication to Captain Arthur Filipps, commanding the war-ship *Santo Antonio e São José,* to the following effect :—The Captain-General of the Royal Fleet has ordered that you should receive from the Stores Department a day's ration of fresh meat for to-day, and a similar one for every day that you are on board, delivered on the proper days, you always supplying the customary list of your crew. GOD preserve

X

Your Excellency. Office, 23rd August 1778. (Signed) João da Costa d'Atayde Teive, Aide-de-Camp.

To Captain Arthur Filipps.

[*Ibid.*, fol. 208.]

No. 33.

August   Monday, 24   1778.

Occurrences.

To Captain Arthur Filipps.

A communication sent to Captain Arthur Filipps, commanding the warship *Santo Antonio e São José*, to the following effect : — The Captain-General of the Royal Fleet orders that immediately upon receiving this letter you cause the men set forth in the annexed list, signed by me, to be got ready, and, together with the proper communication, to cause them to be delivered on board the warship *Santo Antonio e São José*,[1] to Captain José de Mello. This I communicate to you in order that you may execute it. God preserve you. On board of the war-ship *Nossa Senhora dos Prazeres*, on the 24th August 1778. (Signed) João da Costa d'Athaide Teive, Aide-de-Camp.

To Captain Arthur Filipps.

[1] Undoubtedly a clerical error. The vessel in question was the *S. José e Mercés*, which was then refitting.

Upon paying off the ship of war *Santo Antonio e São José* her crew was found to be as follows:—

Paying off list of the warship *Santo Antonio e São José.*						
	Officers	Commissioned		8	42	
		Chaplains		2		
		Commissariat		2		
		Warrant		29		
		Blacksmith		1		
	Volunteers			5	5	
	Crew	Able-bodied seamen		199	339	488
		2nd rate		128		
		Cabin boys		12		
	Infantry of the 1st Fleet	Officers	Commissioned	3	66	
			Non-commissioned	5		
		Drummer		1		
		Soldiers		57		
	Artillery of the Court	Officers	Commissioned	0	36	
			Inferior	3		
		Drummer		1		
		Soldiers		32		

which number of 488 men, together with 14 who came on shore ill, makes the total of 502 men which the said ship of war had on board when she returned to this port, and is 9 men more than she took out.

[*Ibid.*, fol. 208 and 209.]

No. 34.

September	Tuesday, 8	1778.

OCCURRENCES.

Arrival of the war-ship *N. S. de Belem*, Captain Antonio Januario do Valle.	At two o'clock p.m. His Majesty's war-ship *Nossa Senhora de Belem* crossed the Bar, coming from Rio de Janeiro by Pernambuco, under the command of Captain Antonio Januario do Valle, and anchored at four o'clock.

[*Ibid.*, fol. 211.]

Note by General Jacintho Ignacio de Brito Rebello.

The first ten documents (Nos. 1-10) contain the negotiations which preceded the entrance of Arthur Phillip into the Portuguese Royal Navy, his departure from England and arrival in Portugal, and the Decree by which he was made a Captain, in accordance with his agreement.

As soon as he had been appointed to be Captain on the 14th of January 1775 (No. 10) we see (No. 11) that on the 17th of that month he was ordered to go on board the line of battle ship *Nossa Senhora de Belem* as second Captain.

On the 25th he obtains leave to go to Salvaterra (No. 12), where the Court then was, for the purpose, it is but reasonable to suppose, of taking leave of His Majesty, and soliciting the necessary letters of recommendation which would obtain for him the sole command of a vessel upon his arrival at the Colony.

On the 6th of February the ship tried to cross the Bar (No. 13), but could not do so, and she only got away on the 9th (No. 14).

The documents do not inform us as to the vessel's port of destination, but it appears (No. 34) that when she returned on 8th Septr. 1778 it was from Rio de Janeiro, and she came by Pernambuco.

On the 20th of August she had been preceded by the *Nossa Senhora dos Prazeres* and the *Santo Antonio and São José*, the latter of which was commanded by Capt. Arthur Phillip (No. 31).

Thus we see that Capt. Phillip, upon arriving in Portugal, sailed at once to the Brazils, where he remained in service for more than three years, the exact time which elapsed between his crossing the Bar of Lisbon outwards and his again crossing it on his return being three years, six months and twelve days.

When Capt. Phillip first embarked as second Captain of the *Nossa Senhora de Belem*, Antonio Januario do Valle, his Chief, was one of the officers of the Portuguese Navy of best repute. Soon after the ship reached the Brazils, the Viceroy, wishing to strengthen the Fleet, armed some merchant vessels, one of which was the *Nossa Senhora do Pilar*. She was converted into a 26-gun frigate and placed under the command of Arthur Phillip, and on the 27th January 1776 was sent to look out for prizes in the south, for which reason she did not take part in the unfortunate engagement of the 19th February (Nos. 17, 18). Later on Phillip was sent with two more frigates to the River Plate, but soon afterwards the latter were withdrawn for repairs. Though left single-handed, his small vessel was found to be sufficient to keep the Spaniards within bounds (Nos. 20, 21 and 27).

At the close of the year he went to Saint Catherine's to take in firewood (No. 23), and found there, it is to be presumed, the order requiring him to join the Fleet which was defending that Island, in consequence of the preparations which were being made in Spain for the despatch of a powerful armament and a large body of troops to attack the Portuguese possessions. Unfortunately, upon the first news of the arrival of the Spaniards, on the 16th February 1777, the Chief of the Fleet, Robert MacDonell, raised his anchors and set sail, in spite of Arthur Phillip's efforts to persuade him to stay and fight. On the 20th, after the Spaniards had anchored in the harbour of the Island, the Chief held a Council, at which he only presented the orders which he had at first received—not to risk his Fleet—and kept back the later ones. Arthur Phillip's reply shews what his opinion was (Nos. 24, 25 and 27).

After the Fleet had reached Rio de Janeiro it was again sent out as soon as it was ready, and, meeting some Spanish vessels, gave chase. José de Mello, in the *Nossa Senhora dos Prazeres*, and Arthur Phillip, in the *Pilar*, took the lead. A *setia* was captured, with important documents on board, and the Fleet again put into Rio de Janeiro with the prize (No. 26).

Ordered again to leave the port, they chased a large Spanish vessel, and again José de Mello and Arthur Phillip were to the front. The latter, owing to the small size of his vessel, was able to get very close without inspiring distrust, and poured in a broadside. All night the chase continued, and in the morning the Spanish vessel, finding herself surrounded by the Fleet, lowered her flag. She was the *Santo Agostinho*, a 70-gun ship. Again the Fleet returned to Rio de Janeiro, where the prisoners were landed, a fresh crew provided, and the captured vessel placed under the command of Capt. Phillip. The Fleet then sailed for manœuvres, but nothing is known of what was done by it (No. 26).

When the preliminaries for the Treaty of Peace had been signed at Saint Ildefonso, on the 1st October 1777, the captured vessels were returned, and, among them, the *Santo Agostinho*. On the 16th February 1778, the Viceroy, acting upon orders from home, broke up the Fleet, ordering MacDonell to haul down his flag and return to Lisbon in either a ship of war or a merchant vessel, as he might think best. In consequence, he handed over the ship of the line *Santo Antonio and São José*, which had been the Flag-ship, to Capt. Phillip, who, accompanying José de Mello, sailed in her with a Convoy to Europe in May 1778. The Viceroy's despatch (No. 30), addressed to the

Minister of the Marine upon this occasion, is a crown of glory for Capt. Phillip, and shews how much he was esteemed by his comrades and chiefs.

Further information as to these events will be found in Varnhagen's *History of the Brazil.*

INDEX

S

T

THE END

Colston & Coy. Limited, Printers, Edinburgh